ENGLISH GRAMMAR

Routledge English Language Introductions cover core areas of language study and are one-stop resources for students.

Assuming no prior knowledge, books in the series offer an accessible overview of the subject, with activities, study questions, sample analyses, commentaries and key readings – all in the same volume. The innovative and flexible 'two-dimensional' structure is built around four sections – introduction, development, exploration and extension – which offer self-contained stages for study. Each topic can also be read across these sections, enabling the reader to build gradually on the knowledge gained.

English Grammar:

❑ presents the basic concepts and key terms of English grammar in a clear and systematic way
❑ encourages readers to evaluate critically the knowledge they already have, particularly in areas that are problematic for them as learners, and to build up and trust their own intuitions about the language
❑ uses a range of international real texts to illustrate concepts and theories, from sources such as newspapers, novels and academic texts discussing English grammar
❑ is accompanied by a companion website featuring audio files of authentic spoken English, and further activities.

Written by an experienced teacher and researcher, this accessible textbook is an essential resource for all students of English language and linguistics.

Roger Berry teaches English Grammar and Applied Linguistics at Lingnan University in Hong Kong.

ROUTLEDGE ENGLISH LANGUAGE INTRODUCTIONS

SERIES CONSULTANT: PETER STOCKWELL

Peter Stockwell is Professor of Literary Linguistics in the School of English Studies at the University of Nottingham, UK, where his interests include sociolinguistics, stylistics and cognitive poetics. His recent publications include *Language in Theory*, Routledge 2005 (with Mark Robson), *Cognitive Poetics: An Introduction*, Routledge, 2002, *The Poetics of Science Fiction, Investigating English Language* (with Howard Jackson), and *Contextualised Stylistics* (edited with Tony Bex and Michael Burke)

SERIES CONSULTANT: RONALD CARTER

Ronald Carter is Professor of Modern English Language in the School of English Studies at the University of Nottingham, UK. He is the co-series editor of the forthcoming *Routledge Applied Linguistics* series, series editor of *Interface*, and was co-founder of the Routledge *Intertext* series.

OTHER TITLES IN THE SERIES:

Introducing English Language
Louise Mullany and Peter Stockwell

Language and Power
Paul Simpson and Andrea Mayr

Language and Media
Alan Durant and Marina Lambrou

World Englishes 2nd Edition
Jennifer Jenkins

Practical Phonetics and Phonology 2nd Edition
Beverly Collins and Inger Mees

Sociolinguistics 2nd Edition
Peter Stockwell

Pragmatics and Discourse 2nd Edition
Joan Cutting

Psycholinguistics
John Field

Grammar and Vocabulary
Howard Jackson

Stylistics
Paul Simpson

Language in Theory
Mark Robson and Peter Stockwell

Child Language
Jean Stilwell Peccei

Researching English Language: A Resource Book for Students
Alison Sealey

English Grammar: A Resource Book for Students
Roger Berry

ENGLISH GRAMMAR

A resource book for students

ROGER BERRY

Routledge
Taylor & Francis Group

LONDON AND NEW YORK

First published 2012
by Routledge
2 Park Square, Milton Park, Abingdon, Oxon, OX14 4RN

Simultaneously published in the USA and Canada
by Routledge
711 Third Avenue, New York, NY 10017

Routledge is an imprint of the Taylor & Francis Group, an informa business

British Library Cataloguing in Publication Data
A catalogue record for this book is available from the British Library

Library of Congress Cataloging-in-Publication Data
Berry, Roger, 1951–
English grammar: a resource book for students / Roger Berry.
    p.   cm.
  1. English language–Grammar. I. Title.
  PE1112.B456 2011
  428.2–dc22
                                    2011016984

ISBN: 978–0–415–56108–2 (hbk)
ISBN: 978–0–415–56109–9 (pbk)

Typeset in Minion Pro by
Graphicraft Limited, Hong Kong

MIX
Paper from
responsible sources
FSC® C004839

Printed and bound in Great Britain by the MPG Books Group

CONTENTS

HOW TO USE THIS BOOK

The *Routledge English Language Introductions* are 'flexi-texts' that you can use to suit your own style of study. The books are divided into four sections:

A Introduction – sets out the key concepts for the area of study. The units of this section take you step-by-step through the foundational terms and ideas, carefully providing you with an initial toolkit for your own study. By the end of the section, you will have a good overview of the whole field.

B Development – adds to your knowledge and builds on the key areas already introduced. Units in this section might also draw together several areas of interest. By the end of this section, you will already have a good and fairly detailed grasp of the field, and will be ready to undertake your own exploration and thinking.

C Exploration – provides examples of language data and guides you through your own investigation of the field. The units in this section will be more open-ended and exploratory, and you will be encouraged to try out your ideas and think for yourself, using your newly acquired knowledge.

D Extension – offers you the chance to compare your expertise with key readings in the area. These are taken from the work of important writers, and are provided with guidance and questions for further thought.

You can read this book like a traditional textbook, 'vertically' straight through each unit from beginning to end. This will take you comprehensively through the broad field of study. However, the *Routledge English Language Introductions* have been carefully designed so that you can read them in another dimension, 'horizontally' as a *strand* across the numbered units. For example, Unit A1 corresponds with B1, C1 and D1 as a coherent strand; A2 with B2, C2 and D2, and so on. Reading across a strand will take you rapidly from the key concepts of a specific area, to a level of expertise in that precise area, all with a very close focus. You can match your way of reading with the way that you work best.

The index of terms at the end, together with the suggestions for further reading, will help keep you orientated. This textbook has a supporting website with an extensive reference section, additional activities, a further reading list and annotated weblinks to online corpora www.routledge.com/cw/berry.

FIGURES AND TABLES

Figures

Tables

ACKNOWLEDGEMENTS

The author and publisher wish to thank all mentioned below for permission to reproduce copyright materials.

While every effort has been made to find the copyright holders of materials used in this volume, the publishers would be happy to hear from any they have been unable to contact and will make any necessary amendment at the earliest opportunity.

Michael Swan, 2005, 'What is grammar for?', Chapter 1, in *OILS: Grammar*, Oxford: Oxford University Press, pp. 4–7. © Oxford University Press. Reproduced by permission of Oxford University Press.

David Lee, 2001, 'Count and mass nouns.' Chapter 8 in *Cognitive Linguistics*. South Melbourne: Oxford University Press, pp. 137–145. Reproduced by permission of Oxford University Press Australia. © Oxford University Press, www.oup.com.au.

Roger Berry, 1998, 'Determiners: a class apart?' In *English Today*, 14/1, pp. 27–34. © Cambridge University Press, reproduced with permission.

David Lee, 2001, 'Space.' Chapter 2 in *Cognitive Linguistics*. South Melbourne: Oxford University Press, pp. 18–24. Reproduced by permission of Oxford University Press Australia. © Oxford University Press, www.oup.com.au

Michael Lewis, 1986, 'Future time – a summary'. Chapter 17 in *The English Verb*. Hove: Language Teaching Publications, pp. 139–146.

Carter and McCarthy, 2006, 'Hedging and Boosting' from *Cambridge Grammar of English*, Cambridge: Cambridge University Press, pp. 279–284.

John Sinclair, 2001, 'Words and Phrases', Chapter 5 in *Corpus, Concordance, Collocation*, pp. 67–79. Oxford: Oxford University Press. © Oxford University Press. Reproduced by permission of Oxford University Press.

Lynn M. Berk, 1999, Section on 'Semantic roles of the subject', pp. 14–21/23 in *English Syntax: from Word to Discourse*. New York: Oxford University Press.

Carter and McCarthy, 2006, The 'Chapter' on Speech Acts, *Cambridge Grammar of English*, Cambridge: Cambridge University Press, pp. 680–84.

Michael Lewis, 1986, section on Conditional Sentences, *The English Verb*, pp. 148–150, Hove: Language Teaching Publications.

Dave Willis, 1994, the section on The Second Conditional, pages 59–60 of 'The Lexical Approach', in M. Bygate, A. Tonkyn and E. Williams, *Grammar and the Language Teacher*, Hemel Hempstead: Prentice Hall International.

Michael Halliday, 2004, Section 2.6 on Subject, Actor, Theme, pages 53 and 55–58 in *An Introduction to Functional Grammar*, 3rd edition, London: Arnold. Reproduced by permission of Hodder Education.

Ann Hewings and Caroline Coffin, 2004, 'Grammar in the Construction of Online Discussion Messages' (pp. 137–43 only), in *Applying English Grammar*, Caroline Coffin, Ann Hewings and Kieran O'Halloran (eds.), London: Arnold. Reproduced by permission of Hodder Education.

The publishers and author would also like to thank the following for their assistance in the reviewing process: Crayton Walker, Juan Santana Lario, María Sanz Casares, Zhiming Bao, Jonathan White, Maria Estling Vannestål, Marina Kolokonte, Keith Taylor, Jackie Lee, Marta Carretero, Magnus Levin, Göran Wolf as well as other anonymous reviewers.

The author would like to express his gratitude to Lingnan University for the leave granted to him for the writing of this book.

PREFACE

TO TEACHERS/LECTURERS. This book is intended for students of English who need an introduction to its grammar, whether as part of a degree in English or as preparation for teaching the language. It contains four strands:

the **Introduction** sections each describe a key area of grammar, starting with word classes and moving on through phrases to clauses and sentences.

the **Development** sections focus in more detail on one area usually related to that in the Introduction and often involving a re-evaluation of traditional accounts.

the **Exploration** sections enable students to apply what they have learnt and to hone their analytic skills by examining concordance lines or authentic texts connected to one particular area.

the **Extension** sections are built around selected readings on issues related to the previous sections, with the aim of taking students beyond the bounds of descriptive grammar into related approaches and theories.

The book may be used 'vertically' (e.g. by doing all the Exploration sections first) or 'horizontally'.

Activities are offered throughout, not just in the Exploration sections; comments containing suggested answers are usually placed at the end of each section. A number of boxes on Terminology, Variation in English and Non-Standard Forms complement the main text. Extra information (including further activities) can be found on our website at www.routledge.com/cw/berry.

TO STUDENTS. This book has the following objectives:

1) to provide you with a thorough grounding in the most important areas of English grammar, which you will be able to apply in further studies in English.
2) to help you to understand how English 'works' as a system, not as a jumble of isolated rules.
3) to encourage you to approach issues such as correctness, formality and variation realistically, in order to demonstrate that grammar is not always a matter of wrong and right, or black and white.
4) to show the connection between meaning and grammar, or rather between grammatical form and grammatical meaning. While it is sometimes necessary

to focus on one or the other, there are numerous examples of how a change in one results in a change in the other.

5) to equip you with strategies to deal with areas of English grammar that are not covered on the course so that you can become 'your own grammarian'.

6) (if you have learnt English at school) to help you to re-evaluate the simplified and sometimes misleading notions that are common in English language classrooms.

7) to enable you to exploit your intuitions about English to make sense of what you know.

Section A
INTRODUCTION

APPROACHES TO GRAMMAR

A1.1 The trouble with 'grammar'

'Grammar' is not an easy word to use. In order to understand one of the problems associated with it try the following activity:

Activity A1.1

> Fill in the gaps.
>
> 1. *Linguistics is the study of* _____.
> 2. *Phonetics is the study of* _____.
> 3. *Semantics is the study of* _____.
> 4. *Grammar is the study of* _____.

Comment

The generally accepted answers to the first three are 'language', 'pronunciation' (or 'speech sounds') and 'meaning', though you may not know the last one unless you have studied linguistics. As for sentence 4, you may have written something like 'structure' or 'rules', but these apply to other areas as well as to grammar; pronunciation has rules and structure, for example. Another possible answer is 'morphology and syntax' but these are also unfamiliar terms (see below). The best answer is that grammar is the study of 'grammar'. In other words grammar is both the name of the study (a branch of linguistics) and the object of study (a part of language). So while elsewhere we can distinguish the study from the object (e.g. phonetics and pronunciation) we cannot with grammar.

This is just one of the problems associated with the meaning of the word 'grammar'. But there are more, as the next activity shows:

Activity A1.2

> Consider the word 'grammar' in the following sentences. Is the meaning the same? If not, what is the difference?
>
> 1. *I make too many mistakes in grammar.*
> 2. *Many grammars of English are published every year.*
> 3. *Traditional grammar relied heavily on the concept of 'parts of speech'.*

Comment

Sentence 1 relates to the distinction discussed above. But sentences 2 and 3 are something new. The former refers to books about grammar while the latter implies one particular theoretical approach to it, in other words suggesting that there is no one correct way to study grammar.

There is also no absolute agreement about the scope of grammar, i.e. what it includes. In the past it could mean the whole of language study, not just a part. Even nowadays it is common to find books with 'grammar' in their title which deal with subjects such as spelling, punctuation, pronunciation and style. In addition there is no clear agreement on whether topics such as word-formation should be included.

We can summarise all these competing meanings in terms of a number of distinctions. Is grammar:

a) a part (level) of language OR the study of that part (compare 'pronunciation' and 'phonetics')
b) the study of that part OR the study of all of a language (e.g. including punctuation etc.)
c) the study OR an account of that study, as contained in a book (e.g. 'Greenbaum's Grammar')
d) the study OR a theory about that part of language (e.g. 'generative grammar')?

For some it can be any or all of these. To reflect this confusion there is a distinction in the grammar of 'grammar', in that one of the meanings is count (we can say 'a grammar' or 'grammars' when talking about books) while the others are noncount ('grammar').

A1.2 Defining grammar

This book involves several of the options listed above. It aims to show how to study grammar and it also involves, inevitably, some theory. Principally, however, it is about the first part of distinction a) above: one particular part of language. But what part is that? Let's attempt a definition.

The first attempt below tries to define grammar in terms of its component parts:

1) *Grammar = morphology* (how words are made up) + *syntax* (how sentences are made up)

This does not help much, of course, since morphology and syntax are more abstract concepts than grammar; if you know what they mean then you are likely to already know what grammar means. And this approach to definition does not give the whole story. It is not very helpful to know that a bike is composed of two wheels, a frame, a saddle, handlebars, etc. We need also to ask what grammar 'does' – what its purpose is.

Let's try an illustration. Imagine that you are going to a foreign country and you want to learn the language. Unfortunately, there are no speakers of that language around and no courses for learners; the only resource available is a bilingual dictionary. Diligently, day by day, you work your way through it, and at the end of a year you feel you know it by heart. Confidently you travel to the country where this language is spoken. How successful at communicating do you think you will be?

Well, you can probably communicate basic ideas using single words, but most of your hard-won vocabulary is useless; how could you ever use a word like 'scorn' on its own? You are probably even able to put two words together e.g. 'drink water', but this could mean many things, and there is no consistent distinction between this and 'water drink'. (This in fact is what very young children are able to do.) This is before we consider whether your pronunciation is intelligible and whether you can under-stand what people say back to you. Despite your vast knowledge of vocabulary, there is something very important missing: grammar.

So we might attempt a second definition as follows:

2) *Grammar is what turns words into language.*

For me this is insightful, but it is slightly problematic; for most linguists there is a level of grammar below the word (just as for some, there is a level above the sentence, the normal limit of grammar). But the basic idea is sound, so let's try to develop it. There are a number of factors we need to consider:

❑   language is essentially a means of meaningful communication
❑   grammar is the means by which linguistic forms (words, parts of words, the relationships between words, and so on) express that meaning
❑   grammar is composed of rules that operate systematically
❑   grammar operates in both directions: from meaning to form (production) and form to meaning (comprehension)

So here is a third definition:

3) *Grammar is the system of rules that enables users of a language to relate linguistic form to meaning.*

A1.3 Types of grammar

Now that we have defined our 'subject matter', we still need to consider different approaches to it, or different types of grammar. We can make three distinctions:

1) primary (operational) vs secondary (analytic)
When we say we know the grammar of a language it could mean one of two things. Either we know it perfectly because it is our first language (our L1) and we have learnt all the rules unconsciously, or we know *about* the grammar because we have been given rules by teachers or read about them in books. The two are not the same. Someone can have an extensive (secondary) knowledge of grammar but be unable to use those rules when speaking. To take one example: many learners of English 'know' consciously the rule about third person '-s' but do not apply it when they speak, which leads to errors such as 'he think'.

The difference is not simply between knowing an L1 unconsciously and studying a second language (L2) consciously. In the past it was common for schoolchildren to be taught something about the grammar of English as their L1. On the other hand, many people learn an L2 without studying it consciously and even those who do learn it in a formal situation may acquire some primary knowledge as well as secondary; in other words, they have intuitions about the grammar. Very often these intuitions may contradict what they have read or been told; the primary and secondary grammars do not agree. In this book you are encouraged in the activities to apply your intuitions, your primary grammar, even though it may be limited.

The choice of terms here is deliberate. Primary grammar comes first, before a secondary knowledge of grammar; there are many languages, whose secondary grammar has not been described, but of course they still have (primary) grammar, otherwise their speakers could not use them to communicate. And secondary grammar is usually (but not always – see below) an attempt to capture the rules of primary grammar. But these attempts are incomplete; even the longest grammars of English (which nowadays come to almost 2,000 pages) cannot cover all the rules that are inside a native-speaker's head.

2) descriptive vs prescriptive

This distinction refers to two approaches to secondary grammar: should we, in our grammatical accounts, describe how English is used by its speakers (descriptive), or offer rules on how some people *think* it should be used (prescriptive)? In the past many prescriptive rules were made up about English which bore no relationship to native speakers' primary grammar; they were influenced by the grammar of Latin (which is very different to English).

Although prescriptive rules are less commonly found nowadays, and are mainly an obsession for native speakers of English, you may have heard some in your studies, for instance the 'rule' that you should not say '*If I was rich . . .*' but instead '*If I were rich . . .*'. This is nonsense; native speakers say '*If I was rich . . .*' all the time, though if they want to sound very formal they may say '*If I were rich . . .*'. While prescriptive rules offer an illusion of 'correctness', descriptive rules tend to be not so black and white; they may talk about tendencies or something being appropriate in one situation but not in another. So do not always expect to find absolute certainty in grammar.

3) pedagogic vs scientific

This distinction is to do with the target audience of the grammar. Is it for learners and teachers in the classroom (pedagogic) or for linguists who are studying it (scientific)? The rules that learners are given by teachers tend to be simplified into a form that can be easily understood; they are also isolated from another (i.e. they do not form a system, as described above). Scientific grammar is much more complex and extensive, but it is systematic; this course is an introduction to it.

While pedagogic and scientific grammar are both types of descriptive, secondary grammar, pedagogic grammar has some prescriptive influence. Learners want guidance and so a teacher may simplify the facts; for example, she might tell students not to use *want* in the progressive. Sometimes, however, the simplification goes wrong and has little connection to the scientific 'facts', as the next activity shows.

Activity A1.3

> Consider this rule of pedagogic grammar:
>> *'You should use "any" in negatives and questions and "some" in positive sentences.'*
>
> Is it true? Can you think of exceptions?

Comment

While this 'rule' may help to understand sentences such as

> *I've got <u>some</u> money* and
>
> *I haven't got <u>any</u> money*

it is not hard to find exceptions:

> *Would you like <u>some</u> tea?* (as an offer; it would be strange to say *any*)
>
> *I haven't stolen <u>some</u> of the money, I've stolen all of it* (with *some* stressed; if we say *I haven't stolen <u>any</u> of the money* the meaning is completely different)
>
> *<u>Any</u> teacher can tell you that 'any' can be used in positives.*

In other words, *some* can be used in questions and negatives and *any* in positives, and both can be used in the same context with a different meaning, which makes this a fairly useless rule. A refinement of the pedagogic rule says that when we ask a question expecting the answer *yes*, we can use *some*. This is an improvement but it is still far from the scientific rule which talks about 'asserting' the existence of something (with *some*), or not (with *any*), and relates this to other pairs of words which share this distinction (*sometimes* and *ever*, *already* and *yet*); see the reading in D3. The point is that the difference between *some* and *any* is to do with meaning, not grammar.

We can show the relationship between these different types of grammar in a diagram:

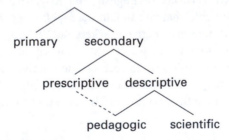

Figure A1.3.1 The relationship between different types of grammar

Activity A1.4

> Think about the following statements and decide if you agree with them.
>
> 1. If you are a native speaker of a language then you know its grammar.
> 2. Nobody knows all the grammar of a language.
> 3. What learners of a language are taught about its grammar is usually simplified and sometimes wrong.
> 4. Grammar is not always a matter of correct facts; it is often a question of tendencies and appropriateness. Something may be right in one situation but not in another.

Comment

Statements 3 and 4 express the philosophy of this book. As for 1 and 2, it depends on which type of grammar we are thinking about. Statement 1 is correct if we are thinking of primary grammar, as is 2 if we are thinking about secondary grammar.

NOTE. From now on, most comments are placed at the end of the section, rather than after their activity.

NOUNS

A2

A2.1 Defining nouns

Nouns are an open word class (see B1); new nouns are being devised almost every day, it seems. A recent example is *chocoholic*. Nouns are by far the most numerous word class; they also tend to make up more of a text than other open word classes.

⭐ **Activity A2.1**

Look at the paragraph above. How many nouns are there? (Do not count repetitions.)

The traditional notional definition of noun goes something like this:
    'a noun is the name of a person, place or thing'
You can probably see some problems with this already. First, there is the question of what we mean by 'name'; we will see another situation below where this word is needed. More importantly, many nouns have nothing to do with people, places or things, for example, nouns referring to abstract concepts such as *love, beauty, pain, war,* or nouns referring to actions, such as *singing, laughter, fight.*

⭐ **Activity A2.2**

Look at these nouns and decide if they fit the above definition:
    arrival, bomb, carpet, death, description, joke, science, teacher, tree, walk

---

As the activity shows, the notional definition is generally not very helpful. Because of this we look for <u>formal</u> features to help us to identify nouns. In this approach, a noun is a word which

a) changes its form for singular and plural and for the genitive: *dog, dogs, dog's, dogs'* (see below for an explanation of these terms)
b) can act as the head of a noun phrase (*new <u>information</u>*) and can be preceded by a determiner such as *some*: *some <u>people</u>*

Point b) is dealt with mainly in A3. Here we will concentrate on a) and related matters.

Activity A2.3

Glob is a word you won't find in a dictionary because it is invented. Look at these sentences and work out if it is a noun.

1. *There are two globs on your shoulder.*
2. *Her feelings were a mixture of embarrassment, anger and glob.*
3. *It is always useful to have a glob around.*
4. *You can glob all you like; I'm not coming.*
5. *He is a glob teacher.*

Did you use the notional or the formal definition to decide? If you used the formal one, which point(s)?

A2.2 Number: singular and plural

The change in form between singular and plural, or rather the choice between the two, is called 'number'. This is a word you already know, but here it is being used in a slightly different way, as a technical term.

Number is an obligatory choice in English (unlike some languages). Nouns must be either singular or plural: *table/tables*. However, not all nouns in English have both a singular and plural (and this means that on its own it is not always a reliable test of whether a word is a noun). There are some nouns which only occur in the singular; we will look at them later in this section.

Plural nouns

There are also some nouns that only occur as plurals; here are some examples:
   binoculars, clothes, glasses, jeans, scissors, shorts, trousers, underpants
They look just like any other plural, but it is not possible to remove the '-s' to make a singular form; 'clothe' is not acceptable. And it is not possible to use a number in front: 'two clothes', though a plural quantifier is possible: *many clothes*. In other cases a singular is possible but it has a different meaning, for example, *a short* means a strong alcoholic drink in a small glass. Where needed, a counting expression, such as *a pair of*, can be used to make them countable:
   a pair of scissors
As you can see from the examples above, several plural nouns refer to items of clothing or tools, but there are many others:
   arms, authorities, congratulations, contents, goods, grounds, surroundings, thanks, troops
See the Website Reference A2.1 for more examples.

Try to turn the underlined plural nouns into the singular, adding *a* if necessary. What effect does this have? Use a good dictionary if you are not sure.

1. On arrival you will need to pass through immigration and <u>customs</u>.
2. She took off her <u>glasses</u> and looked him straight in the eye.
3. The house is surrounded by extensive <u>grounds</u>.
4. You are always in our <u>thoughts</u>.

✪ Activity A2.4

Problems with number

In addition to plural nouns, there are other problems with number:

❏ there are words that look plural, in that they seem to have an added -*s*, but which in fact are singular, for example, *measles, news, mathematics*. You can tell this by looking at the following verb if the noun is a subject:
   The <u>news</u> <u>is</u> very bad.
See the Website Reference A2.2 for more examples.

❏ there are words which look singular but are plural: *cattle, police, people*
   The <u>police</u> <u>have</u> been informed.
These are similar to the plural nouns above.

❏ there are some nouns referring to groups of people, called 'collective' nouns, which can be plural or singular, depending on whether they are regarded as a single group or as a collection of individuals: *committee, enemy, family, government, team*
   Her *family has produced many politicians.*
   Her *family have threatened to disown her.*
The plural is the normal choice with the names of football teams because they are regarded as a collection of individuals:
   Manchester United <u>are</u> coming to play here.
See the Website Reference A2.3 for more examples.

The relationship between nouns (as subjects) and verbs is called 'agreement'. It is discussed in more detail in A8.

The meaning of number

What is the difference in meaning between singular and plural? The answer seems to be simple: it is 'one' of something vs 'more than one'. But as we saw with collective nouns, it is often possible to see some things in two ways. And there are some nouns that seem to contradict this principle. Thus some plural nouns, such as scissors and trousers, are clearly referring to one item (although originally they were made of two parts). Section A8 deals with more cases where the issue of number is not so simple, where grammar and meaning are in 'disagreement'.

A2.3 The formation of plurals

Plurals are formed from the singular form of nouns. Most plurals are formed regularly by the addition of *-s* or *-es* in writing (and replacing a final *-y* after a consonant with *-ies*), and by the addition of /-s/, /-z/ or /-ɪz/ in speech. Here are some examples of regular plurals:

cat/cats	/-s/	*dog/dogs*	/-z/
story/stories	/-z/	*watch/watches*	/-ɪz/

Note that the written and spoken additions do not always coincide; *judges* only has *-s* in spelling to show the plural, but adds /-ɪz/ in pronunciation. The rules are explained in the Website Reference A2.4.

Irregular plurals

You probably already know that a few nouns have irregular plurals. 'Irregular' means that the form of the plural cannot be predicted from the singular. The most common are:

> *children* (from *child*), *feet* (*foot*), *men* (*man*), *mice* (*mouse*), *teeth* (*tooth*), *women* (*woman*)

Then there are a number of words referring to animals that have a 'zero' plural, for example *sheep*, *deer*. There are also a few nouns ending in *-f* or *-fe* which form their plural with *-ves* in writing, for example *knife*, *leaf*, *life*, *thief*, *wife*, *wolf*; in pronunciation the /-f/ changes to /-vz/. See the Website Reference A2.5 for more examples of all of these types.

Words borrowed from foreign languages (typically Latin, Greek and French) are another source of irregular plurals. Here are some examples (singular/plural):

- ❑ *criterion/criteria*
- ❑ *crisis/crises*
- ❑ *curriculum/curricula*
- ❑ *stimulus/stimuli*
- ❑ *chateau/chateaux*

See the Website Reference A2.6 for more coverage.

In addition there are a number of words that have two possible plurals, one regular and one irregular, for example *hoofs/hooves*. The Website Reference A2.7 has more examples.

Number does not only relate to nouns; it also affects pronouns (see B2) and verbs (see agreement in A8).

A2.4 The genitive

This is the other way in which nouns change their form; it is also called the 'possessive' form. The genitive is formed by adding *-'s* to the singular and an apostrophe to the plural:

(singular) *cat*	genitive:	*cat's*
(plural) *cats*	genitive:	*cats'*

The pronunciation of both is exactly the same as for the regular plural, and there are the same three possible pronunciations (see the Website Reference A2.4).

In many cases there is hesitation over whether to spell words as a genitive or plural (since the pronunciation is the same), especially if the head noun (see A3) is no longer mentioned, for example:

I'm going to the butcher's/butchers. (where *shop* is not mentioned)

And an apostrophe is sometimes used to mark an unusual plural form:

I've got no 10's but two 20's.

The genitive is really a feature of the noun phrase (see A3) rather than nouns. If the noun phrase has postmodification (that is, some words following which affect its meaning – see A3), or involves coordination (see A9), the ending is attached to the last noun:

the manager of the team's decision (the manager's decision, not the team's)

Will and Emma's car

Meaning and use of the genitive

The genitive is used to modify another noun; it is part of a noun phrase and has the same position and function as determiners (see B3):

Where's the cat's blue bowl?

Cats' paws suffer many injuries.

The meaning is often said to involve possession (*John's car*), but there are many other relationships that are shown (which is why 'genitive' is a better name than 'possessive').

Look at the following noun phrases and work out the relationship between the genitive and the following noun:

1. *Roger Federer's defeat*
2. *the man's death*
3. *John's sister*
4. *Mary's lover*
5. *the writer's reputation*
6. *the planet's atmosphere*

⭐ **Activity A2.5**

The genitive and 'of' phrases

The genitive is sometimes said to be equivalent to postmodification of a noun with an *of* phrase:

the man's death / the death of the man

but there are situations where both can sound strange:

the day's start (?) vs *the start of the day*

the car of John (?) vs *John's car*

There are a number of factors or tendencies that affect the choice. With animate nouns (that is, those referring to people or animals) the genitive is most common, as in the activity above, particularly when it is indicating an underlying subject (for example,

Peter's decision), but there are situations where it is used with inanimate nouns to refer to times and places, or to part/whole relationships:

> *next year's fashions, London's attractions, the table's surface*

The *of* construction is more common with long noun phrases:

> *the success of the youthful English cricket team* (rather than *the youthful English cricket team's success*)

Another use of the genitive is in a construction called the 'double genitive' where it is part of an *of* phrase:

> *He's a friend <u>of John's</u>.*

Compared to *He is John's friend*, this construction allows a determiner, usually *a*, to be added to the head noun, as in the example. (Of course, it is also possible to say *a friend of John*, without the genitive, but this sounds less idiomatic.)

A2.5 Common and proper nouns

We can make two important distinctions between types of noun. The first is between common and proper nouns. Common nouns make up the great majority of nouns in a language; they are the words we are mostly dealing with in this section and the rest of the book, for example all the nouns in Activities A2.2 and A2.3 above. Proper nouns are the 'names' of unique people, places, geographical features, organisations, and so on; they have no lexical meaning (and generally do not appear in dictionaries). In writing we can recognise proper nouns because they start with a capital letter, for example:

> *London, Leicester Square, Kilimanjaro, Microsoft, Congress, Fred Smith, India*

One formal feature is that they tend to appear with no determiner or modification, though actually *the* commonly precedes certain types of proper noun: rivers (*the Thames*), mountain ranges (*the Alps*) and so on (and is also capitalised in a few cases: *The Hague, The Times*). It is more accurate to say that proper nouns do not allow any contrast in determiners. However, there are situations where they are found with determiners or modification (or in the plural):

> *There are <u>two Mark Browns</u> in my class.*
> *They say he's <u>the next Maradona</u>.*
> *He remembered <u>an England of green fields and endless summers</u>.*

We say that these nouns have been converted into common nouns (even though the capital letter is retained).

A2.6 Count and noncount nouns

The second important distinction is between count and noncount nouns. A large number of nouns in English cannot have a plural or be preceded by *a*, for example:

> *advice, air, fun, luck, milk, weather*

You cannot say, for example, 'an advice' or 'two advices', 'a luck' or 'two lucks'. Nouns which can have a plural or a singular with *a* are called count nouns; they constitute the majority of nouns.

To some extent the grammar here follows logic. Nouns referring to things that are easily divisible into units are count; those that are conceived as a mass are noncount;

thus *water* is noncount while *river* and *lake* are count. There is also a tendency for count nouns to refer to concrete things (which we can see or feel), and noncount nouns to be abstract, but there are exceptions:

abstract count nouns: *idea, statement, thought, description*
concrete noncount nouns: *bread, butter, milk, money, sugar*

And some nouns are unexpectedly noncount, for example *advice* and *information*. This even applies to concrete nouns such as *furniture*; there is no plural 'furnitures' (see D2). Where it is necessary to count such noncount nouns, counting expressions can be used, for example, *a piece of* advice, *a loaf of* bread, two *items of* furniture.

Work out whether these nouns are count or noncount:
accident, dream, equipment, homework, ice, journey, programme, progress, travel

There are many nouns in English which can be both count and noncount. Section C2 deals with this.

VARIATION IN ENGLISH

In some varieties of English, certain nouns have a different count status. For example, *staff* can be a count noun so it is possible to say 'a staff', whereas in standard English you would say 'a member of staff'.

TERMINOLOGY

Why do we say (in scientific grammar) 'count' and 'noncount' rather than 'countable' and 'uncountable'? To illustrate this let's consider a riddle:

'What can be counted but also cannot be counted?' (a)

The answer is: 'money'. How is this possible? Well, in the general sense it is of course possible to count money. You can flick through a wad of notes saying '10 dollars, 20 dollars, 30 dollars', etc. But in the linguistic or grammatical sense it is not possible; you cannot say 'one money, two moneys' etc. The apparent paradox can be rephrased in this way:

'You can count money but you can't count money.' (b)

By using italics (or some other convention) to indicate a linguistic or lexical item we can make things clearer:

'You can count money but you can't count *money*.' (c)

But this would not be obvious in speech. And we need to realise that the two uses of the verb 'count' are very different. One has the ordinary, lexical meaning; the other has a technical meaning, in the sense of being able to make a word plural and/or put numbers and the indefinite article in front. If we now use an adjective instead of the verb we get:

'Money is countable but *money* is uncountable.' (d)

Now while this might be an acceptable statement in pedagogic grammar, we need to go one stage further to distinguish the two uses, and for this purpose we use special terms, 'count' and 'noncount', for the technical, grammatical meaning, while leaving 'countable' and 'uncountable' for normal use. Thus

'Money is countable but *money* is noncount.' (e)

Many terms are like this; when you are studying grammar (rather than learning about it in a language class) you need terms that are precise in meaning and distinctive in form.

Comments

Activity A2.1: there are seven: *noun, word, class, day, example, chocoholic, text*. If the repetitions are included, then 13 of the 44 words in the paragraph are nouns.

Activity A2.2: there are four which fit the definition: *bomb, carpet, teacher, tree*.

Activity A2.3: even though you do not know the meaning of *glob* in each case, you probably worked out that it is a noun in 1, 2 and 3. In 1 the evidence is that it has *two* in front and has an *-s* added (for plural) – points a) and b); in 2 the clue comes from the fact that is in the company of two other nouns, *embarrassment* and *anger* – point b). In 3 it is preceded by *a*, a determiner – point b). In 4 you probably realised that it is a verb, while in 5 it is not so easy to determine; it could be a noun or adjective, but none of the three tests works for it. So even the formal definition is not perfect.

Activity A2.4: all of these words exist in the singular but with different meanings that do not make sense here, or are unidiomatic.

Activity A2.5: as you can see, the genitive marks all sorts of relationships between two nouns, usually involving people. In 1 and 2 there is an underlying verbal relationship, where the genitive marks the object of an underlying verb ('someone defeated Federer') or the subject ('the man died'); or a personal relationship (3 and 4); or an associated feature or attribute (5 and 6).

Activity A2.6: *accident, dream, journey* and *programme* are count; the others are noncount. Note the difference between *journey* and *travel*, though they both refer to basically the same idea. There are other pairs of words like this, for example a *difficulty* and *trouble*.

A3 NOUN PHRASES AND DETERMINERS

A3.1 Noun phrases

In A2 we looked at nouns as a word class. But when we want to study texts and analyse sentences (for example, to identify subjects and objects), we need to recognise a larger unit: the noun phrase. A noun phrase is a noun and all the words that 'go' with it. It can consist of just a noun:

<u>Money</u> is bad for you.
<u>People</u> are strange.
<u>London</u> is a fantastic place.

And a pronoun can also function as a noun phrase:

<u>She</u> is my best friend.

But usually there is more than one word.

Noun phrases can consist of up to four parts, as in the diagram:

DETERMINER	PREMODIFIER	HEAD	POSTMODIFIER
all the	*tall*	*girls*	*with red hair*

Figure A3.1.1 The four parts of a noun phrase

The last three parts are dealt with below. Determiners, as a distinct word class, are given a fuller treatment afterwards.

Heads

The head is the central part of a noun phrase; it is the only part which is obligatory, though if it is a singular count noun, there must be a determiner with it: *a* table or *that* table, not simply 'table'. Heads are usually nouns, but can sometimes be adjectives (*the <u>poor</u>*); see B3. The head is the word that changes for number. It agrees with the determiner and any following verb (if the noun phrase is the subject).

Premodifiers

The function of premodifiers is to add information about the head noun; to 'modify' or limit its meaning. So the reference of *red roses* and *science students* is more restricted than that of *roses* and *students*.

Typically premodifiers consist of one or more adjectives:

<u>big</u> business; *<u>small</u> change*; *a <u>beautiful</u>, <u>red</u> dress* (see A4 for more on adjectives.)
However, nouns are also common:

a <u>newspaper</u> reporter; *a <u>paper</u> cutter*; *<u>climate</u> change*.
When a noun is used as a premodifier, it can be related to a noun phrase with a postmodifying prepositional phrase (see below under postmodification): *a reporter <u>for a newspaper</u>*.

Activity A3.1

> Look at the noun phrases below and say whether the underlined premodifiers are adjectives or nouns.
>
> 1. *<u>business</u> communication*
> 2. *(a) <u>summery</u> dress*
> 3. *(a) <u>car</u> driver*
> 4. *<u>modern</u> communication*
> 5. *(the) <u>summer</u> term*
> 6. *(a) <u>brown</u> <u>paper</u> bag*

There is no absolute limit to the number of premodifiers in one noun phrase:

the great big British breakfast tradition

It is also possible to show an object–verb relationship by using a hyphen in a compound premodifier:

a flesh-eating virus, a power-sharing agreement ('an agreement to share power')

But for more complex structural relationships with a noun phrase a postmodifier (see below) must be used.

 Activity A3.2

The phrase an English teacher is ambiguous. What are the two possible meanings, and how can you explain them in terms of premodification and different word classes?

 Activity A3.3

What is the difference between health food and healthy food?

Postmodifiers

The postmodifier position is where extensive and complex information about the head is given. It can consist of:

- a prepositional phrase (see A4): the woman in a long dress; a friend of the director
- an adjective phrase: a man capable of anything (see A4)
- a clause, especially a relative clause: a decision which was greeted with surprise (see B10)
- a non-finite clause: a memorial dedicated to the victims (see A10)
- an adverb: the first time around, a long way back

Postmodification with prepositional phrases is the most common type.

There is a special type of postmodification where the preposition is determined by the noun, and the prepositional phrase is seen as necessary to complete its meaning. Here are just a few examples:

I have great admiration for her.

This isn't the solution to our problem.

It affected his relationship with his children.

They expressed surprise at the announcement.

There is a widespread belief in reincarnation.

Such prepositional phrases are sometimes called 'complements'. Many such nouns are typically used with one particular preposition. For example, it would be strange to use a different preposition with belief. This use should not be confused with prepositional phrases that are independent of the noun (see adverbials in A8) e.g.

This is a widespread belief in government circles.

Complements are also found with adjectives (see A4) and can take the form of clauses rather than prepositional phrases (see A10).

TERMINOLOGY

In some approaches to English grammar the term 'complement' has a much wider interpretation.

Combinations involving more than one of the above types of postmodification are possible. In such cases noun phrases can become extremely long:

   . . . *a man <u>in a red overcoat who was holding a gun in his left hand</u>*.

Here the noun phrase, whose head is *man*, contains several other noun phrases: *a red overcoat*, *a gun*, and *his left hand*, all with their own head nouns. This is the concept of recursion. Sentences may be composed of very long noun phrases involving several instances of such recursion; we will see examples of this in C10.

   Another type of postmodification is 'apposition': this is where a noun phrase is placed next to another to show a relationship of identity. (Clauses can also be used in apposition to a noun phrase – see A10.) This is particularly common with a proper noun followed by a description or explanation of it:

   <u>Malcolm Fox</u>, <u>the boy's father</u>, was delighted.

   For almost a hundred years after her death, <u>Emma Hamilton</u> (1765–1815), <u>Nelson's celebrated mistress</u>, was airbrushed from the official record.

 Activity A3.4

Identify the head noun and postmodifier in the noun phrases below, all taken from this section. Remember that one way to identify a head is to pluralise (or 'singularise') a noun phrase if possible and to see which word changes.

1.   *postmodification with a particular preposition*
2.   *the following prepositional phrase*
3.   *a very inefficient and limiting system of communication*
4.   *very long noun phrases involving several instances of such recursion*

A3.2 Determiners

Determiners are a closed word class (see B1). They are words which come first in the noun phrase and which 'determine' the noun. By 'determine' we mean that they show what kind of reference the noun has; *<u>this</u> tree* (the one near me) as opposed to *<u>that</u> tree* (the one near you) or *a tree* (one you do not know about). The reason why they come first in the noun phrase is that they specify the most general features of nouns such as their nearness to the speaker/listener, their definiteness, their ownership, their quantity, etc.

   Determiners thus allow nouns to have a potentially unlimited number of referents, to be re-used continually. We could imagine a primitive people who live in a world where there are only proper nouns, where every object (not just the people and places) has to have its own name. Every time a new object is encountered a new noun is needed, even if it is, say, a stream just like the one near their cave; they would not be able to say 'Look, another stream'. This would be a very inefficient and limiting system of communication. Determiners are what make the difference between human language and such a system.

Activity A3.5

> Identify the determiners in the above paragraph. Look at the list of classes below if you are not sure.

Classes of determiners

Determiners can be divided into a number of separate sub-classes:

a) demonstratives: *this, that, these, those*
b) possessives: *my, your, his, her, its, our, their* (see B2)
c) articles: *the* (definite), *a/an* (indefinite) (see B3 for more about them)
d) interrogatives: *which, what, whose* (*Whose* money was stolen?) (see B9)
e) relatives: *whose* (the boy *whose* money was stolen) (See B10)
f) *wh-ever* words: *whatever, whichever* (*Whatever* choice you make will be wrong.)
g) quantifiers: *all, any, both, each, either, enough, every, few, little, much, many, no, several, some*
h) personal pronouns: *us, we, you* ('*you* people').

Activity A3.6

> Which of the above classes can also be pronouns? Which cannot?

It is not always easy to decide which words are determiners. There are several classes of words whose status as determiners is debatable, numerals (numbers) in particular. In fact, there are two classes of numerals:

a) the cardinal numerals: *one, two, three*, etc. These seem to be most like quantifiers (but precise ones as opposed to vague ones), since they can function as determiners (e.g. *two friends*) and pronouns (e.g. *two* (*of them*) *are coming*); compare this with *some*. They can also combine with definite determiners (*my two friends*) or have plural inflections like nouns: *They arrived in twos and threes.*
b) the ordinal numerals: *first, second, third*, etc. plus *next* and *last*. They are also preceded by definite determiners: *the second week* and can function as nouns: *A third of the class was missing.*

In other words, numerals are very hard to classify, and it may be best to put them in a separate word class.

We also need to bear in mind that the genitive of nouns (A2) occupies the same position in noun phrase structure as determiners, e.g. *John's money*.

The ordinal numerals look very similar to adjectives. The strongest argument for including them in determiners is that they can precede other determiners: *the first few weeks*. But there seems to be an adjective element to some other determiners as well, in that they

- ❏   have comparison: *fewer/fewest, less/least*
- ❏   can be modified by adverbs: *very few/many*
- ❏   and can appear (formally) as predicatives (see A8): *their excuses were many*

The division between adjectives and determiners is therefore not entirely clear in structural terms, just as that between pronouns and determiners is not clear in membership terms.

Some cases where two determiners occur together need to be treated as single determiners. This applies to *a few* and *a little*, as their grammar shows:

a few drinks (*a* is otherwise not possible before a plural head noun)

a little money (*a* is not possible before a noncount noun)

Many a is similar since it only precedes singular count nouns (not plurals): *many a battle*.

Number and agreement with nouns

With determiners it is important to know which type of noun they go with. Some pairs of quantifiers are distinguished according to whether they 'agree with' plural count or noncount nouns: *many chairs* vs *much furniture*, *few loaves* vs *little bread*. Demonstratives, on the other hand, have a straightforward singular/plural distinction: *this/that chair/furniture, these/those chairs*.

Some as a quantifier is used with both plural count and noncount nouns (*some coins, some money*), but it can also be used with singular count nouns:

Some woman was looking for you.

Here it is not a quantifier referring to a vague or unknown number or quantity, but indicating an unknown individual.

Some quantifiers are semantically plural but grammatically singular: *each, every, many a*. The distinction in meaning between *each, every* and *all* is particularly subtle. All three are used to refer to the total members of a group, but are different in their number agreement; *all* goes with plural nouns:

All children have fears.

Each/every child has fears.

Each tends to pick out each member of a group singly (and there may only be two), while *every* talks about them together (and there must be at least three):

I've marked all the exam papers. (as a whole)

I've marked almost every exam paper. (some idea of separate marking)

'I've marked almost each paper.' (not possible)

There are also structural differences; for example, *every* is one of the few determiners that cannot be used as a pronoun, while *all* can be used in front of other determiners: *all these arguments*.

See the exploration in C3 and the reading in D3 for more issues to do with determiners.

Comments

Activity A.3.1: 1, 3 and 5 are nouns, 2 and 4 are adjectives, while in 6 there are both. Note that an adjective premodifier comes before a noun premodifier. (By the way, in the phrase *adjective modifier*, the word *adjective* is actually a noun modifier!)

Activity A3.2: In one meaning *English* is an adjective premodifier, meaning someone from England. In the other *English* is a noun premodifier, meaning the language. The same ambiguity would be possible with many nationality/language words such as *German, French, Chinese*, which can all be nouns as well as adjectives.

Activity A3.3: The two look very similar and the meanings are similar, too, but there is a difference. *Healthy food* is food that has the quality of being good for you. It is gradable and comparable (see A4), so some food can be 'very healthy' or 'healthier'. *Health food*, however, is a type or class of food (designed to be good for health, but not necessarily so – 'health food' isn't always 'healthy food'). Some adjectives and all nouns used as premodifiers have this function of classifying, as opposed to expressing a quality. So, for example, a 'foreign' investor is distinct from a local one.

Activity A3.4: The head nouns are *postmodification, phrase, system* and *phrases*. Everything after them in 1, 3 and 4 constitutes the postmodifiers, which contain other noun phrases: *a particular preposition* in 1, *communication* in 3, and *several instances* and *such recursion* in 4. Note that the postmodifier consists of a prepositional phrase in 1 and 3 and a non-finite clause in 4 (*involving . . .*).

Activity A3.5: There are seven (not counting repetitions): *a, every, the, its, their, another* and *such*. There are also a number of noun phrases which have no determiner, for example *human language*.

Activity A3.6: The answer is that most can. As a result, it can be argued that determiners are not a separate word class. This issue is discussed at length in the article in D3 (in the section entitled 'Troubles for linguists').

A4   ADJECTIVES, ADVERBS AND PREPOSITIONS

In A2 we dealt with the most numerous word class, nouns, and in A3 with another word class closely connected with nouns: determiners. Here we will deal with three more word classes: adjectives, adverbs and prepositions. Other word classes are dealt with in B2 (pronouns), A5 (verbs), A6 (auxiliaries) and A9 (conjunctions).

A4.1 Adjectives

Adjectives are an open word class (see B1). In notional terms they are often said to refer to qualities and attributes. But we can argue that nouns also do this. Whether we say 'The mountain is <u>high</u>' or 'The <u>height</u> of the mountain . . .' we are talking about an attribute of the mountain.

> Identify the adjectives in this sentence, noting the criteria you used:
> *No other nation can produce a book collector on quite the heroic scale of Sir Thomas Philips, who amassed the greatest private library the world has ever seen.*

 Activity A4.1

As usual, we must turn to formal characteristics for a useful, applicable definition. A word is an adjective if it meets all or some of the following conditions:

- ❑ it can be used as a premodifier in noun phrases: *a <u>red</u> car*. This is called the 'attributive' use of adjectives
- ❑ it can be used as a subject and object predicative (see A8): *Her car is <u>red</u>. I painted it <u>red</u>*. This is called the 'predicative' use of adjectives
- ❑ it has comparative and superlative forms: *happier/happiest*
- ❑ it is gradable: *very happy*
- ❑ it occurs in postmodification: after indefinite pronouns (e.g. *something <u>red</u>, nothing <u>interesting</u>*), with certain adjectives (e.g. *the only information <u>available</u>*), and in special phrases (e.g. *the president <u>elect</u>*).
- ❑ (rarely) it is the head of a noun phrase after the definite article: *the <u>poor</u>* (see the Website Reference A3.1 for more adjectives used in this way).

Of these it is the first four characteristics that are most important in recognising adjectives. These are discussed in pairs below.

Attributive vs predicative

Most adjectives can be used in both positions, e.g. *It's <u>good</u> food* (attributive) and *This food tastes <u>good</u>* (predicative). However, a number of adjectives only occur as premodifiers of nouns, e.g. *an <u>utter</u> fool, the <u>chief</u> troublemaker, my <u>former</u> boss, a <u>lone</u> traveller*. You cannot say 'my boss is former'. These are called attributive adjectives. And some only occur after verbs such as *be*, e.g. *afraid, asleep, unwell*, e.g. *She's unwell*, not 'she's an unwell person'. These are called predicative adjectives. (See the Website Reference A4.1 and A4.2 for more adjectives used in these ways.)

Predicative adjectives tend to refer to situations that are not lasting, whereas attributive adjectives refer to more permanent characteristics. This explains why you cannot talk about 'an unwell person' or 'an afraid person'; but you can say *a sick person* or *a frightened person*.

Sometimes an adjective which can be used in both positions may change its meaning:

Attributive: *My old friend . . .* (referring to the length of the friendship) vs
Predicative: *My friend is old.* (referring to someone's age)
Attributive: *My late husband . . .* (he's dead) vs
Predicative: *My husband is late.*

Gradability and the comparison of adjectives

Many adjectives are 'gradable'; that is, the 'quality' they refer to can have different degrees, and so they can be used with a wide range of adverbs that are sometimes called 'intensifiers', such as *very, quite, rather, fairly, pretty, so, too, how, incredibly, completely*:

very happy, too expensive, how big

One such adverb is placed after the adjective: *happy <u>enough</u>.*

One very obvious feature of some adjectives is that they can change their form, like nouns and verbs; they have special endings, or inflections. The two forms that we are talking about here are the comparative and superlative, for example:

basic form: *tall*
comparative: *taller*
superlative: *tallest*

The inflections *-er* and *-est* are added to the end (or *-r* and *-st*, if the word already ends in *-e*, and *-ier* or *-iest* to replace a final *-y* if preceded by a consonant). This changing of form is known as the 'comparison' of adjectives.

Not all adjectives have inflectional comparison; many, generally longer adjectives have 'phrasal' comparison (i.e. more than one word), using *more* and *most* as adverbs to modify them:

basic form: *beautiful*
comparative: *more beautiful*
superlative: *most beautiful*

The rule that is usually given for deciding between the two possibilities is as follows:

❑ one-syllable adjectives have inflectional comparison, as with *tall*
❑ adjectives with three (or more) syllables have phrasal comparison, as with *beautiful*
❑ two-syllable adjectives are variable; those ending in *-y, -ow, -er, -ere, -ure* may inflect (*wealthier, shallower, cleverer, sincerer, securer*), but they can also have phrasal comparison. This choice also applies to a number of other two-syllable adjectives (*politer/more polite*), otherwise phrasal comparison is the norm.

Section C4 investigates this in some detail and finds that these 'rules' often do not apply. For example, some one-syllable adjectives can have phrasal comparison and some three-syllable adjectives can have inflectional comparison.

Two adjectives have irregular forms for comparison: *good* (*better, best*) and *bad* (*worse, worst*). Two others have irregular alternatives to the regular forms: *far* (*farther/ further, farthest/furthest*) and *old* (*older/elder, oldest/eldest*).

The comparison and gradability of adjectives are related. Obviously, if we can talk about a quality that has different degrees (*very large, quite large*) then we can also use it in comparisons (*larger*). Some adjectives, however, have one but not the other (see, for example, *glad* in Activity A4.2 below); and many adjectives, e.g. *electric*, *national*, have neither possibility.

Two types of adjective that are particularly noteworthy are *-ed* and *-ing* adjectives:

an <u>interesting</u> story

a <u>bored</u> listener

These are derived from the equivalent participles (see A5), but we can tell they are adjectives first by their attributive position and by the fact that they may be gradable (*very interesting*) and can have comparison (*more interesting*).

The meaning of comparative and superlative forms

The three forms of adjectives are often introduced in teaching materials with a picture of three children or buildings, or trees, as in this diagram:

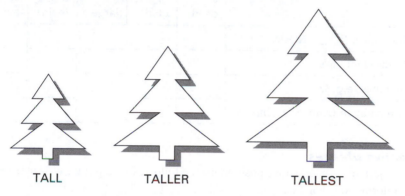

TALL   TALLER   TALLEST

Figure A4.1.1 The meaning of comparatives and superlatives 1

This may give the impression that they describe three different degrees of tallness, but this would be incorrect. The meaning of *tall* is established in <u>absolute</u> terms, whereas *taller* and *tallest* are established <u>relatively</u>. Thus it is perfectly possible to be 'taller' or 'tallest', but not 'tall', as these examples show.

She's <u>taller</u> than him, but I wouldn't say she's <u>tall</u>.

He's the <u>tallest</u> in his class, but I wouldn't say he's <u>tall</u>.

So this diagram is also accurate:

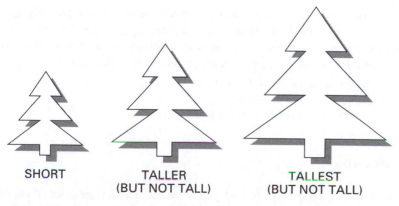

SHORT   TALLER   TALLEST
           (BUT NOT TALL)   (BUT NOT TALL)

Figure A4.1.2 The meaning of comparatives and superlatives 2

We should not forget that there are other ways of making comparisons using adjectives: . . . *(not) as tall as* . . . , . . . *less tall than* . . . , . . . *least tall* . . .

Activity A4.2 ✪

> How 'adjectival' are these adjectives? Look at the adjectives in the table below and put a tick where the property applies. Use your intuitions (or a dictionary).

Table A4.1.1 How 'adjectival' are adjectives?

	a. dead	b. glad	c. large	d. main	e. aware
1. Attributive: 'a ____ NOUN'					
2. Predicative: 'he's ____'					
3. Gradable: e.g. 'very ____'					
4. Comparative (with *-er* or *more*)					

Adjective phrases

Many adjectives in predicative position can be followed by a phrase or clause to give more information. For example:

> I'm <u>happy</u> <u>for you</u>.
> I'm <u>happy</u> <u>that he's finally found someone</u>.

And some have to be:

> I'm <u>fond</u> <u>of her</u>. (Not 'I'm fond.')
> They're <u>unable</u> <u>to come</u>.

These phrases or clauses which complete the meaning of the adjective are sometimes called 'complements'. (See A3 and A10 for more on complements.) Many adjectives are typically associated with a particular preposition in such phrases, e.g., *fond of* or *dependent on*.

Adjective phrases can also occur as postmodifiers of nouns: *a plan <u>bound to fail</u>*. Such cases can be related to a relative clause (*a plan <u>which is bound to fail</u>* – see B10).

Adjective phrases are also common with comparatives and intensifiers to give more information about the basis of comparison or 'intensification'.

> She's <u>happier than she has ever been</u>.
> We're <u>as happy as it's possible to be</u>.
> The difference is <u>too small to worry about</u>.

A4.2 Adverbs

Adverbs are an open word class (see B1). They consist of a number of sub-classes, some of which are only loosely connected to the others (for example, the intensifiers described above). They have been called a 'ragbag' – a place for putting unwanted things. Isolated systems of words, such as *yes* and *no*, *please*, and *not*, are usually included in adverbs, though they have little in common with them. As a result they are much harder to define than other word classes.

Traditionally adverbs have been thought of as words derived by the addition of -*ly* to adjectives that modify the meaning of verbs in terms of their manner, time and place. However, there is a vast range of meanings conveyed by adverbs, and not all of them modify verbs. We have already seen one such case: intensifiers, used to modify adjectives: *very happy*. And a lot of adverbs, even those to do with manner, time and place, do not end in -*ly*.

Put your hands <u>together</u>.

I <u>soon</u> realised he wasn't coming.

Put the money <u>there</u>.

⭐ **Activity A4.3**

Identify the adverbs in these sentences:

1. *Have they arrived yet?*
2. *Even my mother likes her slightly.*
3. *He's not quite ready.*
4. *I was only looking at it.*

Form and function

As regards their form, unlike the other three open word classes (nouns, adjectives, verbs), adverbs do not have any inflections that can be used to identify them, apart from a few endings of limited application, such as -*wards* (e.g. *afterwards*), -*ways* (e.g. *sideways*) and -*wise* (e.g. *lengthwise*). The -*ly* inflection is not a reliable indicator, partly because, as mentioned, many adverbs do not end in -*ly*, but also because many words ending in -*ly* are adjectives, for example:

costly, daily, deadly, friendly, kindly, kingly, likely, lively, lonely, lovely, ugly, weekly

These do not add -*ly* to form adverbs; you cannot say 'she spoke lovelily/friendlily'.

In addition, there are some adverbs that have the same form as adjectives, for example, *late, early, fast, straight, dead*:

We arrived late. It's dead easy.

Just as with the corresponding adjective, these may form comparatives and superlatives where appropriate with -*er* and -*est*:

He arrived later/earlier than expected.

Otherwise comparison is formed using *more* and *most*: *more politely*.

We should also note that there are some '-ly' adverbs that are not related in meaning to adjectives even though they appear to be, e.g. *hardly, lately, largely*:

I hardly know him.

Since adverbs do not have any distinctive morphological features, we need to refer to their structural role for identification. Adverbs have two main grammatical functions:

❑ as the modifier of another word, as we saw above with intensifiers, e.g. of adjectives (*He's very happy. He's a very happy man.*), other adverbs (e.g. *very quickly, only now*) or pronouns and noun phrases (e.g. *They won't like it, especially her*).

❑ as the adverbial element in a clause: *We walked slowly.* See A8 for more on adverbials, especially their position in the sentence.

Activity A4.4

> Write two sentences for each of the following words, one where they are adverbs and one where they are adjectives: *harder, kindly, later, fast, well.*

NON-STANDARD FORMS

In non-standard usage, particularly American, some 'adjectives' are used as adverbs; in some cases the '-ly' adverb would not be an appropriate alternative. Here are some examples:

> *That's real cool.* (*Really cool* is also possible.)
> *He's doing fine.* (*Finely* would sound strange.)
> *We clean forgot.* (= 'completely'; *cleanly* would not be possible.)
> *Take it easy.* (In this fixed expression *easily* would sound strange.)
> *They guessed right.* (*Correctly* would be similar in meaning, but not *rightly*.)

Section B4 deals with different types of adverb; another type, adverb particles, is dealt with in B7.

A4.3 Prepositions

Prepositions are a closed word class (see B1). Although the name suggests that they are placed in front of something (i.e. noun phrases), their actual grammatical function is to relate two parts of a phrase or clause together, usually

❑ a verb and a noun phrase (*Look at the bus*)
❑ a noun phrase inside another noun phrase (*the man in the leather jacket*)
❑ an adjective and a noun phrase (*afraid of snakes*)

With the following noun phrase they constitute prepositional phrases, which play an important part as adverbials in clause structure (see A8): *They sat on the floor.*

They are generally thought of as 'little' words, and they supply many of the function words that make grammar possible, such as *of* and *to* (see A1 and D1). However, not all of them are 'little', e.g. *concerning, throughout.* And it is convenient to recognise phrasal prepositions (not to be confused with prepositional phrases); that is, prepositions consisting of more than one word, such as *according to, in front of, on top of, in spite of.*

The basic meanings of prepositions are to do with time and space. For example, we can identify the following basic spatial meanings for these three common prepositions:

- ❏ *on* is to do with a surface: *The picture is <u>on</u> the wall.*
- ❏ *in* is to do with an area or volume (or the idea of containment): *He's <u>in</u> Canton.*
- ❏ *at* is to do with a point: *She's <u>at</u> Canton.* (= the airport, or station).

See David Lee's paper in D4 on these three prepositions and how they indicate spatial relationships. However, many other meaning relationships are possible: causation, means, purpose, benefit, etc. One preposition may have many of these different ideas, as the next activity shows.

⭐ **Activity A4.5**

Match the following sentences with the meanings of *for*:

a)	*I did it <u>for</u> her.*	1)	support
b)	*He was fined <u>for</u> speeding.*	2)	purpose
c)	*They're <u>for</u> the government.*	3)	cause
d)	*He's the Member of Parliament <u>for</u> Oldham.*	4)	period of time
e)	*She writes <u>for</u> a magazine.*	5)	benefit
f)	*Knives are <u>for</u> cutting.*	6)	representing
g)	*We stayed <u>for</u> a week.*	7)	occupation

Comments

Activity A4.1: There are three: *heroic, greatest, private*. You probably know these words already, but the position of all of them in front of nouns, as well as the ending on *greatest*, would have helped. Note that one, *private*, can also be a noun, and that *book*, although it is a premodifier, is actually a noun. *Other* is classified as an adjective by some grammarians but is best treated as a postdeterminer (see A3).

Activity A4.2: There is not a hard and fast answer for all of the boxes, and some people may disagree; some suggestions are below. In 1b, *glad* may occur in the attributive position in a few expressions (*glad rags, glad tidings*) but generally it is not possible ('a glad day'); it is a predicative adjective (unlike *happy*). And many people would not agree that *dead* is gradable; see C4 for more on this. The borderline between attributive and predicative adjectives is not always clear. *Aware* is definitely predicative but can it be used attributively? Can you say *he's an aware person*? Similar uncertainty applies to *key*, which used to be attributive only (*a key decision*) but can now be heard predicatively (*That decision was key*). So this factor may change over time.

We should note that gradability and comparison are not always the same, e.g. for *glad*: *I'm very glad* but *I'm more glad/gladder than I was* (?)

We can conclude that some words are more 'adjectival' than others. A word such as *large* is said to be a 'prototypical' (or core) adjective because it has all the features, while *main* would be a 'peripheral' adjective.

Table A4.3.1 How 'adjectival' are adjectives? Suggested answers

	a. dead	b. glad	c. large	d. main	e. aware
1. Attributive: 'a ___ NOUN'	/	x?	/	/	?
2. Predicative: 'he's ___'	/	/	/	x	/
3. Gradable: e.g. 'very ___'	?	/	/	x	/
4. Comparative: with *-er* or 'more'	?	?	/	x	/

Activity A4.3: The adverbs are *yet* in 1, *even* and *slightly* in 2, *not* and *quite* in 3, and *only* in 4.

Activity A4.4: Here are some possible answers, adverbs preceding adjectives:
   He works harder than anyone. / This is a harder problem than the others.
   Would you kindly leave the door open? (= please) / She has a kindly face.
   Ask me that later, please. / We'll take the later ferry.
   She runs fast. / She's a fast runner.
   He acted his part well. / I don't feel well.

Activity A4.5: The links are a5, b3, c1, d6, e7, f2 and g4.

VERBS AND THEIR FORMS

Verbs are an open word class (see B1). In terms of grammar (rather than lexis) they are the most important word class because they are the central element in clauses (see A7); each full clause must have a verb, and they determine what other elements will be present. In this book, auxiliary verbs are treated as a separate word class ('auxiliaries') as they are a closed class (see A6). It is main (or lexical) verbs that are the topic of this section.

   Traditionally, verbs are said typically to denote actions. There are two problems with this. First, nouns such as *running, singing, fight* or *laughter* also denote or imply actions. Second, many verbs are not to do with actions. They can also be to do with events, processes, states, relationships, and so on:
   The building <u>collapsed</u>.
   It <u>snowed</u> yesterday.
   I <u>want</u> some chocolate.
   I <u>have</u> three sisters
In other words, verbs do not just denote actions.

> **Activity A5.1**
>
> Identify the verb forms in the paragraph above beginning 'Traditionally . . .'. Don't worry about repetitions.

As regards formal features, verbs can be recognised by the following characteristics:

❑ they inflect for tense, for the third-person singular, and for the -*ing* and -*ed* participles
❑ they agree with, and usually follow, the subject when there is no auxiliary ('agreement' – see A8)
❑ they form verb phrases, either on their own or in combination with auxiliaries, where they represent the 'head' (see A6)
❑ they precede objects

It is the first point, their inflections, that is of interest in this section.

A5.1 Verb forms

Verbs have fairly extensive inflectional morphology; they have more possible regular variations than either nouns or adjectives. In addition there is much more irregularity. Verbs can have between three and eight different forms (or parts).

> **Activity A5.2**
>
> Can you guess which verb has the most forms? Can you list the forms and label them?

TERMINOLOGY

Two of the labels above may have surprised you. Instead of '-*ing* participle' and '-*ed* participle' you may be familiar with 'present participle' and 'past participle'. However, I have dropped these terms because there is nothing 'present' or 'past' about the forms they represent. The present and past nature of verb phrases is conveyed by the tense forms, not by the participles. Even though '-*ed* participle' is not entirely accurate (because not all such forms are formed with -*ed*), it is still a better label.

Regular and irregular verbs

There is an important distinction between 'regular' and 'irregular' verbs. Regular verbs have four forms; if the basic form is known, the other three can be predicted from it. These three are:

❑ the third person singular, which is formed by adding -*s* or -*es* to the basic form (see B2 for a discussion of person);

❑ the *-ing* participle, which is formed by adding *-ing* (and deleting silent *e*);
❑ the past tense and *-ed* participle, which have the same form, namely with the addition of *-ed* or *-d*.

See the Website Reference A5.1 and A5.2 for the rules governing the spelling and pronunciation of regular verb forms.

The table below shows the forms of one typical regular verb, *like*, with those of one irregular verb, *know*, as well as those for *be*, for comparison.

Table A5.1.1 Forms of regular and irregular verbs

	REGULAR	IRREGULAR	'BE'
a) basic form: infinitive	*like*	*know*	*be*
present			*am, are*
b) 3rd person singular *-s* present	*likes*	*knows*	*is*
c) past	*liked*	*knew*	*was, were*
d) *-ing* participle	*liking*	*knowing*	*being*
e) *-ed* participle	*liked*	*known*	*been*

Irregular verbs have between three and five forms (and eight in the case of *be*). The third person singular and *-ing* participle are predictable, as with regular verbs. However, the forms of the past tense (usually) and *-ed* participle (always) are not predictable. This explains why we have to list three forms when trying to remember how to use irregular verbs. Here are a few examples:

basic form	past tense	*-ed* participle
see	*saw*	*seen*
go	*went*	*gone*
fly	*flew*	*flown*
buy	*bought*	*bought*
show	*showed*	*shown* (or *showed*)

There are about 150 irregular verbs in English (more, if we count archaic forms). Some are them are rare (e.g. *forsake, forsook, forsaken*), but many of them are very common, such as those above. A list is given in the Website Reference section.

There are a number of ways to make some sense out of this irregularity. If we divide up the verbs according to the differences between the basic form, past tense and *-ed* participle, there are five patterns:

A. where all three forms are the same:
    put, put, put
    spread, spread, spread
    This occurs with some verbs ending in /d/ or /t/.
B. where the base and the past tense are the same. This is very rare.

C. where the base and *-ed* participle are the same:
> *come, came, come*
> This is quite rare.
D. where the past tense and *-ed* participle are the same
> *have, had, had*
> *find, found, found*
> *lead, led, led*

Note that the two forms, though the same, are not predictable from the basic form. This type of irregular verb is very common.
E. where all three forms are different
> *drink, drank, drunk*
> *speak, spoke, spoken*
> *blow, blew, blown*

As exemplified by types A and D above, the past tense and *-ed* participle forms of most irregular verbs are the same.

Another way to categorise irregular verbs is according to vowel changes, for example:

> *swim, swam, swum*
> *sing, sang, sung*
> *sink, sank, sunk*

but this is limited, and there are verbs which look deceptively similar: *swing, swung* (not *swang*), *swung*.

Some verbs vary between regularity and irregularity. Thus *speed* has the regular form *speeded* for both past tense and *-ed* participle as well as *sped*; *spill* likewise has both *spilt* and *spilled* and *leap* has *leaped* and *leapt*. Such verbs are all indicated in the Website Reference section.

VARIATION IN ENGLISH

Gotten is preferred in American English to the British English *got* as the past participle of *get*.

A5.2 Finite forms vs non-finite forms

We make one basic distinction between verb forms: between 'finite' (or 'tensed') forms and 'non-finite' (or 'non-tensed') forms. The three finite forms are the present, third person singular *-s* and past tense forms; they are the ones to do with tense.

The three non-finite forms are the infinitive, and *-ing* and *-ed* participles. (There are four if we distinguish the bare infinitive from the *to* infinitive, e.g. *love* and *to love*.) The reason for distinguishing them is that non-finite forms cannot make a verb phrase on their own (see A6); they are 'unfinished' and need a finite form to complete them. Finite (complete) forms, by contrast, may stand on their own. Since tense is an obligatory choice in English, all verb phrases must be either present or past.

So, although the present and infinitive have the same form (except in the case of *be*), it is important to distinguish them. For example, the two following sentences seem to be identical apart from the addition of *will*:

a)   *I have it*
b)   *I will have it*

But in fact what is really happening is that one finite form in a), the present tense *have*, is being replaced by another, *will*, in b), and it is the non-finite infinitive, *have*, in b) that is being added. See C5 for another example of this.

This distinction will be important when we discuss verb phrases in A6 and clauses in later sections.

A5.3 The 'future tense'

Activity A5.3 ✪	So far we have seen two tenses: past and present. How many other tenses are there in English?

Activity A5.4 ✪	Look at the verb forms below. Which refer to future time? What is the difference in meaning between them? (i.e. what meaning do they have in addition to 'future'?) 1. You <u>will do</u> as you are told. 2. The train <u>leaves</u> in 15 minutes. 3. I'm <u>seeing</u> him tonight. I'<u>ll tell</u> him then. 4. They'<u>re going</u> to sell their house. 5. (knock on door) That'<u>ll</u> be Yoyo.

Not all of the forms above exclusively refer to the future. If we say *it's raining* or *it rains* then the time reference is normally present or general. If we compare *it's going to rain* with *it'll rain*, in the latter, there is a personal element involved: promise or prediction, while the former suggests the speaker is looking at dark clouds.

So we can offer the following reasons why there is no future tense in English:

❏   tense in English (present/past) is marked by inflections; if we wanted to 'invent' a future tense we would need to take *-ll* and attach it to the end of verbs: 'it rain'll'
❏   *will* and *shall* grammatically belong with the modal auxiliaries (see B6)
❏   *will* doesn't always refer to future time, and when it does, there is always another meaning, e.g. prediction, command or promise
❏   though *will* is very frequent, other forms have as good a claim to be a future tense, e.g. *be going to*. (See the reading in D5.)

Thus there are various ways of referring to future time in English, but nothing that can reasonably be called a future tense. And if *will* is not a marker of the future tense, then *would* is not a marker of a conditional tense. So what we are left with is two tenses: past and present.

A5.4 Other verb forms

There are two other (finite) verb forms that you need to be familiar with: the imperative and the subjunctive. The imperative (e.g. <u>*Sit down!*</u>) is identical in form with the infinitive; it is explained in B9.

The subjunctive is the name given to certain 'unexpected' finite verb forms which are the remnants of a once extensive system in English. It is found nowadays only in a few situations:

❑ after conjunctions such as *if, if only* and *as though*, and the verb *wish*, to express a hypothetical idea:
> *If I <u>were</u> rich . . .*
> *It's as though he <u>were</u> looking for trouble.*

This is a formal use. The expected form, *was*, is also possible.

❑ after certain verbs, such as *recommend, suggest, advise*, and after adjectives such as *important*, to suggest a future 'desired' state or action (the 'mandative' subjunctive):
> *I suggest he <u>leave</u> immediately.* (instead of the expected *leaves*, which is also possible)
> *It is important that you <u>be</u> there on time.* (instead of *are*, which is also possible)

This is also formal.

❑ in certain fixed phrases expressing wishes:
> *God <u>save</u> the Queen. Long <u>live</u> the King.*

Except for the verb *be*, the subjunctive is only noticeable in the third person singular, where the *-s* ending is not used. With *be*, the present subjunctive is the same for all persons ('be'), as is the past subjunctive ('were').

Comments

Activity A5.1: The forms are: *are*, said, denote, are, denote, imply, are, (to) do, can*, be, (to) do.* Those marked with an asterisk are auxiliaries.

Activity A5.2: The verb is *be*. The eight forms are:

be	infinitive
am, are, is	present tense forms
was, were	past tense forms
being	*-ing* participle
been	*-ed* participle

As can be seen, *be* makes several distinctions in present and past tense forms that other verbs do not make.

Activity A5.3: The answer is 'none'. You may have come to a total of eight, twelve, or even sixteen forms (if the 'conditional' is known to you), but English basically has only two tenses: present and past. You may have suggested 'perfect' and 'continuous' forms, and in pedagogic terms it is acceptable to talk about the 'present perfect' or 'past continuous' <u>tenses</u>. But in scientific grammar the ideas of perfect and continuous are covered by another concept, 'aspect', which is dealt with formally in A6 and semantically in B5.

What may surprise you most is to be told that there is no future tense in English. The claim that there is a future tense in English is based on a 'fallacy' (a fundamentally incorrect belief), that time and tense are equivalent, that because there are past, present and future 'times', there should be past, present and future 'tenses'. Time is a notional category; tense is a grammatical, linguistic category. There is no one-to-one relationship between the two. For one thing, the future is very different from the past and present, in that it is not certain, which means that when we refer to the future we are involving other ideas, such as predictions, promises or plans, rather than facts.

Activity A5.4: All of the underlined verb forms refer to the future apart from *-ll* in 5, which indicates a current deduction, based on the evidence of the knock on the door (and perhaps Yoyo's known propensity for lateness). In 1 *will* has the idea of an order; in 2 the present tense refers to a future event in a fixed schedule; in 3 the present continuous suggests a current plan or arrangement for the future, while *-ll* has the idea of a promise. In 4 the selling of the house is made to seem a matter of course.

A6   AUXILIARIES AND THE VERB PHRASE

In A5 we looked at verb forms. But, as with nouns and noun phrases, there is a larger unit that we need to recognise when looking at the organisation of clauses and sentences: the verb phrase. Similar to noun phrases, verb phrases consist of a verb and all the other words that 'go with it'. But in this case, the words that can 'go with' verbs are limited to the auxiliaries (with the possible exception of adverb particles – see B7), and the length of verb phrases is strictly limited.

The major difference between tense and aspect (see B5 for their meanings) is that tense is only morphological in nature (i.e. it affects the form of words), while aspect is formed with the use of extra words – the auxiliaries.

A6.1 Auxiliaries

Auxiliaries are a closed word class. They can be divided into two sub-classes:

❑ modal auxiliaries: *will, would, shall, should, may, might, can, could, must*. They are
   discussed at length in B6
❑ primary auxiliaries: *be, have, do.*

The primary auxiliaries are also main verbs, and like them (but unlike the modals) have a full set of verb forms, as described in A5. The use of *do* as a primary auxiliary in the formation of negatives is dealt with in A7. The rest of this section is concerned with the use of *be* and *have* in the construction of verb phrases involving aspect and the passive.

A6.2 Verb phrase structure

Verb phrases are composed of a verb and up to four auxiliaries. The auxiliaries are all optional; only the main verb element – equivalent to the head of noun phrases – is obligatory (except in the case of ellipsis – see B11).

   They sang.
   They are singing.
   They have sung.
   It is sung.

The primary auxiliaries *be* and *have*, in conjunction with the participles, are used to form the three aspects (perfect, progressive and perfect progressive) as well as the passive forms of verbs.

   Verb phrases in English may seem very chaotic, but in fact they are constructed according to a very systematic set of principles. In order to construct correct verb phrases, you need to know three things:

1. The forms needed for each verb phrase; thus
        have + *-ed* participle for the perfect aspect
        be + *-ing* participle for the progressive aspect
        be + *-ed* participle for the passive
2. The order of the auxiliary elements:
        MODAL then PERFECT then PROGRESSIVE then PASSIVE
3. The principle of 'jumping endings', by which the participle ending is placed not with its own auxiliary but with the following auxiliary or main verb; it 'jumps over'. For example, the (present) perfect of *look* is formed by the use of *have* plus the *-ed* participle. But we do not say 'I had look' (with the *-ed* participle of *had*); rather we say *I have looked*, where the *-ed* participle has jumped to the end of *look*.

Here is a table showing these three principles at work to form the most complex verb phrase, consisting of four auxiliaries plus verb: for example, *will have been being sung* (This, by the way, is very rare; most verb phrases are simpler.) Note how the participle endings have all jumped over the following auxiliary or verb.

Table A6.2.1 Verb phrase structure

	MODAL (auxiliary 1)	PERFECT (auxiliary 2)	PROGRESSIVE (auxiliary 3)	PASSIVE (auxiliary 4)	main verb
		have + -ed	*be + -ing*	*be + -ed*	
example	*will*	*have*	*been*	*being*	*sung*
verb form		*= infinitive*	*= -ed participle*	*= -ing participle*	*= -ed participle*
finiteness	finite	non-finite	non-finite	non-finite	non-finite

We should note the confusing nature of English here: the fact that *be* potentially appears twice in verb phrase structure, as does the *-ed* participle. In speech there is also the fact that *been done* sounds like *being done*. In addition, the primary auxiliaries are often contracted, which can lead to further confusion (see A7).

We can use these three principles to understand why certain verb phrases are incorrectly constructed. Let's take an example: 'They are been found.' You can tell that this is wrong, but why? Let's analyse the text:

TEST:	*are*	*been*	*found*
FORMED BY:	*be* + present	*be* + *-ed*	*find* + *-ed*
ENDINGS UNJUMPED:	*be* + *-ed*	*be* + *-ed*	*find*
REPRESENTS:	PASSIVE	PASSIVE	VERB

Figure A6.2.1 Analysis of incorrect verb phrase structure 1

The problem, then, with this verb phrase is that it consists of a double passive.

> Look at the three sentences below. Two are incorrect and one is correct. Say which one is correct and explain why the other two are incorrect using the above principles of verb phrase structure.
>
> a) *They have being found.*
> b) *They have been being found.*
> c) *They are having found.*

A6.3 Verb phrase combinations

In A5 the question 'How many tenses are there in English?' was posed, with the perhaps surprising answer '2'. If we rephrase the question as 'How many verb phrase combinations are there in English?' we get the following calculation:

2 (for the (simple) tenses) × 2 (for the progressive) × 2 (for the perfect) = 8
(excluding modals and passives)

For example, for the verb *see* (using *he* as subject) we have the following possibilities:

he sees (present simple)   *he is seeing* (present progressive)
he has seen (present perfect)   *he has been seeing* (present perfect progressive)
he saw (past simple)   *he was seeing* (past progressive)
he had seen (past perfect)   *he had been seeing* (past perfect progressive)

The first form in the above verb phrases is the finite one: the one that shows the tense and person, regardless of whether it is a verb or auxiliary (see A5).

If we include passives, then the number of verb phrase combinations doubles to sixteen.

  Activity A6.2

Supply the following verb phrase forms for the verb 'take'. Use 'he' as subject.

1.   *present (simple) passive:*
2.   *present progressive passive:*
3.   *present perfect passive:*
4.   *present perfect progressive passive:*
5.   *past (simple) passive:*
6.   *past progressive passive:*
7.   *past perfect passive:*
8.   *past perfect progressive passive:*

Activity A6.3

Name the verb phrase forms in the sentences below. Use the following formula (brackets show the optional elements):

PRESENT or PAST, (PERFECT), (PROGRESSIVE), (PASSIVE)

1.   *They have been laughing.*
2.   *We are being laughed at.*
3.   *They had been being laughed at.*
4.   *I have never laughed so much.*
5.   *You were laughing all the time.*
6.   *We are been laughing.*

A6.4 The passive voice

All verbs can have perfect forms, and all verbs (with some restrictions – see the discussion of stative verbs in B5) can have progressive forms. But not all verbs can have passive forms. This is because they need to be transitive, with an object. Transitivity is examined more fully in C6 as a characteristic of verbs.

Intransitive verbs such as *happen* have no object and cannot have a passive: 'It was happened to me'. A few transitive verbs such as *have* and *cost* do not normally have a passive: 'Two cars are had by him.' 'Ten dollars are cost by the ticket.'

Some verbs are very common in the passive, for example:

It was <u>alleged</u>/<u>claimed</u> that . . .

Be born (*I was born in 1964*) only occurs in the passive.

The passive is formed from its counterpart 'active' sentence by making the object into the subject, transforming the verb as shown above, and expressing the original subject (if needed) in a prepositional phrase beginning with *by*:

Shakespeare wrote Macbeth. (active)

<u>Macbeth</u> <u>was written</u> <u>by Shakespeare</u>. (passive)

Passives can be 'reduced' so that only the *-ed* participle remains in a 'non-finite' or 'participle' clause (see A10), for example:

It sounds reasonable, <u>put</u> like that.

If <u>noticed</u>, it will cause trouble.

If we paraphrase we can see the hidden passives: . . . *when it <u>is put</u> like that; If <u>it is</u> noticed*. See C5 for more on reduced passives.

There are three reasons for using the passive:

- ❏ so that the original subject does not have to be mentioned, either because it is known, or obvious from the context, or thought undesirable to mention, e.g.:

  He's been arrested (by the police presumably)

  In fact, most passives do not have a *by* phrase.
- ❏ to avoid having a long subject
- ❏ to change the 'information structure' of a clause:

  Macbeth? Wasn't it written <u>by Shakespeare</u>?

  Here the use of the passive allows 'Shakespeare' to be presented as new information at the end of the clause.

These last two reasons are explained more fully in A11.

Get is sometimes used in place of *be* as an auxiliary for the passive.

I finally <u>got</u> promoted.

This sounds informal; it can also have the idea that the subject is somehow responsible for the action, rather than an affected party.

Comments

Activity A6.1: b) is correctly formed; it represents the present perfect progressive passive of *find*. Here is an analysis of the other two:

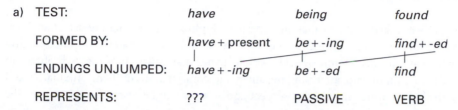

a)	TEST:	*have*	*being*	*found*
	FORMED BY:	*have* + present	*be* + *-ing*	*find* + *-ed*
	ENDINGS UNJUMPED:	*have* + *-ing*	*be* + *-ed*	*find*
	REPRESENTS:	???	PASSIVE	VERB

Figure A6.4.1 Analysis of incorrect verb phrase structure 2

The problem here is that there is no aspect form that is represented by *have* + *-ing*.

c)	TEST:	*are*	*having*	*found*
	FORMED BY:	*be* + present	*have* + *-ing*	*find* + *-ed*
	ENDINGS UNJUMPED:	*be* + *-ing*	*have* + *-ed*	*find*
	REPRESENTS:	PROGRESSIVE	PERFECT	VERB

Figure A6.4.2 Analysis of incorrect verb phrase structure 3

This contains the correct forms for both progressive and perfect, but they are in the wrong order. If they were ordered correctly we would get the verb phrase *have been finding*.

Activity A6.2:

1. he is taken
2. he is being taken
3. he has been taken
4. he has been being taken
5. he was taken
6. he was being taken
7. he had been taken
8. he had been being taken

Activity A6.3:

1. present perfect progressive
2. present progressive passive
3. past perfect progressive passive (though it sounds strange)
4. present perfect
5. past progressive
6. This is a trick question – it is not a correctly formed verb phrase. (Can you work out why?)

A7   VARYING THE VERB PHRASE

In A6 we looked at the formation of basic verb phrases, involving the use of auxiliaries to form progressive and perfect aspects, as well as the passive, in combination with tense. In this section we will look at further manipulation of the verb phrase in order to form interrogatives and negatives and combinations of them. Auxiliaries and verbs behave differently in this respect and so they will be discussed separately. The place of contractions is also examined.

TERMINOLOGY

You may be familiar with the term 'question' rather than 'interrogative'. However, the meaning of 'question' is fairly vague in popular usage, so it is normal to use 'interrogative' instead, as it refers precisely to the forms that are being described below. There is also a difference between form and function here. Interrogatives function as questions, but not all questions are interrogative in form, e.g.

> *It's raining?* (a declarative question)

(In writing the question mark is the only indicator of a question; in speech this would be matched by a rising intonation.) Here we are interested in sentences that change their structure. Declarative questions are discussed in B9.

A7.1 Negatives and interrogatives

Negatives and interrogatives with auxiliaries

If there is a modal or primary auxiliary in the verb phrase then negatives are formed by placing *not* after the auxiliary; if there is more than one auxiliary, it is placed after the first one:

> *I am not lying.* (the negative of the present progressive)
> *You have not done it.* (the negative of the present perfect)
> *They will not do it.* (the negative of the modal *will*)
> *It was not being done.* (the negative of the past progressive passive)

When *not* is placed after *can* it is usually written as one word: *cannot* (*can not* is also found in American English).

Interrogatives are formed by the 'inversion' of the auxiliary and the subject – that is, by swapping their positions:

> *Can you do it?* (the interrogative of *You can do it.*)
> *Have they finished it?* (the interrogative of *They have finished it.*)

(Note that inversion has other limited functions in English; see A11.)

This section only deals with one type of interrogative/question, the so-called *yes/no* questions, since they are the direct counterparts of positive (declarative) sentences. Other types, such as *wh-* and tag questions, are dealt with in B9.

Negatives and interrogatives with verbs

Historically, English formed the negative and interrogative of verbs in the same way as for auxiliaries: by adding *not* and by inverting respectively. You may sometimes encounter archaic forms such as *I know not, I like it not*.

However, in modern English, verbs are not allowed to invert with the subject and cannot have *not* placed after them (for an apparent exception to this see pro-forms in B11). If there is no auxiliary, a 'dummy' auxiliary, *do*, is introduced into the verb phrase. This is then used for inversion and for attaching *not*:

> *Do you* know?
>
> I *do not* know.

In this situation, *do* is the finite verb form (see A5). So any third person or tense ending is transferred to it (as *does* or *did*) and the verb is changed to the infinitive. Thus

> She *likes* it.
>
> I *hated* it.

become

> She *does not like* it and *Does she like* it?
>
> I *did not hate* it and *Did you hate* it?

It is also possible to use *do* for emphasis, i.e. to say

> She *does like* it. I *did hate* it.

These might be used to contradict suggestions that 'she does not like it' or that 'I did not hate it'.

When they are used as verbs, *be, do* and *have* behave differently from each other. *Be* is treated like an auxiliary (i.e. there is no need for *do*):

> We *are* strong. We *are not* strong. *Are we* strong? (Not 'Do we be strong?')

Though it may sound strange, *do* uses the dummy auxiliary *do*:

> I *did* it. I *did not do* it. *Did I do* it?

Have can function either way. It is common with *do*:

> We *have* the time. We *do not have* the time. *Do we have* the time?

It rarely behaves like an auxiliary; if it does then in the negative a contraction would be usual:

> We *haven't* the time (rather than *We have not* . . .). *Have we* the time?

Activity A7.1

Turn the following sentences into the corresponding negative and interrogative.

1. *I have been unwell.*
2. *They believed me.*
3. *I do yoga once a week.*
4. *He should have listened to me.*

Negatives with modals

The interaction of modal auxiliaries with negatives produces some strange results. For example, *must not* is not the negative in meaning of *must*. We can see this if we compare it to the corresponding semi-modal, *have to*; thus

> I *do not have to* do it.

does not mean

    I <u>must not</u> do it.

The former means there is a lack of obligation, while the latter means there is an obligation not to do it. In other words the negation is transferred to the following verb. We can also see this if we ask a question about obligation:

    <u>Must I</u> come? – No, you <u>don't have to</u>. (Not *No, you must not.*)

Other modals behave in the same way. *May*, for example, has both types of negation:

    You <u>may not</u> smoke. (= negation of permission, 'you are not allowed to smoke')

    They <u>may not</u> be here. (= negation of *be*, 'it is possible that they are not here')

Similarly, *can't have* is the 'negative' of *must have* when used extrinsically (see B6) to express a negative possibility:

    He <u>must have</u> done it. – No, he <u>can't have</u>. (= 'it is not possible . . .)

A7.2 Contractions

As we have already seen in A6 and B6, in spoken English (and informal written English) it is normal to 'contract' *not* and certain auxiliaries. The following contractions are common:

Table A7.2.1 Common contractions

	BE			HAVE			Modals		Negation
full form	*am*	*are*	*is*	*have*	*has*	*had*	*will*	*would*	*not*
contracted form	*-'m*	*-'re*	*-'s*	*-'ve*	*-'s*	*-'d*	*-'ll*	*-'d*	*-n't*

The auxiliary contractions are joined to the subject of the verb: *He's* . . . etc. Note that *-'s* and *-'d* appear more than once as contractions, so *He's done* is potentially ambiguous. It could represent *He has done* or *He is done*, though other factors will clarify the situation.

    The auxiliary contractions, apart from *-'s*, are normally used only after subject pronouns (including *there*); thus

    The dog<u>'s</u> outside. (= *is*)

    The cat<u>'s</u> broken the vase. (= *has*)

    We<u>'d</u> already finished. (= *had*)

    He<u>'d</u> like to eat it. (= *would*)

However, *the dog<u>'d</u> like to eat it* would be unlikely.

    Note also that *does* can also be contracted in casual spoken English: *What's he mean?* Here *-'s* stands for *does*. Thus all three primary auxiliaries can be abbreviated to *-'s*.

    The negative contraction *-n't* may be used with all auxiliaries (e.g. *haven't*, *wouldn't*), apart from *am* and *may* ('mayn't' is occasionally found; 'amn't' is not). There are three irregular forms: *won't*, *shan't* and *can't* (rather than 'willn't', 'shalln't' and 'cann't'). Negative contractions are also found with *be* and (sometimes) *have* when used as main verbs: *She isn't happy / They haven't a clue* (though *They don't have / haven't got a clue* would be more usual).

Thus in negatives of auxiliaries there are two possibilities: to contract the auxiliary

She's not coming.

or to contract the negative

She isn't coming.

But it is unusual to contract both: 'She'sn't coming'.

Activity A7.2

Expand these contractions into their full forms:

1. *She's satisfied.*
2. *We'll be there soon.*
3. *I'd rather stay at home.*
4. *I couldn't've done it without your help.*
5. *She's satisfied the examiners.*

NON-STANDARD FORMS

1. *Ain't* is very common in speech and transcriptions as a non-standard contraction of the present forms of both *have* and *be* combined with *not*:

    It ain't gonna happen. (= *isn't*; it also stands for *aren't*)

    I ain't done it. (= *haven't*; it also stands for *hasn't*)

    This happens also when *be* is a verb as well as an auxiliary (as it is in the above examples):

    She ain't here.

2. Many dialects of English have a rule that allows for double negation, for example:

    I ain't done nothing.

    The standard version of this would be:

    I haven't done anything.

A7.3 Combinations of negatives and interrogatives

It is, of course, possible to have both a negative and an interrogative in the same sentence. However, there are two ways of doing it:

1. Invert only the auxiliary with the subject; keep *not* after the subject.

    Can you not wait? Do you not know her?

    This is formal.
2. Invert both auxiliary and *not* with the subject; this only happens if *not* is contracted.

    Can't you wait? Don't you know her?

    This is far more common, particularly in spoken English.

There is one irregular contracted negative/interrogative form: *Aren't I . . .* (alongside *Am I not . . .*).

We can show how negatives, interrogatives and contractions systematically interact in the form of a diagram:

Varying verb phrases

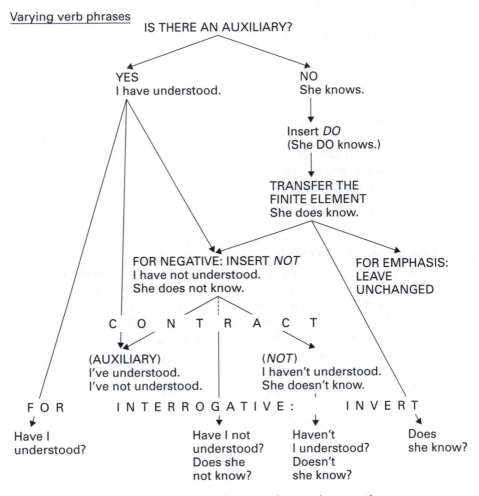

Figure A7.3.1 Interaction of negatives, interrogatives and contractions

This shows that interrogative inversion does not operate on auxiliary contraction. The dotted line indicates that contraction is bypassed.

Activity A7.3 ⊛

> Take the sentence *She is coming* and process it in the same way.

A7.4 Transfer of negation

Some verbs, when used in front of other verbs, may behave something like auxiliaries, in that negation is transferred to them when they are followed by a negative clause or infinitive. Thus

> He seems <u>not to know</u> me. (formal)
> I plan <u>not to attend</u>. (formal)
> We thought <u>you weren't coming</u>.

could also be expressed as

> He <u>doesn't seem</u> to know me.
> I <u>don't plan</u> to attend.
> We <u>didn't think</u> you were coming.

The meaning is the same. *Not* negates the idea of *know*, *attend* or *coming*, not *seem*, *plan* or *think*; the subjects are indeed 'seeming', 'planning' and 'thinking'.

Comments

Activity A7.1:

1. *I have not been unwell. Have you been unwell?*
2. *They did not believe me. Did they believe me?*
3. *I do not do yoga once a week. Do you do yoga once a week?*
4. *He should not have listened to me. Should he have listened to me?*

Activity A7.2:

1. ... *is* ...
2. ... *will* ... Some grammarians say that *'ll* can also represent *shall*; a tag question (see B9) can suggest this: *We'll help them, <u>shall</u> we?* but also *We'll help them, <u>will</u> we?*
3. ... *would* ... (see B6)
4. ... *could not have* ... It is unusual to have a double contraction like this.
5. ... *has* ...

Activity A7.3: You should end up with the following possibilities:

She is not coming.	She's coming.
She's not coming.	She isn't coming.
Is she coming?	Is she not coming?
Isn't she coming?	

CLAUSES AND CLAUSE ELEMENTS

A8

A8.1 Clauses

So far in the Introduction sections we have talked about word classes and their associated phrases. In this section we now move on to a larger unit: clauses, which are built up from phrases.

The semantic definition of clauses is that they contain one complete idea; there is something to this – but it is not easy to establish (it is also offered as a definition for the sentence), so we need to look for more reliable, formal properties of the clause. These include the following:

❑ they contain at least a subject (except with imperatives) and a verb
❑ there is one, and only one, finite verb form (unless there is coordination – see A9)
❑ other elements are permitted according to the patterns of the verb

There are some structures which are called clauses but which do not fulfil all three characteristics: 'non-finite clauses' and 'verbless clauses'. These share some of the features of clauses (see A10), but here we are talking about full, or 'finite' clauses.

A8.2 Clause elements

We can identify five different elements that go to make up clauses. So far we have encountered three of them: subject, verb and object. But there are two more that we need to identify – predicatives and adverbials. All five are dealt with one by one below; their abbreviations are shown in brackets.

Subject (S)

Subjects can consist of a noun phrase (including pronoun):

   The house stands on top of a hill.
   _It_ has excellent views.

Clauses themselves can also be the subject in other clauses (see A10):

   What you did is unforgivable.

The subject in English has a wide range of possible semantic roles. It is typically thought to represent the agent or the 'doer' of an action, but often this is not the case. Possible roles for subject include:

❑ the experiencer (_I_ saw)
❑ the 'locative', or the place of action (_This book_ talks about . . .)
❑ in a passive, the thing or person 'affected' by an action (_He_ was abandoned . . .)

The reading in D8 gives a more detailed discussion of the roles that subjects can play in clauses.

There are three formal properties that we can use to identify subjects:

❑ typically, they are the first element in a clause, as above, though they can be preceded by adverbials
❑ they invert with auxiliaries to form interrogatives (as we saw in A7)
❑ most importantly, they determine the form of the finite verb in the present tense.

This last point is known as 'subject-verb agreement' (or 'concord'). When the verb is in the present tense there is a special 'third-person -_s_' ending (see A5) that is used when the subject is singular and is a third-person pronoun (*he, she, it*), a noun phrase or a clause, for example:

<u>He</u> seems alright.

However, subject-verb agreement is not always straightforward. We saw in A2 a number of cases where it can appear that subject/verb agreement is inconsistent, for example:

The team <u>has/have</u> decided not to play.

Such collective nouns, however, are not exceptions to the rule, as the noun can be considered either plural or singular. But there are other cases where the noun phrase (A3) and verb do not 'agree', for example with time periods or quantities:

Ten <u>years</u> <u>is</u> a long time.

Here the noun phrase 'ten years' is treated as a single unit, not a collection of ten separate years. Such cases of 'notional' agreement are common. Co-ordinated noun phrases normally have plural agreement, but can have singular if treated as one entity:

<u>Their defeat and subsequent surrender</u> mean<u>s</u> that the war is over.

There is another situation where agreement is problematic. This is where a post-modifying noun in the subject noun phrase influences the verb because it is closer, rather than the head, for example:

He is the only <u>one</u> of the <u>students</u> who <u>know</u> the answer.

Here the head of the subject noun phrase is *one*, so the verb should be *knows*, but, because of the proximity of *students*, the plural form is chosen. This is not considered correct by many people.

There is one situation where agreement does not depend on the subject. This is when the subject is 'existential' *there*, in which case the number of the following noun phrase determines the verb form, for example:

There <u>are</u> many <u>cases</u> of absentee landlord<u>s</u>.

Note, however, that *there* is still the subject because it inverts with the verb: *Are there . . .* See A11 for more on this construction.

NON-STANDARD FORM

In spoken English it is very common to use contracted *is* with existential *there*, regardless of whether the following noun is singular or plural:

There<u>'s</u> many ways of doing it.

Verb (V)

The verb is the central element in a clause. It determines what other elements can occur in the clause, e.g. objects and predicatives. It even influences the choice of subject in a few cases (e.g. *it* with *rain*). Much more detail about types of verb is given in B8. Note that 'verb' as a clause element is not quite the same as 'verb' as a word class, as discussed in A5; here we are referring to the whole of the verb phrase.

Object (O)

The idea of object was introduced in A6, and the concept of transitivity, on which it depends is investigated in C6.

> Identify the objects in these sentences.
>
> 1. *They've found my credit card.*
> 2. *He became a teacher.*
> 3. *I hate work.*
> 4. *She runs every day.*
> 5. *We saw you at the show.*

Objects can consist of a noun phrase, pronoun, or another clause:

> <u>the man</u>.
>
> *I know* <u>*him*</u>.
>
> <u>what you mean</u>/<u>that you like her</u>.

With personal pronouns the objective case is used – *him* in the above example (see B2).

Usually objects come directly after the verb. There are three types:

1. Direct (Od)

    as in the three examples in Activity A8.1 above. Traditionally, direct objects are said to indicate the thing or person (or 'patient') affected by, or directly involved in, the action (*I hit* <u>*him*</u>, *We saw* <u>*them*</u>), or something that results from the action (the 'resultant'): *I wrote* <u>*it*</u>. But in fact they cover a wider range of semantic roles.

2. Indirect (Oi)

    Typically, indirect objects indicate the human recipient or beneficiary of an action:

    > *I wrote* <u>*them*</u> *a letter.*
    >
    > *I gave* <u>*her*</u> *a good reference.*

    When it co-occurs with a direct object, the indirect object comes first, as in the above examples. Usually indirect objects do not occur on their own, but with some verbs this is possible (although there is an implied object), for example:

    > *You can pay* <u>*me*</u> *now.* ('the money')

    Indirect objects can be related to prepositional objects with a change of structure; see below.

3. Prepositional (Op)

    Prepositional objects are preceded by prepositions. In some cases these are part of prepositional verbs, for example:

    > *I can't stop* <u>*looking at her*</u>.

    In other cases prepositional objects can be related in meaning to indirect objects (with a change in word and no preposition). Thus

    > *I threw the ball to* <u>*him*</u>.
    >
    > *We bought a bike for* <u>*her*</u>.

    are related in meaning to

    > *I threw* <u>*him*</u> *the ball.*
    >
    > *We bought* <u>*her*</u> *a bike.*

    The preposition in these related cases is *to* (indicating a recipient) or *for* (a beneficiary). There may be a slight difference in emphasis between the indirect and prepositional versions (see A11 for an explanation), and in some cases no corresponding sentence is possible (see Activity A8.2 below).

Testing for objects

All three types of object may become the subject in a passive (see A6):

> *A bike* was bought for her. (related to a direct object)
> *She* was bought a bike. (related to an indirect object)
> *I* was laughed at. (related to a prepositional object)

When we ask questions about the object we use WHO (or WHOM) and WHAT:

> *Who* did you buy a bike? (*Whom* . . .)
> *What* did you buy him?
> *Who* did she laugh at? (*At whom did she laugh?*)

This can be useful in distinguishing objects (especially prepositional objects) from adverbials (see Activity A8.5 below). It should be noted that alternatives with *whom* are very formal.

★ **Activity A8.2**

Change the underlined prepositional objects into the related indirect object. Bear in mind that *for* and *to* do not always indicate a recipient or beneficiary.

1. *I told the story <u>to everyone</u>.*
2. *We found a job <u>for her</u>.*
3. *She has explained the problem <u>to me</u>.*
4. *I said something wrong <u>to her</u>.*
5. *We put this question <u>to her</u>.*

Now do the reverse: change the underlined indirect objects into prepositional objects.

6. *Her aunt sent <u>her</u> a present.*
7. *I wrote <u>her</u> a letter.*
8. *I wrote <u>her</u> a reference.*
9. *He asked <u>me</u> a question.*

★ **Activity A8.3**

Sometimes turning a sentence into the passive can help us to understand its clause structure. Look at the following sentence:

> *We elected <u>her</u> <u>class representative</u>.*

You can see that there are two noun phrases underlined in it after the verb: *her* and *class representative*. Try to make each one the subject of a passive.

Predicative (P)

Predicatives (sometimes called complements) can consist of a noun phrase, adjective phrase or clause:

	<u>a teacher</u>.
He is	<u>very happy</u>.
	<u>what we need</u>.

There are two types: subject predicative (Ps), as in the above examples, and object predicative (Po) as in these examples:

> I painted the wall <u>black</u>.
> She considers me <u>her friend</u>.

Subject predicatives occur after 'link' verbs such as *be, become, look, appear*, etc.; object predicatives occur after the object of 'link transitive' verbs. See B8 for more on these. Both types of predicative indicate a relationship of equivalence or description. With object predicatives, we can show the relationship with a paraphrase involving a link verb:

> After painting <u>the wall was black</u>.
> She considers that <u>I am her friend</u>.

Predicatives can look like objects since they come after verbs or objects. And they are usually questioned in the same way, with *who* or *what*:

> <u>Who</u> are you? I am <u>her friend</u>.
> <u>What</u> are you? I am <u>a teacher</u>.

In one situation, however, subject predicatives can be questioned using *how*, namely when the answer is an adjective:

> <u>How</u> is she? <u>Better</u>.

To distinguish objects and predicatives, the passive test (as in Activity A8.3 above) can be used. Working out how many separate entities are involved in a clause can also help. Objects and subjects are two different entities, whereas with subjects and their predicatives, or objects and their predicatives, there is only one entity: *the black wall*, or *me, her friend*. There is one apparent exception, with reflexive pronouns, e.g. *I hurt myself*, but here the subject and object, though co-referential, are regarded as separate entities.

Activity A8.4 ★	This is an old joke. A man leaves a hotel and asks the porter 'Can you call me a taxi?' 'Yes, sir,' replies the porter. 'You're a taxi.' Can you explain this 'misunderstanding' in terms of clause elements?

Adverbial (A)

Adverbials can consist of:

- ❏ an adverb phrase: *He left <u>very quickly</u>.*
- ❏ a prepositional phrase: *I left it <u>on the table</u>.*
- ❏ a clause: *I fell asleep <u>because I was tired</u>.* (See A10 for more on this.)
- ❏ a noun phrase: *I'll see you <u>next week</u>.*
- ❏ a non-finite clause: *<u>Recovering his composure</u>, he turned and left.*

They can occur several times in a clause:

> <u>Breathing heavily</u>, I <u>slowly</u> walked <u>to the car</u>.

As in the above example they can be placed in a number of positions: the start, middle and end of clauses. In the 'middle' position they can be placed after the first auxiliary in the verb phrase:

> I was <u>slowly</u> walking to the car.

They usually express circumstances surrounding the clause, and so are not so closely related to verb patterns (see B8). Indeed, in most cases they are optional, and so are not included in basic clause patterns listed below. However, there are a few situations where they are obligatory:

I lay <u>on the grass</u>.

He put it <u>in his pocket</u>.

Here *on the grass* and *in his pocket* are necessary to make a clause; you could not say 'I lay' or 'I put it'.

The term 'adverbial' is similar to 'adverb', intentionally so, but they are different. The former is a clause element while the latter is a word class. While many adverbials are made up of adverb phrases, many consist of other units (e.g. prepositional phrases, as in the examples above). Equally, many adverbs (such as *very*) cannot be adverbials. However, there is a strong link, especially in the wide range of meanings that they cover: place, time, manner, reason/purpose, speaker attitudes and sentence relations.

When we ask a question about an adverbial we use *wh-* words such as *when, where, how, why* (and *how long*, but not *what*):

Where did he put it?

This can help to distinguish adverbials from predicatives and objects (especially prepositional objects).

Adverbials, as well as predicatives, can occur after the verb *be*:

The snake was <u>behind the fridge</u>. (Where . . . ?)

⭐ **Activity A8.5**

Use *wh-* questions to identify whether the underlined noun phrases are objects or adverbials (with the preposition included where appropriate).

1. We'll meet <u>this evening</u>.
2. We started <u>the day</u> with a strong coffee.
3. He looked into <u>the room</u>.
4. I'll look into <u>the matter</u> later.

Basic clause patterns or structures

We can use different combinations of the five clause elements to analyse the structure of any basic clause in English. This gives a total of seven patterns (ignoring the repetition of optional adverbials):

a) SV: *We laughed.*
b) SVO: *I found it.*
c) SVP: *She looked sick.*
d) SVA: *He was lying on the grass.*
e) SVOO: *I bought him a drink.*
f) SVOP: *We painted it black.*
g) SVOA: *I put it in his pocket.*

See C8 for practice on this.

Comments

Activity A8.1:
Sentences 1, 3 and 5 have objects: *my credit card*, *work* and *you*. *A teacher* in 2 is a predicative; *every day* 4 and *at the show* in 5 are adverbials – see below.

Activity A8.2:

1. *I told everyone the story.*
2. *I found her a job.*
3. Not possible, even though *explain* seems similar to other verbs with two objects. 'She has explained me the problem' is incorrect.
4. 'I said her something wrong' is wrong. *Say* does not allow this pattern.
5. 'We put her this question' is not possible.
6. *Her aunt sent a present to her.*
7. *I wrote a letter to her.*
8. *I wrote a reference for her.* Note how *for* is used here for a beneficiary and *to* in 7 for a recipient.
9. *He asked a question of me.* (This is a rare case where *of* is the preposition involved when a prepositional object can be linked to an indirect one.)

From this we can see how it is important to know which patterns a verb allows (see B8).

Activity A8.3: Turning *her* into the subject of a passive we get:
   She was elected class representative.
But if we try to do the same with *class leader* we get nonsense: 'Class leader was elected her (by us)'!? This shows that *class representative* is not an object, unlike *her*. It is, in fact, a 'predicative'.

Activity A8.4: In the man's request, *me* is an indirect object and *a taxi* is a direct object; the structure intended is SVOiOd. We can see the meaning if we change the indirect object to a prepositional one: *Can you call a taxi for me?* However, the porter (deliberately) misinterprets it as SVOdPo, where *me* is regarded as a direct object and *a taxi* an object predicative; a paraphrase would be *Can you say that I am a taxi?* In the first interpretation *call* is a ditransitive verb, in the second a link transitive verb (see B8 for more on these). The meaning of *call* is different in the two interpretations as well – another example of meaning and grammar changing together.

Activity A8.5:
1. When . . . 2. What . . . 3. Where . . . 4. What . . . Sentences 1 and 3 have adverbials, 2 and 4 have objects. *Look into* in 4 is a prepositional verb (see B6).

TYPES OF SENTENCE

A9.1 The sentence

Traditionally, the sentence is the highest unit of analysis in grammar. Sentences are composed of clauses, clauses of phrases, phrases of words, and words of morphemes (the smallest unit). But at each level of analysis, a higher unit may consist of only one unit of the lower level. So a phrase may consist of one word, as we have seen in a number of places. Indeed, it is possible for a sentence to consist of just one morpheme: *Listen!* In some approaches it is also maintained that there is a level of analysis above the sentence; see B11 for more on this.

Defining the sentence is not easy. One traditional, notional, definition is that sentences express one complete idea, but this has also been suggested for clauses. But when we try to define sentences formally, there is another problem: the popular idea of what a sentence is differs from the grammatical one. Most people, when asked, would say that a sentence is something that starts with a capital letter and ends with a full stop, question mark or exclamation mark.

There are two things wrong with this popular definition. First, it does not really help us to understand what a sentence is – why people put a full stop in a certain place and not elsewhere (and why, with a few exceptions, people agree on where full stops should go). Second, and more importantly, it can only be applied to writing, not speech. It is a 'graphological' definition. Speech is just as valid a medium as writing, but there are no capital letters or full stops in it.

We could attempt a parallel 'phonological' definition, which would apply to speech. It might go something like this: a sentence is a string of words that follows certain intonation patterns (e.g. falling for declaratives and *wh-* word interrogatives, rising for *yes/no* interrogatives). But this would be difficult to apply and would have many exceptions.

What we need is a grammatical definition, which would apply regardless of the medium, and there is one:

'A sentence is a string of words that follows the rules for forming clauses and combinations of clauses.'

The rules for forming clauses – in which the verb pattern plays the central role – were addressed in A8 and B8. The main aim of this section is to discuss the rules for the combination of clauses. The combination of clauses is a universal feature of English, whether spoken or written, and we need to explain how it happens. However, some grammarians have pointed out that it is not easy to separate some types of speech into sentences; an extreme claim is that the sentence is a graphological concept, but this book maintains that the grammatical definition offered above is valid. Grammatical sentences differ from graphological sentences in a number of ways. For example, in grammatical terms, the semi-colon also forms a sentence boundary. We will consider the issue of whether speech has sentences in A12.

A9.2 Types of sentence

In order for us to talk about grammar at the sentence level, it helps to make a number of distinctions:

1. *Major* (or regular) *sentences* vs *minor* (or irregular) *sentences*. The purpose of this distinction is to distinguish the type of sentence we are interested in, namely major sentences. Minor sentences are incomplete; they lack some important element. There are various types; thus to a question such as *When will she come?* we might get the following responses:

> *In the afternoon.* (a prepositional phrase)
> *Before her sister does.* (a subordinate, adverbial, clause – see A10)
> *Tonight.* (an adverb/adverb phrase)
> *Next week.* (a noun phrase)

These responses all have some grammar, but not on the sentence level, in that they constitute adverbials in terms of clause elements. They are sometimes called 'fragments', since they can be seen as part of a major sentence. We can construct a major sentence for all of them using the original question, for example:

> *She will come <u>in the afternoon</u>.*

There is one other type of minor sentence, so-called 'non-sentences', for example:

> *No smoking. / Silence!*

Such non-sentences are typical of signs and headlines. Although they may have some grammar at the phrase level (e.g. the fact that there is a determiner preceding a noun in *No smoking*), they are different from fragments in that it is not certain what the equivalent major sentence should be: *Smoking is not allowed* (?), *There is no smoking here* (?).

Activity A9.1

> Say whether these newspaper headlines are major or minor sentences.
>
> 1. *Ailing Maggie in hospital.* (*ailing* = 'sick')
> 2. *Save our schools by restoring teachers' authority.*
> 3. *End to reading classes.*
> 4. *How your money is spent by the state.*

---

2. *Simple sentences* vs *multiple sentences*. This distinction applies to major sentences. A simple sentence is one consisting of only one clause, while a multiple sentence consists of more than one clause. Since we have already dealt with the construction of clauses in A8, this section is mainly interested in multiple sentences, i.e. how clauses are combined.

3. *Compound sentences* vs *complex sentences*. These are two types of multiple sentence, reflecting the two main ways in which clauses are combined. They are discussed below.

This diagram shows the relationship between the various kinds of sentence described above:

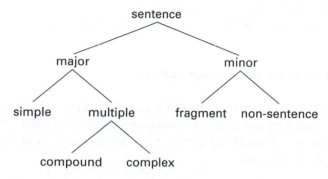

Figure A9.2.1 The relationship between different types of sentence

Activity A9.2

Look at this short paragraph taken from the text in C9 and answer the question underneath. The numbers in brackets indicate graphological sentences.

> *(1) Here is how I came to love my mother. (2) How I saw in her my own true nature. (3) What was beneath my skin. (4) Inside my bones.*

There are four graphological sentences, but how many grammatical ones are there?

Multiple sentences

Multiple sentences are those where two or more clauses are combined. There are two types of combination: co-ordination and subordination. With co-ordinated clauses, two or more clauses of equal importance are joined, in series; a co-ordinating conjunction (see below) is usually inserted, for example:

> *She works hard, has an enquiring mind <u>and</u> is popular with her colleagues.*

Here there are three clauses. Such sentences are called 'compound', and the clauses are called 'main'.

The other type of clause combination is subordination. In this, one clause of lesser importance, a subordinate clause, is added to a main clause:

> *I like him <u>because he is different</u>.*

In this example the subordinate clause can be regarded as an adverbial of the main clause. Such sentences are called 'complex'.

Main clauses are sometimes called 'independent' clauses, because it is thought that they can stand on their own, while subordinate clauses cannot. While this would apply to the example above (*I like him*), it does not apply to all cases:

> *He said <u>that he wasn't coming</u>.*

Here we cannot just say *He said*, because *that he wasn't coming* is the object and the verb *say* requires an object. Subordinate clauses always represent a part of the main clause, either as a clause element, as above, or as part of a clause element, as in this example:

> *Where did you put the pen <u>I lent you</u>?*

Here *I lent you* is part of the object *the pen I lent you*.

Complex sentences can become quite complicated especially in some kinds of writing, and it is possible to find both types of combination in the same sentence, i.e. compound-complex sentences (see C10).

The different types of subordinate clause are described in some detail in A10.

A9.3 Conjunctions and subordinators

The conjunction is the last word class that we will encounter. Conjunctions are a closed class; their function is to join two clauses together and show the meaning relationship between them. There are two types of conjunction, parallel to the two types of clause combination:

❏ coordinating: *and, but, or*
❏ subordinating, e.g. *when, if, although, because, since, before*, etc. Some consist of more than one word: *as soon as, so that*.

There are also a number of other words that are used to introduce subordinate clauses:

❏ *that*: *I know <u>that</u> you don't like him.* (see A10)
❏ *wh-* words: *I know <u>what</u> you mean.* (see A10)
❏ relative pronouns (see B10)
❏ *if* and *whether* in indirect questions (see B12): *I wonder <u>if/whether</u> she's coming.*

These are sometimes called 'subordinators'; the term can be extended to include all subordinating conjunctions.

Although they are used differently, conjunctions cover similar meanings to linking adverbs and some prepositions. All show the connection in meaning between two ideas. Thus:

    but (coordinating conjunction)
    although, though, yet (subordinating conjunction)
    however, nevertheless, yet (linking adverbs)
    despite, in spite of (prepositions)

all cover the idea of 'concession', that is where two ideas are somehow contradictory, and the second one would not be expected from the first. However, conjunctions create a closer connection than linking adverbs because they are in the same sentence.

Activity A9.3

> The four graphological sentences below illustrate the same basic meaning relationships using different grammatical means: a co-ordinating conjunction in 1, a subordinating conjunction in 2, a linking adverb in 3 and a preposition in 4. Work out

a) how many grammatical sentences there are in each case;
b) what type of sentences there are (simple vs multiple, compound vs complex).

1. *He's stubborn but I still like him.*
2. *I still like him although he's stubborn.* (or *Although . . .*)
3. *He's stubborn; however, I still like him.*
4. *In spite of his stubbornness I still like him.*

As well as joining clauses, co-ordinating conjunctions can be used to join smaller units, for example, phrases:
He's <u>clever</u> <u>and</u> <u>hard-working</u> with it.
Should I see <u>a doctor</u> <u>or</u> <u>a dentist</u>?
or parts of phrases:
I was <u>laughing</u> <u>and</u> <u>crying</u> at the same time.
And can also join two subordinate clauses:
We'll leave <u>when the job is done</u> <u>and</u> <u>when we've been paid</u>.
The boundary between conjunctions and linking adverbs can sometimes be hard to draw. First, linking adverbs such as *so* and *yet* are often used as conjunctions:
The party was getting boring <u>so</u> we left. (Or *. . . boring. So we left.*)
Second, co-ordinating conjunctions are often used to introduce simple sentences, where they have the appearance of linking adverbs, as in this example (at the start of a paragraph) from the Amy Tan text in C9:
<u>And</u> then my mother cut a piece of meat from her arm.
In a prescriptive approach (see A1) it is said that this is wrong, that 'you shouldn't start a sentence with *and*', but this is common in creative and other types of writing. In this book, the approach taken is that this is a graphological sentence (because this is what the writer wants), rather than a grammatical sentence. Grammatically it belongs to the previous sentence, but this does not imply that it is 'incorrect'. See C9 for more discussion of such 'sentences'.

 Activity A9.4

How would you describe the use of *however* in this sentence?
We wrote to the company on August 18, however we have received no reply.

Sometimes clauses are joined without a conjunction. Tag questions are one example (see B9); 'echoes' at the end of sentences are another:
She's got a lot of nerve, <u>she has</u>.
And spoken English quite often has strings of clauses with no explicit connection. (See A12 and C12 for more on this.)

Comments

Activity 9.1: Only (2) is a major sentence. (4) is a subordinate clause – see A10. *Your money is spent by the state* would be a major sentence but the addition of 'how' shows that it is only a clause element, a fragment which could be reconstructed as

This article shows how your money is spent by the state.

Activity A9.2: There is only one grammatical sentence, based on (1), which has the clause structure SVPs, where the predicative is a clause. (2), (3) and (4) are all fragments; (2) and (3) are merely further predicative clauses based on (1), while (4) echoes the prepositional phase (*beneath my skin*) that is part of (3). The whole paragraph could be rewritten as:

Here is how I came to love my mother, how I saw in her my own true nature, what was beneath my skin, inside my bones.

Note that, although (2) and (3) begin with *wh-* words, they are not interrogatives; they are subordinate clauses (see A10). The whole constitutes a major, multiple, complex sentence. See C9 for more practice on this.

Activity A9.3:

(1) consists of one multiple, compound sentence.
(2) consists of one multiple, complex sentence.
(3) has two simple sentences; the semi-colon is equivalent to a (grammatical) sentence break.
(4) consists of one simple sentence; the prepositional phrase carries the same basic meaning as one of the clauses in the other sentences.

Activity A9.4: However is essentially a linking adverb, but here it used like a coordinating conjunction (= *but*). This usage is quite common, in particular in business communication, but it is considered by many to be incorrect, an example of what is called a 'run-on' sentence.

A10 SUBORDINATE CLAUSES

As we saw in A9, subordinate (sometimes called 'dependent') clauses cannot stand alone as major sentences. For example:

Because she is generous.

This is an example of a minor sentence or fragment (see A9).

There are different types of subordinate clause (not to be confused with the different clause types in B9). Some represent a clause element, some a part of a clause element. One of the latter types, relative clauses, is dealt with in detail in B12.

In this book the term 'clause' generally refers to full, finite clauses: those that have all their 'parts' (especially the subject and the finite verb). However, we also need to deal with clauses that are incomplete in some way – non-finite and verbless clauses – since they possess some of the characteristics of clauses.

A10.1 Finite subordinate clauses

Nominal clauses

'Nominal' is the adjective for 'noun'. Nominal clauses are another type of subordinate clause; they take the place of noun phrases, as the subject, object or predicative of a clause; they begin with *wh-* words or *that*:

(subject)	*What I like best* is swimming.
	That she is brilliant is well-known.
(object)	*I know what you like.*
	where you're going.
	how we can do it.
	that you're unhappy.
(predicative)	*This is what I like best.*

Sometimes the use of a nominal clause as the subject may sound unusual; in A11 we will see more common alternatives.

The type of object and predicative possible in a nominal clause is determined by the verb pattern. *Know* in the above examples has a wide range of nominal clause constructions as direct object.

Nominal clauses also appear as the object of reporting verbs:

She said that she is retiring next year.

'What are you doing?' I asked.

I told her what you like.

When *that* introduces an object nominal clause, it may be omitted:

I know you're unhappy.

She said she is retiring next year.

In this case the subordinate clause has no overt marker. Such clauses are said to be 'contact' clauses; they are discussed again in B10.

Adverbial clauses

Adverbial clauses function as adverbials in the main clause. They are introduced by subordinating conjunctions:

She got the job because she has a lot of experience.

The adverbial clause here answers the question *'Why (did she get the job)?'* We should analyse the clause pattern of the above sentence as SVOA, not SVO + clause.

Other adverbial clauses answer the question *when*:

I left before the concert finished. (*When . . . ?*)

Not all subordinate adverbial clauses can be related to *wh-* questions, however:

Although he's rich, he has few friends.

Another test for adverbial clauses is to substitute them with a prepositional phrase or an adverb:

> She got the job _for that reason_.
> I left _then_.
> _Despite his wealth_, he has few friends.

Adverbial clauses, like adverbials, are generally optional in clauses and can be placed in more than one position. Here are some alternatives to the above examples:

> He has few friends _although he's rich_.
> _Because she has a lot of experience_ she got the job.

In B5 we noted that subordinate clauses with time conjunctions, such as _when_, _before_, _after_, mark future time with the present tense, even though the main clause may have a future time marker such as _will_:

> I'll leave before the concert _finishes_.

This also applies to clauses introduced by _if_ (so-called 'conditionals'):

> I won't go if the weather's bad.

See the two readings in D10 for more on the topic of conditional sentences.

| Activity A10.1 ✪ |

> The following sentence is ambiguous. Can you explain this using the difference between nominal and adverbial clauses, plus the concept of transitivity?
>
> > _Tell me when the concert finishes._

Appositive clauses

The above subordinate clauses function as clause elements. There are three types of subordinate clause that do not: appositive clauses, complement clauses (see below) and relative clauses. Relative clauses are dealt with in B10; the general concept of apposition is discussed in A3.

Appositive clauses are introduced by _that_ (which can be omitted), and form the postmodification of noun phrases. They are associated with abstract nouns such as _fact_ and _news_.

> The fact _that you are here_ proves it. (Also _The fact you are here_ proves it.)
> The news _that he has recovered_ has cheered everyone up.

In these examples we could omit _the fact_ and _the news_ and still have a complete sentence.

Complement clauses

Subordinate clauses can also appear as complements of adjectives (as we saw in A4) and nouns (see A3), that is, as part of their phrases. They are introduced by _that_ (which can be omitted):

> I'm _afraid_ that we'll be late. (Also I'm _afraid_ we'll be late.)
> I'm _sure_ that you'll find it satisfactory.
> There is a _fear_ that the recession will cause more job losses.
> The _belief_ that it prevents ageing is widespread.

Complement clauses preceded by a noun look like appositive clauses, but they are different since we cannot omit the preceding noun. To say 'That it prevents ageing is widespread' is meaningless. We can also paraphrase them with a related verb in place of the noun followed by a nominal clause:

They _believe_ _that it prevents ageing_.

Complement clauses also look similar to relative clauses introduced by _that_ (see B10), but we can see the difference in these two examples:

Somewhere, there is _a report_ _that no one has read_. (relative)

There is _a report_ _that fighting has broken out_. (complement)

Here _that_ is not a structural part of the complement clause, while it is in the relative clause. We can still say _fighting has broken out_, whereas _no one has read_ is incomplete because _that_ supplies the object.

Work out whether these clauses with _that_ are nominal, complement or appositive.

1. _That the government is corrupt is well known._
2. _The idea that we should leave our homes is outrageous._
3. _She made a statement that the allegations were false._
4. _The boss claimed that we were responsible._

✪ Activity A10.2

A10.2 Incomplete clauses

Non-finite clauses

Non-finite clauses are clauses which lack a subject and a finite verb form; however, we still call them clauses since they have some clause structure.

They are introduced by the three non-finite verb forms; thus we can divide them into three types:

- ❏ infinitive clauses: _I saw her _leave the room__.
- ❏ _-ing_ (participle) clauses: _I heard someone _shouting for help__.
- ❏ _-ed_ (participle) clauses: _I got the watch _repaired in town__.

Each non-finite clause in these examples has its own clause structure. _The room_ is the direct object of _leave_, _help_ is the prepositional object of _shout_, and _in town_ is an adverbial related to _repaired_.

We can also identify the role that the clause plays in the main clause. In the above cases it is part of the pattern of the verb; in each case the non-finite clause constitutes the object predicative with a link transitive verb (_see_, _hear_ and _get_). As with finite clauses the particular verb may determine what kind of non-finite clause is possible (see B8).

_Wh-_ words can also appear in _to_ infinitive clauses:

I know { _what to do._
where to go.
how to do it.

Compare these with the parallel examples under nominal clauses above.

Although there is no overt subject in non-finite clauses, it can be worked out from the subject or object of the main clause:

I want to leave. (*I will leave.*)

I want her to leave. (*She will leave.*)

A non-finite clause itself may be the subject of the main clause:

To live so long must be terrible.

Making money is easy.

In these cases the subject of the non-finite verb is not identifiable, but it is not important.

Participle (*-ing* and *-ed*) clauses can be part of the postmodification of a noun:

I noticed a boy lying on the grass.

I read a book called The White Hotel. (a reduced passive)

These can be related to finite relative clauses (see B10) containing a relative pronoun and a form of the verb *be*:

I noticed a boy who was lying on the grass.

I read a book which is called The White Hotel.

In this case they are part of one element of the main clause.

There is another situation where non-finite clauses function as a clause element themselves. This is where they are loosely attached to the main clause as adverbials, for example:

To cut a long story short, I've lost everything.

Shaken by this experience, he decided to resign.

Using this principle, we can solve many problems.

Note the comma in writing that separates them from the rest of the sentence. In the last two of these examples the identity of the unmentioned subject of the non-finite verb can be found in the main clause. The *-ed* participle suggests a passive meaning (*he was shaken by this experience*), while the *-ing* participle suggests an active meaning (*we use this principle . . .*).

-ing clauses can be preceded by prepositions, i.e. they can be part of prepositional phrases, for example:

On hearing this, the crowd gave a big roar.

By applying early, you increase your chances of success.

Verbless clauses

Verbless clauses have no verb as well as no subject. They are introduced by certain subordinating conjunctions and function as adverbials in the main clause.

Although sleepy, she still managed to finish her homework.

Slippery when wet.

As with non-finite clauses we can still see some clause structure, despite the lack of subject and verb. Thus *sleepy* and *wet* in the above examples can be classified as subject predicatives, as a full paraphrase indicates: *Although she was sleepy . . . , . . . when it is wet.* In the following example *in doubt* functions as an adverbial:

If in doubt, consult your doctor. (*If you are in doubt . . .*)

Other conjunctions which can appear in this position include *whether, while, whenever, though, once, as if.*

> **★ Activity A10.3**
>
> Expand the following non-finite and verbless clauses (underlined) into full finite clauses.
>
> 1. *If possible, place all plastic in a separate container.*
> 2. *I heard someone singing in the shower.*
> 3. *The man, described as being 6 foot tall, is in his late forties.*
> 4. *They stood there as if shell-shocked.*
> 5. *Once lost, your reputation can never be fully recovered.*

Comments

Activity A10.1: In one meaning *when it stops* is the direct object of a ditransitive *tell* (i.e. it is a nominal clause); it represents the information that the speaker wants to know (for example, when a horrific scene in a film is over). In the other meaning *when it stops* is an adverbial clause (and *tell* is monotransitive) referring to the time of the telling; i.e. *Don't tell me now, tell me when it stops.* The two related questions would also show the difference: *What/when did she tell you?*

Activity A10.2: (1) is nominal (as subject), (2) is appositive, (3) is complement and (4) is nominal (as object).

Activity A10.3:

1. *If it is possible* . . . Note that the subject here is not the same as that in the main clause.
2. *. . . someone who was singing . . .*
3. *The man, who was described . . .*
4. *. . . as if they were shell-shocked.*
5. *Once it is lost . . .*

REDESIGNING SENTENCES

A11.1 Word order in English

English is said to be an SVO language. That is, transitive clauses tend to have the basic order of SUBJECT – VERB – OBJECT. Other languages are the same, but other basic word orders are common: SOV, VSO. (When we say O here, we are also thinking about predicative and adverbial clause elements, which, like the object, typically follow the verb.)

Activity A11.1 ✪ Think of a language you know well. What is its basic word order?

We should not forget either that there are many other word order rules in English that we have seen throughout this book, for example, the rule that adjectives precede the noun they modify, or that prepositions come first in prepositional phrases (because there are some languages where they come last and are called 'postpositions').

Compared to other languages English is said to have a fixed word order, but this is not entirely true. This section looks at a number of situations where clause elements are rearranged, where there is a difference from the basic word order. We have already seen a number of situations where the word order in English is different:

- ❏ passives (although strictly speaking the order is still S-V)
    Your question will be answered soon.
- ❏ interrogatives, where the verb phrase is split up so that the first auxiliary can invert with the subject, as in
    Will you answer my question?
- ❏ relative clauses, where the object relative pronoun can be first in the clause
    (. . . *the question*) *that no one could answer . . .*
- ❏ interrogatives and nominal clauses, where a *wh-* word may represent the object or adverbial of the clause:
    What were you thinking?
    How are they feeling?
    What you did is unforgivable.

Inversion

The inversion of subject and auxiliary (with the use of *do* if needed) is not exclusive to interrogatives. It is also used in negative constructions when the negative word or phrase is placed at the start of a sentence (= 'fronted' – see below):

Not only did we win, we also played well.
Nowhere else can you find such beauty.
I haven't paid my rent. Nor have we.

You would not say 'Not only we won . . .', but an unfronted version is possible without inversion: *We not only won . . .* This also applies with words that have a negative idea, such as *seldom* (= 'almost never'):

Seldom have I seen such bravery.

Another formal situation where subject/auxiliary inversion occurs is in sentences indicating a hypothetical conditional idea:

Had I known, I wouldn't have come.
Were he to come, he would not be welcome.
Should you change your mind, there would be a financial penalty.

They can be paraphrased as 'If I had known . . .', 'If he were to come . . .' (or 'If he came . . .'), and 'If you should change . . .' (or 'If you changed . . .'). *Were* after *he* is another example of the subjunctive (see A5). These are all formal constructions.

Another clause-initial element that leads to subject/auxiliary inversion is *so*:

So disappointing <u>have the results been</u> that. . . .

There is another type of inversion in English, where the subject changes places with the whole verb phrase after another element has been fronted. It is most common when an adverbial of place has been fronted:

<u>In the middle</u> was situated a large table.

<u>Opposite him</u> sat the Queen.

(not *Opposite him did the Queen sit* with subject/auxiliary inversion.) Both examples are AVS. Such inversion allows the arrangement of sentences to fit the information principle (see below). 'Uninverted' (SVA) versions are of course also possible:

A large table was situated in the middle.

The Queen sat opposite him.

Such when fronted also triggers subject/verb inversion:

Such has been the demand for our products that . . .

This kind of inversion is also found in some reporting clauses when the object quote has been fronted:

'Don't sit down,' <u>said the teacher</u>. (see B12 for more on quoting)

A11.2 Reasons for redesigning sentences: three principles

<table>
<tr><td>

Look at the following sentence:

   Amy had never seen in stores underwear that would fit someone who was the size of fat Bev.

What is unusual about the word order here? Can you describe what is happening and explain why?

</td><td>⭐ **Activity A11.2**</td></tr>
</table>

The above activity shows one reason for changing word order in English: to place a long noun phrase at the end of a sentence. This is sometimes called the principle of 'end weight': anything 'heavy' should be placed at the end.

The general aim for using an unusual word order – apart from the cases of grammatical expediency listed above – is to make communication more effective. Thus it makes sense to have long clause elements at the end so that the clause structure can be quickly established. Compare these two sentences:

A sense of doom that affected him all day followed him.

He was followed by a sense of doom that affected him all day.

Here the use of the passive in the second sentence allows a short subject to precede the verb and the long noun phrase (*a sense of doom that followed him all day*) to be placed last, whereas in the first example the listener or reader has to wait till almost the end of the sentence before finding out what its structure is.

Another reason for changing word order is to achieve 'end focus', that is, to place the most important element at the end. This is the element that has the so-called 'nuclear stress' in speech. It may be an element that receives stress because it is being contrasted;

I'm not talking about <u>soccer</u>. (I'm talking about <u>American</u> football.)

Sometimes it is necessary to have more than one focus in a sentence. Then a number of devices such as fronting and clefting (see below) can be used to make use of the beginning in addition to the end of sentences.

A third principle behind the arrangement of sentences is the 'information principle'. As a general rule information at the start of a sentence in English is taken to be 'given' or old, whereas that at the end is regarded as new – particularly if it is focused on. A typical pattern in a text might be where a sentence starts with given information followed by new; then in the next sentence, this new information becomes the given information to which more new information is attached. In the next two sentences the division between given and new is shown by a slash (/):

They / have found a new way of distilling essential oils.

This discovery / could eventually lead to savings in production costs.

This organisation of sentences helps with the 'cohesion' of texts (see B11).

One more reason for using the passive (see A6) is to bring an original object to the front of a clause where it is understood as given information:

Macbeth was written by Shakespeare.

Here, 'Macbeth' would have already figured in the discussion and 'Shakespeare' is the new piece of information. To say *Shakespeare wrote Macbeth* would have different implications.

However, the given/new pattern does not always exist; it is quite possible for there to be no given information in a sentence; see 'existential *there*' below.

These three principles are not hard and fast rules, and sometimes they are in conflict with one another. And there are other reasons, for example, to have the same (or similar) 'topic' in initial position in succeeding sentences. The concept of topic is discussed in the reading in D11; it is called 'theme' there (though some grammarians distinguish the two).

A11.3 Techniques for redesigning sentences

In addition to the passive and subject/verb inversion, as exemplified above, there are a number of constructions used to satisfy these three principles; they are sometimes called 'movement rules'.

'Existential' there

In order to avoid having an indefinite 'subject' in the 'given' position, a sentence starting with *there* can be used:

There is a book on the table.

This places the whole of the noun phrase *a book on the table* in the position for new information. It would sound strange to say *A book is on the table*, though sometimes descriptions do have indefinite noun phrases in initial position:

A battered-looking wooden bedside table and a cheap chair of black-painted metal and faded red plastic comprise the room's remaining furniture.

We need to distinguish this use of *there* from its use as an adverb of place. Both uses are possible in one sentence, as in this example:

There were about 2,000 people there.

The first, existential, *there* could not be stressed; the second could be, and would have to be pronounced a strong form /ðeə/. However, not every case of initial *there* is existential. It can also be the result of subject/verb inversion:

> *There* is your man. (+ AVS, cf. *Your man is there.*)

See A8 for information about subject/verb agreement with existential *there*.

Fronting

In some cases we can simply move to the front of a clause an element that normally comes after the verb. There are two examples of fronted objects in the Amy Tan text in C9:

> *The pain you must forget.*
> *This I knew.*

rather than

> *You must forget the pain.*
> *I knew this.*

We have already seen examples in this section where certain cases of fronting lead to inversion, but generally it does not.

Fronting allows clauses to fit in with the information principle, but also to have two focuses: *This I knew.* In addition, in the first example above the fronting allows this sentence to have the same topic as the previous sentence (*The pain of the flesh is nothing.*)

Fronting is particularly common with adverbials:

> *On Wednesday I'll tell you more about the exam.*

The initial position is normal for linking and comment adverbs (such as *however* and *fortunately*) functioning as adverbials (see B4).

Predicatives can also be fronted:

> *Okay, Monday at 7 it is.* (referring to an agreement to meet)

Fronting looks very similar to subject/verb inversion and the effect can be the same:

> *In the middle a large table is situated.* (fronting)
> *In the middle is situated a large table.* (fronting plus subject/verb inversion)

Fronting is the device used in exclamatives (see B9):

> *How sweet it is!*

 Activity A11.3

> Look for fronted prepositional phrases functioning as adverbials in the above section under 'Fronting'.

Extraposition

We saw in A10 that subordinate and non-finite clauses may be the subject of main clauses. However, such clauses may become quite long, so in order to avoid having long subjects and observe the principle of end-weight, extraposition (sometimes called 'anticipatory *it*') may be used:

> *It is well-known that she is brilliant.*
> *It must be terrible to live so long in such awful conditions.*

Here *it* is a 'dummy' subject, replacing the (non-finite) clause *to live so long*, which has been 'extraposed' to the end of the sentence. It is also possible to say

>   *To live so long in such awful conditions must be terrible.*

But this could sound awkward.

Extraposition can also take place with objects when there is a nominal clause:

>   *I like* it *when you read to me.*
>   *I would appreciate* it *if you could phone me.*

Here *it* refers to the following clauses. It can also be omitted:

>   *I like* when you read to me.

But the use of *it* makes it clearer that the following element is an object, rather than an adverbial, as in

>   *I like* when you read to me *to be lying in bed.*

Activity A11.4 ✪

> There are two cases of extraposition in the above text on 'Extraposition'. Can you find them and convert the sentences to their 'unextraposed' equivalents?

Clefting

Cleft sentences allow different elements to be focused on. There are two types, both involving the addition of a subordinate clause to separate out the less important information. With '*it* clefts' a 'dummy' *it* is used to introduce the sentence, as with extraposition, but then there is a finite form of the verb *be* followed by the focused element as its predicative (*the violence* in the example below). The sentence is completed with a relative clause:

>   *It's* the violence *that I hate most.*

Compare this with a basic clause: *I hate the violence most.* Clefting is the structure that is used when testing for central adverbs in B4: *It was* loudly *that he spoke.*

The other type of clefting is called '*wh-* cleft' (or 'pseudo-cleft'). It uses a nominal clause introduced by *what* to separate out the less important information and place it at the start of the sentence. This nominal clause is the subject of the main clause; it is followed by a finite form of the verb *be* and the focused element as a predicative, as in this example:

>   *What I hate most is* the violence.

Activity A11.5 ✪

> Turn the sentence below into three different *it* cleft sentences using each underlined element.
>
>> *John noticed* the damage later.

Other techniques

The techniques described above are not the only way to redesign sentences in order to satisfy the end-weight, end-focus and information principles. The choice between OiOd and OdOp constructions that we saw in A8 can lead to different end focuses:

>   *I gave them the* money */ I gave the money to* them.

And the concept of 'quantifier float' (discussed in the reading in D3) can be explained with reference to the given/new distinction.

All of my friends / were there.

My friends / were *all* there.

In the second example *all* is part of the new information.

But in fact the most important technique is lexical rather than grammatical, namely to choose a verb which permits the desired arrangement of elements, as in these examples:

The customers *liked* the new design.

The new design *pleased* the customers.

As can be seen, the subject in each case corresponds to the object of the other. In the first example the liking of the new design is presented as new information; in the second it is the pleasing of the customers that is new.

Comments

Activity A11.1: Most European languages are SVO, as is Chinese. Examples of SOV are Japanese, Hindi, Persian and Turkish, of VSO Classical Arabic, Welsh, Irish and Tagalog.

Activity A11.2: The adverbial *in stores* has been placed in front of the direct object (*underwear* . . .). It is unusual to place adverbials between the verb and object, but in this case the object noun phrase is very long; it is postmodified by not just one but two relative clauses:

underwear *that would fit someone who was the size of fat Bev*

so to place the adverbial at the end could be confusing:

Amy had never seen underwear that would fit someone who was the size of fat Bev *in stores*.

In this version it is not clear that *in stores* is actually an adverbial for the main clause (rather than postmodification of *fat Bev*).

Activity A11.3: There are two examples, underlined below.

1. 'In some cases we can simply move to the front of a clause an element that normally comes after the verb.' It is not only *in some cases* that has been 'moved'; another prepositional phrase, *to the front of a clause*, has been placed between the verb and object to prevent it appearing after a lengthy object.
2. 'In addition, in the first example above the fronting . . .'. *In addition*, of course, is a linking adverb.

Activity A11.4:

1. 'It is also possible to say *To live so long in such awful conditions must be terrible.*' The un-extraposed version would be 'To say *To live so long in such awful conditions must be terrible* is also possible', but this sounds very awkward; there is too much before the main verb.
2. 'the use of *it* makes *it* clearer *that the following element is an object*'. Here *it* represents the object, with *clearer* as the object predicative. The unextraposed

equivalent would be 'the use of *it* makes <u>that the following element is an object</u> clearer', but this is not possible since the verb *make* does not allow a *that* clause as an object.

Activity A11.5: The three possibilities are:

    It was John who noticed the damage later.
    It was the damage that John noticed later.
    It was later that John noticed the damage.

The subordinate clause in this last sentence is not, strictly speaking, a relative clause (for example, the antecedent is not a noun, and *that* cannot be replaced by *which*, though *when* is a possible replacement).

A12   GRAMMAR IN SPEECH AND WRITING

A12.1 Variety in English

So far in this book grammar (and the English language) has generally been treated as a uniform phenomenon, as 'one size fits all'. Occasionally some indication has been given that there is variation, for instance:

- between different dialects of English, for example, British and American forms
  e.g. *I have already seen it* vs *I already saw it*
- between formal and informal forms (or rather formal and non-formal forms)
  e.g. *To whom am I talking?* vs *Who am I talking to?*
- between 'correct' forms and forms that are considered by some to be incorrect
  e.g. *Students have fewer chances of finding work nowadays.*
      Students have less chances of finding work nowadays.

But there is much more variety than this.

A12.2 Speech and writing

Another distinction that plays a part in variety is that between speech and writing. However, there are differences within both writing and speech. The grammar used in academic writing is not the same as that in e-mails, nor are conversations the same as prepared speeches.

There are clearly other factors at work, such as formality. So if we compare a typical spoken sentence with a written one

    Lend us a tenner. (=£10)
    I am writing to request the loan of £100.

We would have to note that the former is informal (and could be used between friends from the same social group) while the latter is formal (as in a letter to a bank manager). However, it is not just a matter of writing being formal and speech informal. Speech can also be formal, for example:

I was wondering if I could possibly trouble you to lend me £10?

Another factor involved is planning. Writing tends to be planned, speech not. We can see evidence of the latter in the use of fillers and hesitation markers, such as *sort of, you know, like*, which can be used to fill in gaps while planning takes place:

I was <u>like</u>, sitting there minding my own business . . .

I was <u>sort of</u> thinking that we might go out tonight.

He's the owner of that, <u>you know</u>, big shop in the centre of town.

A third factor is the amount of variation within the two modes (rather than between). Writing is more permanent and therefore more vulnerable to prescriptive forces (see A1). Certain grammatical forms are much more easily stigmatised in writing, for example the use of multiple negation (see A7). As a result, writing has become more standardised, and speech retains much more variation, particularly between different dialects but also within them. Many spoken forms are difficult to render into writing, except as parody.

A final factor is the nature of participation. Writing is typically a solitary process, whereas much of speech, in the form of conversation, is two- or multi-sided, involving two or more participants simultaneously, with such interactional properties as feedback, interruptions and so on.

However, modern technology has made writing potentially almost as interactive as conversation. Indeed, technology is responsible for breaking down several of the traditional divisions between speech and writing, such as formality in the case of emails and other forms of computer-mediated communication.

A12.3 Basic differences: intonation and punctuation

In this book, grammar is treated as being neutral to speech or writing; rules have been specified without mention to either, for example for the definition of the sentence in A9, where the traditional writing-based definition was rejected. Admittedly, the role of writing (e.g. in the shape of spelling and punctuation) is occasionally given some attention; see, for example, the use of commas to mark off comment adverbs in B4, but this is only because it is easier to illustrate.

However, there are a number of areas where we cannot ignore the differing effects of the mode on grammar, where there are basic grammatical features in one mode that cannot be mapped onto features in the other mode. For instance, there may be different morphological arrangements in speech and writing; the regular plural morpheme in English, which has two written but three spoken forms (as we noted in A2), would be an example.

The main difference between speech and writing is the use of intonation (and other suprasegmental features such as stress) in the former and punctuation in the latter. The two sometimes correspond; for example, a question mark in writing with a yes/no question can be equated to a rising intonation in speech:

Are you coming?

And a word space may correspond to a double stress pattern to distinguish a premodifier + noun from a compound noun (e.g. *black bird* vs *blackbird*). However, most punctuation has no obvious equivalent in speech. Commas may indicate pauses, but equally they may have a purely grammatical rationale.

There are some features of grammar in writing that are not reflected in speech, for example the difference between the plural, genitive, and genitive plural of nouns (*dogs, dog's, dogs'*), though this does not seem to affect intelligibility. In general, however, intonation is a much more sophisticated tool for marking grammatical distinctions than writing. Different types of tag questions, for example, are distinguished by intonation in speech, as described in B9, while their written form is the same.

A full account of the connection between grammar and intonation (and indeed between punctuation and grammar) is not feasible here. Some references are mentioned in the further reading.

A12.4 Some tendencies in spoken English

Beyond the absolute distinctions described above there are many situations where the difference is more to do with a tendency. For instance, in the written texts studied in C10 and C11, noun phrases tended to become very long, involving multiple layers of subordination. Compared to this, noun phrases in unplanned speech tend to be short, with a limited amount of premodification and postmodification, and with little subordination.

Here are some more specific, typical features of speech.

Contextual ellipsis

B11 discusses one form of ellipsis, where the missing words may be deduced from the accompanying text:

I'll come if you want (me to come).

This can be called textual ellipsis. There is another kind of ellipsis which is very common in informal spoken language, particularly conversation. This is where the start of a clause is omitted, for example:

Hope you are well. (I hope . . .)
(So are you coming?) – Depends on the weather. (It depends . . .)
(Why did he do it?) – Don't know. (I don't . . .)

This is sometimes called 'contextual (or "situational") ellipsis' because there are no textual clues to help supply the missing words. Instead the context – e.g. the fact that two people are talking to each other – can be used to sort out the complete meaning, although knowledge of common phrases also plays a role (e.g. with (*it*) *depends*).

In the above examples, it is the subject that is missing, but the inverted auxiliary in interrogatives can also be omitted:

Tomorrow at 4 be okay for you? (Will tomorrow . . .)
You coming? (Are you . . .)

(Note that these are related to *yes/no* interrogatives, not to declarative questions: *You're coming?*)

Both auxiliary and subject can be left out:

Know what I mean? (*Do you know . . .*)

Got any matches? (*Have you got . . .*)

This can include the verb *be* as well as the auxiliary:

Good to see you yesterday. (*It was good . . .*)

Though ellipsis is most obvious with shortened clauses, where a clause is missing some words, the concept can be extended to minor sentences involving one word answers:

I just passed my driving test. – Fantastic! (*That's fantastic!*)

Note that this is not a case of textual ellipsis. The missing words are not reconstructable from the previous text.

> ⭐ **Activity A12.1**
>
> Try to reconstruct these common elliptical clauses. Can you think of any more?
>
> 1. Get it?
> 2. Told you so.
> 3. Sounds good to me.

Auxiliaries are also omitted in semi-modal expressions (as discussed in B6), often with non-standard spelling:

You gonna get in trouble. (*You're going to . . .*)

We betta watch out. (*We had better . . .*)

I gotta go. (*I've got to . . .*)

When these are used in writing to indicate speech they are intended to sound very informal.

Left and right dislocation (also called 'headers' and 'tails')

This involves making a 'copy' of an important noun phrase, moving it either to the start (left) or finish (right) of the clause and leaving a personal pronoun in its original place:

This film we're going to see – what's it about?

What's it about, this film we're going to see?

This is another technique for moving an element around the sentence (see B11) so that it can be focused on and/or made the topic, or so that a long subject can be avoided: *What's this film we're going to see about?* In real time the initial position may be used because the speaker states the topic before being sure what to say about it, while the final position may be preferred when the speaker starts a question and then realises the subject will be quite long.

New structures

There are some new structures that have become popular in speech recently (but which are frowned on by some older people). Two examples are the use of *go* and *be like* as reporting verbs to introduce direct speech ('quotes'):

And she <u>goes</u> 'What are you up to?'
He<u>'s like</u> 'Keep your hands off!'
Be like can also be used for reporting thoughts:
And I<u>'m like</u> 'What am I doing here?'
This construction can be understood as meaning 'I'm saying/thinking something like . . .'. See B12 for more on reported speech.

Non-standard forms

Elsewhere in this book we discuss a number of cases that are regarded variously (depending on who you talk to) as non-standard, incorrect or acceptable but informal. These include:

❑ agreement following existential *there*: *There's your pills.* (vs *There are your pills*; see A8)
❑ contact relative clauses with the <u>subject</u> deleted: *There's a lot of people think he's crazy.* (See B10.)
❑ the use of *they* to refer back to an indefinite noun phrase (see B2)
❑ non-standard pronouns (for example: *y'all, hisself* – see B2)

Different forms of coordination

In formal written language, when there is a list of coordinated items, the normal 'rule' is to place *and* between the last and last-but-one item.
We need <u>ham</u>, <u>cheese</u>, <u>water</u> <u>and</u> <u>bread</u>.
While variations on this pattern may occur in writing, they are more common in speech, perhaps as a result of planning issues (e.g. speakers may not know which is the last but one item in a list). Variations are found with the repeated use of *and* between clauses, as in this extract from one of the texts in C12:
. . . I – was also in the marching band – <u>and</u> – basically – we had to – perform at football games – at the 4th of July parade of course – <u>and</u> we had to wear these horrible uniforms – . . . – <u>and</u> we had to march in formation out on the football field . . . (See also the reading in D12.)
Another possibility is to omit *and* in phrasal coordination:
<u>Good money</u>, <u>good conditions</u>, <u>long holidays</u> – what else do you want?

Vocatives

Vocatives are words or phrases used in speech to draw the attention of a person or persons to what the speaker is saying. The choice of an appropriate vocative to reflect the relationship between speaker and hearer is also important. Vocatives cover a wide range, from the very familiar (*mum, dude, mate, Jonny*) to the very formal (*Sir, Madam, Dr*). Although they do not function as clause elements, their positioning is of interest. The most frequent position is at the end, as in this example:
Good morning, <u>sir</u>.
But the beginning is also possible:
<u>Emily</u>, can you pass me the towel?

> **⭐ Activity A12.2**
>
> It is sometimes said that emails are a 'hybrid' form, a mixture of written and spoken language. Look at this email and identify features typical of speech.
>
> *Will contact Jonny.*
>
> *Presume you mean Tuesday 2nd November. Would be good to catch up though . . .*
>
> *Make sure you bring your thermals when you get back – heavy frosts the last few mornings . . .*

> **⭐ Activity A12.3**
>
> Investigate the role of *Peter* in the sentence below. Which two of the above tendencies of spoken English could it exemplify? How would this ambiguity in writing be distinguished in speech?
>
> *He's a friend of mine, Peter.*

A12.5 Conclusion

So are spoken grammar and written grammar different phenomena? And is the sentence only relevant for writing?

One extreme answer would be that speech and writing are distinct. The other extreme would be that the grammar of speech is just a subset of (the rules for) the grammar of writing and that it needs no special treatment. However, to follow the first extreme above would be extremely inefficient; most information about the two modes would need to be repeated. To follow the alternative would be to maintain the second-class status of speech and to perpetuate the poor treatment of features that are typical of spoken English. It is accepted that the study of grammar has long had a bias towards the written form (understandably so, since language study originally evolved to study and preserve classic literature).

The approach taken in this book is somewhere in between: that writing and speech have the same grammatical choices (within the constraints of their differing mediums), but that they differ in terms of tendencies (strong ones, in some cases). Moreover, as noted above, the barriers between the two modes are being broken down by new forms of communication (see D12 for more on this).

As regards the status of the sentence, we certainly need some concept to explain how clauses relate to one another in writing. The fact that the sentence is not a purely graphological concept is demonstrated in C9 by the difference between graphological and grammatical sentences established there. Moreover, there are certainly some forms of speech (of the more formal, more planned variety) where sentences can be clearly identified.

However, identifying sentences in all forms of speech is difficult if not impossible, as anyone who has tried to transcribe speech using full stops will know. This difficulty can extend to informal written forms: the ubiquitous use of dashes to connect clauses in emails and other forms of computer-mediated communication is evidence of this.

Comments

Activity A12.1:

1. <u>Do you</u> get (= 'understand') it?
2. <u>I</u> told you so.
3. <u>It</u> sounds good to me.

These and others have become so common that they are almost fixed phrases.

Activity A12.2: In full the text would be (added sections underlined):
> Ok, <u>I</u> will contact Jonny.
> <u>I</u> presume you mean Tuesday 2nd November. <u>It</u> would be good to catch up though . . .
> Make sure you bring your thermals when you get back – <u>there have been</u> heavy frosts the last few mornings . . .

The last line shows a more extensive use of ellipsis, with the subject, auxiliary and verb being omitted. See the reading in D12 for more discussion of the nature of email communication.

Activity A12.3: One possibility is that *Peter* represents a vocative: the person being addressed. The other is that it is a case of right dislocation, implying *Peter is a friend of mine*. In speech there would be different intonation: the vocative would have low flat intonation.

Section B
DEVELOPMENT

WORD CLASSES

B1.1 Classifying words

When we begin to study something unknown, one of the ways that we try to make sense of it is by grouping, or classifying the different phenomena that we encounter. The same was true when people first started thinking about and describing languages: they looked at the basic units – the words – and tried to find ways of putting them into groups. Indeed, in the past this approach was almost the only one used in describing grammar, and it is still important, though we need to supplement it with other approaches.

The eight original classes were derived from the study of Latin and Greek and were traditionally called 'parts of speech'. They were:

❏   noun, adjective, verb, adverb, pronoun, conjunction, preposition, interjection

This list has been adjusted slightly for English (see below) and nowadays a more accurate cover term, 'word classes', is used.

B1.2 Open and closed word classes

This refers to an important distinction between types of word class. Open word classes are those that are open to new members; closed classes are not. For example, it is relatively easy to make a new noun to describe some invention or new behaviour, for example *chocoholic*, but the same is not true of pronouns. Here is a list of the two types, as identified for modern English:

❏   open: noun, adjective, adverb, (main) verb
❏   closed: pronoun, determiner, preposition, auxiliary, conjunction

The division into main verb and auxiliary (verb) is made precisely because of this open/closed distinction.

There are other differences between open and closed classes. Words in open classes tend to be longer and less frequent than those in closed word classes; they also supply more of the meaning or **content** in language. Closed words classes carry less meaning and often supply the **function** words that are mentioned by Swan in the reading in D1. For example, when we say *the capture of the murderer*, the word *of* does not have any content meaning; it merely shows that the following noun, *murderer*, can be considered the object of *capture*.

It is not entirely true to say that the closed classes do not admit new members; for example *you guys* could be added to the class of pronouns (as an informal plural version of *you* – see B2). But the process is much slower.

B1.3 Formal and notional approaches to defining word classes

In the A sections there are two ways used to define word classes and to establish what class a word belongs to. The first relies on the meaning of the word and is sometimes called 'notional'. For example, if we say that a noun is the name of a person, place or thing, this is a notional definition; it tries to cover the meanings of nouns. The problem is that it does not do the job fully. What about nouns such as *laughter*, *statement* or *hatred*? We would have to extend the definition by adding notions such as ideas, feelings, actions etc. until it becomes useless. (And wait: aren't actions to do with verbs?)

The point is, when we identify the word class of a word we do it on the basis of its grammar, not its meaning. In other words, we use a formal definition. For example, if I say to you *I can see you've been durling lately*, you know that *durling* is a verb because of its formal characteristics – the facts that it has the ending *-ing* and comes after *-ve been*.

The table below shows the main word classes of English and their notional and formal characteristics in the order they appear in this book. The formal features are divided into morphological (i.e. inflections) and structural (the words they go with). It will be noted that closed word classes (apart from primary auxiliaries) do not have inflections.

Table B1.3.1 The word classes of English

Word Class (section where it is discussed)	open/ closed	traditional or notional 'definition'	examples	morphological features	structural features
Nouns (A2)	open	words used for the name of a person, place or thing	*man, house, height, Paris*	– plural with *-s* – genitive (apostrophe *-s*)	– the head of a noun phrase – subject, object or predicative of verbs
Pronouns (B2)	closed	words used instead of a noun	*this, who, mine*		– function as a noun phrase – typically no modification
Determiners (A3)	closed	(not a traditional word class) words that 'determine' the following noun	*the, no, every*		– the first part of the noun phrase, before adjectives – obligatory with singular count nouns used as heads – some agree with nouns
Adjectives (A4)	open	words used to qualify the meaning of a noun	*fine, brave, utter, afraid*	– comparative and superlative forms – add '*-ly*' to form adverbs	– modified by adverbs such as *very, so* (gradability) – predicative or attributive – some can be the head of a noun phrase (*the poor*)

Table B1.3.1 (continued)

Word Class (section where it is discussed)	open/ closed	traditional or notional 'definition'	examples	morphological features	structural features
Adverbs (A4, B4)	open	words used to add meaning to verbs	*often, slowly, very*	– some end in '-ly', '-ways' '-wise'	– modify verbs, adjectives and other adverbs
Prepositions (A4)	closed	words that precedes a noun	*in, to, of, in spite of*		– precede noun phrases, relate them to other elements
Verbs (A5)	open	words used to denote an action, event (or state?)	*make, know, buy, sleep*	– inflections for 3rd person -*s*, past tense, -*ed* and -*ing* participles	– agree with their subject (unless imperative) – determine which clause elements are possible – preceded by auxiliaries – precede objects
Auxiliaries (A6)	closed	(not a traditional word class) they 'help' the verb	*have, be, do, can*		– only one form (modals) – used to form aspect and passive of verbs – combine together – precede (main) verbs
Conjunctions (A9)	closed	words used to join two ideas	*and, if, although*		– used to join two clauses together

Fuller formal definitions (and problems associated with them) are given in the individual sections dealing with word classes.

 Activity B1.1 ✪

> Look at the following sentences and try to allocate each word to its word class.
>
> 1. *When I think about it, we should have done better.*
> 2. *Melt the butter in a separate pan.*
> 3. *Double standards abound in the discussion on climate change.*
>
> How many words are from open and closed classes?

B1.4 Problems with word classes

There are a number of general problems with a word-class approach to grammar:

❑ there are classes that we are not sure about (e.g. numerals, interjections);
❑ the distinction between some classes is not always clear, e.g. between pronouns and determiners (see A3), or between adverbs and prepositions (see A4);

❑   many words do not meet all the criteria for membership listed above (e.g. a noncount noun such as *money* does not have a plural or a genitive), so we have a situation in which some words are more typical members of a word class than others. It is nowadays normal to talk of 'core' or 'prototypical' members of a word class, in contrast to 'peripheral' or 'marginal' members. See A4 for an illustration of this with adjectives.

❑   some words are difficult to assign to any class, e.g. *yes* and *no* are generally said to be adverbs, but they have little in common with other members of that word class.

❑   adverbs especially are a problem to define formally. See B4 for more details.

In addition there are many words that can belong to more than one class (e.g. *change, round, back*). This is not necessarily a problem, though; we can use the different word class labels to explain the way such words behave and how they are different from other words. And we will see that such uses often involve a difference in meaning, which corresponds to that in grammar.

A further issue follows on from this: is word class membership an inherent feature of words or a feature that is endowed by particular instances of use; i.e. should we say that *information* is a noun or that it is used as a noun in particular cases? Some linguists would argue that only the second approach is valid. In this book, however, I have generally followed the former, traditional approach; dictionary writers seem to have no problem assigning a word class (or more than one) to words in isolation.

B1.5 Conclusion

For centuries a word class approach was the principal tool for analysing the grammar of European languages, including English (there are, of course, other traditions). In conjunction with the identification of sentence roles (subject, object, etc. – see A8) it *was* grammar. And it still forms the backbone of modern grammatical analysis. However, we have seen it is not a foolproof method for classifying words, and in order to understand how words function in sentences we need to supplement it with further approaches.

Comment

Activity B1.1: Here is a list of the word classes:

pronouns: *I, it, we*	conjunction: *when*
auxiliaries: *should, have*	verbs: *think, done, melt, abound*
determiners: *the, a*	adjectives: *separate, double*
adverb: *better*	prepositions: *about, in, on*
nouns: *butter, pan, standards, discussion, climate, change*	

You may have wanted to call *climate* an adjective (see A3), but apart from that most of the words are fairly easy to assign. This is not always the case (for example, *to* in the previous sentence), as we will see later. As regards open and closed classes, there are 13 instances of each (including some in closed classes – *in* and *the* – which are repeated).

B2 PRONOUNS

B2.1 Definition

Pronouns are a closed word class and their number is quite small. The traditional definition is that they 'take the place of nouns', hence their name. However, there are two problems with this definition. First, many pronouns are not replacing anything, for instance:

> <u>Somebody</u> *must know the answer.*
>
> <u>It</u> *is raining.*

Here *somebody* and *it* are not replacing any noun, and it is difficult to think of nouns that could take their place.

Second, where pronouns do constitute a replacement, it is noun <u>phrases</u> that they are equivalent to, not nouns. In other words, all the words that go with a noun are replaced, as well as the noun.

> *I saw <u>the girl with the long blonde hair</u>.*

is related to

> *I saw <u>her</u>*

and not 'I saw <u>the her with the long blonde hair</u>'.

So for a formal definition of pronouns we can mention two characteristics:

a) structurally they are equivalent to noun phrases (see A3) and can function as subjects or objects (see A8)

b) usually they occur alone, without modification (rare exceptions would be *something new*, or *poor you*); however, quantifiers such as *some* (see A3) are commonly followed by postmodification with an *of* phrase:

> *You can fool <u>some of the people</u> <u>all of the time</u>.*

B2.2 Personal pronouns

The most important class of pronouns are the personal pronouns, both because they are the most common and because they can vary in a number of ways, some of which are unique in English. They vary

❑ for person (first, second and third), e.g. *I*, *you*, *he*
❑ for number (singular and plural), e.g. *I* vs *we*
❑ for case (subjective and objective), e.g. *I* vs *me*
❑ for gender, e.g. *he*, *she*, *it*

These forms are explained below. We can organise this variation into a table showing how the various forms are related to each other; this is called the 'personal pronoun paradigm':

Table B2.2.1 The personal pronoun paradigm

	first	*second*	*third*
singular	I/me	you	he/him, she/her, it
plural	we/us	you	they/them

(The slashes separate the subjective and objective forms (see below), the commas the different genders.)

B2.3 Problems with personal pronouns

The table above is the situation that is usually presented to teachers and learners of English. However, there are problems with all four of the categories mentioned above.

Person

Person is a word you already know, but here it is being used in a different, technical sense. It means the way personal pronouns refer to different participants in the speech/writing situation, in other words, in the act of communication:

❑ the first person refers to the speaker or writer
❑ the second person refers to the listener(s) or reader(s) (sometimes called 'addressee(s)')
❑ the third person refers to all other people and things outside the act of communication.

There are some problems here. For one thing *it*, by definition, is not a 'personal' pronoun. But more importantly, there is a huge difference between the third person and the other two. The reference of the first and second person pronouns can only be identified by specific knowledge of each act of communication; they are 'deictic', just like the words *here* and *there*, *now* and *then*, as in this imagined phone conversation:

> *Who's that?*
> *It's me.*
> *No, it's not – I'm me. You're you. So where are you, you?*
> *I'm here.*
> *No, you're not. I'm here. You're there.*

In contrast, third person pronouns can function as a cohesive device, helping to hold a text together (see B11). It is here that we find the traditional idea of pronouns replacing noun phrases.

> *Is that <u>today's paper</u>? Can I borrow <u>it</u>?*

But as we saw above, this idea of replacement is not always the case, even for third person pronouns.

One other third person pronoun should be added here: *one* (and *ones*), which can act both as a substitute for a head noun:

Which <u>sweet</u> do you want? – I'll take the red <u>one</u>.

and for an indefinite noun phrase:

I need <u>a new car</u>. – Where are you going to find the money for <u>one</u>?

Number and gender

Even though it sounds simple, number is also a problematic category for pronouns. The second person in English has no distinction between singular and plural (it is said to be 'neutralised'), and the third person has the additional distinction of gender, but only in the singular. As for the first person, strictly speaking *we* is not the plural of *I*, because it is very difficult, if not impossible, to have two or more first persons (though two examples would be a document signed by many people beginning *We the undersigned . . .* , or twins speaking simultaneously). Usually *we* means 'I and you' or 'I and he/she/they'. The former is called 'inclusive' *we* because it includes the listener (*What shall <u>we</u> do tonight?*) and the latter 'exclusive' *we* (*<u>We</u>'re going home; what about you?*). *Let's* can only be interpreted as inclusive.

There is another situation where the singular/plural distinction is problematic, where the paradigm is not so neat or accurate, as the next activity shows.

Activity B2.1 ✪

> Fill in the gap with a suitable pronoun; use your intuitions.
> *Anyone can see that, can't _____?*

Case

Most of the personal pronouns have two forms, or 'cases', depending on the role they play in a sentence. The subjective typically occurs as the subject, while the objective typically occurs as the object, hence their names (see A8 for more on these roles):

<u>I</u> like it. They hate <u>us</u>.

The distinction is neutralised for *you* and *it*.

There are a number of issues concerning the choice of subjective or objective. Typically the objective is also used for predicatives (e.g. after the verb *be* – see A8): *It is me.* Some people, however, believe the subjective should be used: *It is I*, though there is no historical reason for this. The objective tends to be used instead of the subjective when the pronoun is first in a coordinated phrase, even though it is the subject:

<u>Me</u> and Darren are having a party tomorrow.

This sounds informal (and wrong to some people) compared with

Darren and <u>I</u> are having a party tomorrow.

Related forms

A number of related forms are sometimes included with the personal pronouns because they seem to follow the same pattern. These are

❑ possessive pronouns: *mine, yours, his, hers, ours, theirs*
    <u>Mine</u> is red.

Its does not exist as a pronoun: 'Is this <u>its</u>?'

The double genitive that we saw with nouns is also common with possessive pronouns: *a friend <u>of mine</u>* (rather than 'a friend of me')

❏   possessive determiners: *my, your, his, her, its, our, their* (see A3)

>   <u>My</u> *car is red.*

The possessive pronouns and determiners correspond to the two uses of the genitive:

>   <u>Will's</u> *is red.* / <u>Mine</u> *is red.*
>   <u>Will's</u> *car is red.* / <u>My</u> *car is red.*

❏   reflexive pronouns, where the subject and object are the same: *myself, yourself, himself, herself, ourselves, yourselves, themselves*

>   *I hurt <u>myself</u>.*

⭐ **Activity B2.2**

Fill in the gap with a suitable pronoun.

If anyone doesn't want to surrender, they could shoot _____ .

NON-STANDARD FORMS

There are several non-standard personal pronouns that you may come across in representations of dialect or historical speech. Here are a few:

a)   old and middle English distinguished singular and plural for the second person. *You* etc., was only plural, while the singular and related forms in writing were: *thou* (subjective), *thee* (objective), *thy* (possessive determiner), *thine* (possessive pronoun), *thyself* (reflexive). A descendant of this, written *tha*, can be heard in the Yorkshire dialect.

b)   a number of dialects of English have second person plural forms: *yiz* (Irish), *youse* (Liverpool), *y'all* (southern American). Another, *you guys*, originally American, is now common in standard British English as well and could be regarded as an informal plural spoken alternative to *you*.

c)   several dialects have *hisself* as an alternative to *himself*. Although it is regarded as ungrammatical, it is quite logical, being formed from the possessive rather than the objective form, like *myself* and *yourself*.

Generic uses

The biggest problem with the traditional paradigm is that it also ignores a whole range of uses of the personal pronouns to describe people in general (i.e. generic reference as opposed to specific – see B3 for more on this). Here are some examples with explanations:

WE: <u>We</u> *now enjoy a better standard of living.*

This use is very typical of politicians who are trying to include everybody (not just their listeners) in their field of reference.

YOU: *It's awful when <u>you</u> can't remember someone's name.*

This is sometimes said to be an informal alternative to *one* (see below), but in fact it is very common and is found in quite formal as well as informal circumstances. By using it speakers try to involve the listener in the generalisation they are making.

THEY: *They say it's going to rain tonight.*
           It doesn't make any difference; they'll still get you.

Here *they* is not referring to or replacing any previously-mentioned noun phrase. It is referring vaguely to people with whom the speaker does not identify – people in positions of knowledge (e.g. the weather forecasters) or power (e.g. the government).

ONE: *One tries one's hardest.*

This is very formal.

B2.4 Other pronouns

There are a number of other important groups of pronouns:

- reciprocal pronouns, which indicate a mutual relationship between subject and object: *each other, one another*
     They hate each other.
- relative pronouns: *who, whom, (whose), which, that, 'zero'*
     That's the man who stole my bike.
  These are discussed in more detail in B10 under relative clauses.
- interrogative pronouns, used in asking questions: *who, whom, (whose), which, what*
     Who is responsible for this?
  These are discussed in more detail in B9.
- demonstrative pronouns: *this, that, these, those* (see B3 on determiners)
     That's enough!
- indefinite pronouns, including quantifiers, e.g. *all, both, some, many, few, a few* (see B3 on determiners), and combinations of *every, some, any, no* and *one, body, thing* (all written as one word except *no one*):
     Everyone will come

B2.5 Conclusion

Even though their numbers are small, pronouns are a complicated word class, especially the personal pronouns. We can try to revise the personal pronoun paradigm to take into account some of the factors that have been described above:

Table B2.5.1 The personal pronoun paradigm revised

	first	*second*	*third*			
			definite			*indefinite*
singular	I/me	you	he/him	she/her	it	they/them
plural	we/us	(you guys)	they/them			

But this fails to capture all their subtlety, for example:

❏ their use for generic reference
❏ the various uses of *one*
❏ the role of non-standard forms
❏ the choice between using personal pronouns in the first place and some impersonal construction (e.g. the passive), which is important in many types of formal writing.

And we need to ask whether this paradigm is a satisfactory model for describing them.

Comments

Activity B2.1: The issue here is how to refer back to indefinite (see B3) pronouns such as *anyone* (or indeed to indefinite noun phrases in general). There are a number of possibilities. Some people would choose *he*, but the objection to this is that the person might equally be a woman. *He or she* sounds very awkward, while the unisex *s/he* is impossible in speech (and rare in writing nowadays). The preferred choice in British English is, perhaps surprisingly, *they*. It may sound illogical, but it has been common in English for a long time. All we need to do is to accept that *they* can have indefinite singular reference (which is less strange than suggesting that *he* can have female reference).

Activity B2.2: The obvious choice is *themselves*, but this is plural while *anyone* is singular. If we follow the logic of the last activity, the answer is *themself* (like *yourself/ yourselves*). This does actually occur, though it is rare:

> *You won't be the first person who gets themself involved in a holiday romance.*
> How natural does this sound to you?

ARTICLES

The articles *a/an* and *the* are rather special members of the determiner word class. In one sense they are different from each other because they belong to the classes of indefinite and definite determiners respectively. However, in each case they represent the basic determiner. Also, they are the two of the most frequent words in English (*the* is in fact by far the most frequent). So they are worthy of special attention.

B3.1 Membership and forms

One of the first questions that we need to ask is: how many are there? You are probably already familiar with the definite (*the*) and indefinite (*a/an*) articles, but some grammarians have proposed a third: the 'zero' article. Having a 'zero' article allows us to say that all common nouns must always have a determiner. It means a simpler rule for the construction of noun phrases, but it is a rather unusual concept; see the article in D3 for more discussion.

Some grammarians also claim that *some* could be considered the plural of *a* (*a dog*: *some dogs*), but the problem is that *some* adds the idea of a number or quantity (although a vague one) to the plural:

There are wolves/some wolves in that forest.

Then there is the fact that *some* can go with noncount nouns: *some money*. So it is best to leave *some* to the quantifiers and stick with just two articles: the definite (used with both singular and plural nouns) and the indefinite (used with singular only).

The main issue is the 'meaning' or uses of the articles, i.e. the difference between definite and indefinite. This is dealt with below under 'reference'.

TERMINOLOGY

Elsewhere in the book these forms are usually referred to as *a* and *the*, but here we need these terms, partly to be able to say that 'the indefinite article has two forms: *a* and *an*'. You could not say '*a* has two forms: *a* and *an*'.

The indefinite article has two forms, both in speech and writing (not to mention the stressed form): *a* /ə/ and *an* /ən/. The choice between them depends on the pronunciation of the following word; the former is used in front of consonant sounds, the latter in front of vowels (see the pronunciation symbols in the Website Reference). It is the only 'word' in English that behaves so.

The definite article also has two unstressed pronunciations, /ðə/ (before consonants) and /ði/ (before vowels), but this is not reflected in the spelling.

B3.2 The concept of reference

Articles do not have any meaning in themselves. But they help with the meaning of nouns by pointing out what kind of reference they have, i.e. what it is we are talking about when we use nouns. There are two distinctions between types of reference that are important in understanding articles:

1. specific vs generic reference
This relates to whether the article picks out a specific instance or instances of a noun, or whether it applies to all possible instances of a noun (i.e. it is generic, or generalising). Most uses of both articles indicate specific reference:

I saw <u>a</u> man / I saw <u>the</u> man / I saw <u>the</u> men.

Here we are talking about a particular individual or group of individuals (not *men* in general).

There are a few uses of articles which indicate generic reference. They are noted in the lists below and are explained under the heading 'Generalising with noun phrases'.

We also need to recognise some uses of the indefinite article which are non-specific, but also not generic, in that they make reference neither to specific individuals nor whole classes.

2. definite vs indefinite reference
The basic difference between the articles is whether they indicate definite reference (*the*) or indefinite (*a/an*). This difference is usually explained in terms of whether something is 'known' ('definite') or not, but we need to refine this idea because it is not just a matter of 'knowing'. Using the articles involves factors such as whether speakers can <u>assume</u> that listeners know what they are talking about. A fuller 'definition' is given below under the heading 'The definite article: specific uses'.

The definite/indefinite distinction applies to other determiners: e.g. possessives and demonstratives (definite), and quantifiers (indefinite). *Which* and *what* as question words have the same definite/indefinite difference as *the* and *a/an*, which explains why people often ask a *which* question when a speaker's assumption is incorrect.

Can you tell me where <u>the</u> post-office is? – *<u>Which</u> post-office do you mean?*

B3.3 The indefinite article

The indefinite article can be regarded as the basic form (the 'default' determiner), to be used with singular count nouns when they are the head of an NP and when there is no reason to use *the* (or any other central determiner). These situations include:

a) *There was <u>a</u> new student in class today* – establishing something (specific reference). This is the most typical use of *a/an*.
b) *It's cold – you'll need <u>a</u> jacket.*   – something not existing = 'any'
c) *Will is <u>a</u> teacher.*   – describing (rather than referring)
d) *<u>A</u> rifle is a dangerous weapon.*   – generic reference (see below)
e) *105 ('<u>a</u> hundred and five')*   – in numbers (and fractions)
f) *twenty miles <u>an</u> hour*   – in rates

★ **Activity B3.1**

Say whether and why the following underlined nouns need the indefinite article.

1. It is _____ new <u>system</u> of communication.
2. They didn't give you _____ good <u>advice</u>.
3. Peter is _____ excellent <u>father</u>.
4. We need _____ better <u>crisis</u> management.

B3.4 The definite article: specific uses

With common nouns *the* is basically used to help the noun refer to a thing or things that the speaker (or writer) thinks the listener (or reader) can locate or identify uniquely, that is, without confusing it or them with other possible referents. This applies in the following cases:

a) *Where's the butter?*   – immediate situation
b) *The President is going to make a speech.*   – larger situation

These two 'situational' uses involve knowledge of one's environment, and they are very common in spoken English. For example, if you are in a kitchen, you could expect *the fridge, the floor, the table* (perhaps), *the light*, etc. If you are in a particular country, you could expect *the government, the economy, the president*, etc. What is sometimes called 'unique reference', as with *the sun* and *the moon*, is just an extension of this.

c) *I ate a cake and a roll; the roll made me sick.*   – direct anaphora
d) *The first time I rode my bike, the machine fell apart.* – coreferential anaphora
e) *The first time I rode my bike, the bell fell off.*   – indirect anaphora

In these three uses 'anaphora' simply means referring back to something earlier in the text. In c) it is the same noun, *roll*, in d) it is the same thing but referred to with a different noun (*bike/machine*), while in e) there is something associated with an already-mentioned noun, something that could be expected (e.g. on a bike: *the seat, the handlebars, the bell*).

f) *The girls sitting over there are my cousins.*   – cataphora

Cataphora means referring forward; in this case it is the postmodification, *sitting over there*, which makes the reference of the noun identifiable.

g) *He's the best person for the job.*   – 'unique' adjectives

Sometimes premodification can be the reason for definiteness. Superlative and similar adjectives (e.g. *next, same, only*), which give an idea of uniqueness, tend to have this effect.

h) *The boy with the fair hair lowered himself down the last few feet of rock and began to pick his way towards the lagoon.* (The first line from the novel, *The Lord of the Flies*, by William Golding.)

This last use may be called the 'pre-emptive' use of the definite article, since the author is trying to create, rather than reflect, the conditions for definiteness. This use is common at the start of stories.

B3.5 The definite article: other uses

Before moving on we should note some other uses of the definite article which are not part of the specific reference described above:

i)   *How shall we get there? Let's take the bus.*   – institutions
j)   *The lion is a dangerous animal.*   – formal generic (see below)
k)   *We must help the poor.*   – generic adjectives (see below)
l)   *You're asking the impossible.*   – = 'something which is . . .'
m)   *The more the merrier.*   – with comparatives
n)   *The Times*   – with proper nouns

Activity B3.2

Read this old joke. It comes from a time when televisions were big solid objects. You may not find it funny but try to work out the two uses of the definite article which the joke relies on.

A. *'I'm fed up with all this fighting on the television.'*
B. *'Why?'*
A. *'I keep falling off.'*

Activity B3.3

Consider this pedagogic rule:

The first time you mention something you use 'a', and the second time you use 'the'.

Look at the following text from an Agatha Christie novel and find all the references (including pronouns) to a dog. Do they support the 'rule'? Why/why not?

1.   *'Did they have a dog?'*
2.   *'I beg your pardon?'*
3.   *'I said did they have a dog? General and Lady Ravenscroft. Did they take a dog*
4.   *for that walk with them on the day that they were shot? The Ravenscrofts.'*
5.   *'They had a dog – yes,' said Garroway. 'I suppose, I suppose they did take him*
6.   *for a walk most days.'*
7.   *'If it had been one of Mrs Oliver's stories,' said Spence, 'you ought to have found*
8.   *the dog howling over the two dead bodies, but that didn't happen.'*

This passage basically does not support the 'rule', even though it is a narrative, where participants are typically introduced and then referred to again. This is the use described in c) above, but note the careful way in which the example is phrased, with two possible referents (*cake* and *roll*).

So generally the rule is not true, because:

1.   *the* is commonly used for first mention (see all the other specific uses described above):

   Where's the sugar?

2. For 'second' mention, pronouns are the logical choice (as in the passage):

    I bought a clock on Friday and on Saturday it stopped going.

    If there is a gap and the reference is not clear then *the* may be used. Writers can also use *the* to avoid repeating a pronoun too much.

3. Lack of specificness can continue into the second mention (as in the passage):

    Darren wants a bike for his birthday but I don't think a bike is a good idea.

B3.6 Generalising with noun phrases

If you want to make a generalisation about all the members of a 'class' there are several ways to do it. The most common way with count nouns is to use a plural noun phrase with no article:

Dogs are our best friends.

Not of course *Dog . . .* because this would be interpreted as a noncount noun (see C2). The equivalent for noncount nouns would be without an article:

Cheese is made from the milk of cows and other animals.

It is also possible to use both the definite and indefinite articles with a singular noun phrase for generic reference, as we saw in the lists above. The indefinite article can be used to pick out a typical member of a class:

A dog is for life, not for Christmas. (We could also say *Dogs are . . .*)

The definite article is often used with musical instruments and dances:

Can you dance the tango?

But it usually has an academic tone, when people are writing about something professionally:

The invention of the wheel was the most important development in transport.

In such cases the responsibility lies with the employer.

This use is quite common in grammatical description (as in this book):

The indefinite article has two forms . . .

The definite article is also used with generic plural noun phrases in two situations:

❑   with generic adjectives, e.g. *the poor, the long-term unemployed* (cf. A3)
❑   with nationality nouns, e.g. *the French, the Chinese*

B3.7 Conclusion

Articles are probably the most difficult words in English for non-native speakers to learn, especially if their first language does not have articles (which means the vast majority of speakers in the world; even when the languages do have articles there are differences in use). And the rules for their use, especially for the specific uses of the definite article are quite difficult, and impossible to apply while speaking (of course, they are not meant to be applied in this way). But this is still no excuse for the inaccuracy of the 'second-mention' rule. Here is a better pedagogic 'rule':

Table B3.7.1 The difference between *the* and *a* with singular count nouns

	known to speaker	known to hearer	'rule'	example
1)	+	+	use *the*	Can I have the car?
2)	+	−	use *a*	I bought a new car today.
3)	−	−	use *a*	I need a new car.

In fact the second and third columns correspond to the two types of reference discussed in this section: specific vs non-specific (known to speaker) and definite vs indefinite (known to hearer).

Comments

Activity B3.1: (1) and (3) require the indefinite article; *system* and *father* are count nouns. In (2) *advice* is a noncount noun, and in (4), though *crisis* is a count noun, it is not the head of the noun phrase; *management* is, and it is noncount.

Activity B3.2: On the first line we think that *the television* means the system of entertainment (institutions; use h) above). But on the last line we realise that it is specific reference to a particular object in the immediate situation.

Activity B3.3: There are several references to a dog. They are (line numbers in brackets):

a dog *(1)*, a dog *(3)*, a dog *(3)*, a dog *(5)*, him *(5)*, the dog *(8)*

Notice how the first four mentions keep the indefinite article, because the dog is not yet established in the story; the first three mentions are questions. It is only with the fourth mention that the dog becomes established (i.e. has specific reference); it is now available to be referred to as definite (as the speaker and listener know that they are talking about the same thing). But in the fifth mention, instead of the definite article, the definite pronoun *him* is used. Only after a little gap is the definite article used with the noun to remind us what is being discussed.

TYPES OF ADVERB   **B4**

As was said in A4, adverbs have different types and functions, and it is hard to capture them all in one description. Here is a list of some prominent types of adverb; it is not exhaustive.

Central adverbs

These are the adverbs of time, manner and place described in A4 that are traditionally regarded as being the most typical. They 'modify' the verb or whole sentence:

I quickly left the room. (manner, answering the question 'how?')
She'll arrive shortly. (time, answering the question 'when?')
He lives locally. (place, answering the question 'where?')

We can also mention here frequency adverbs such as *always, often, usually, sometimes, rarely, seldom, never,* which answer the question 'how often?'

It seldom rains here.

One feature of such adverbs is that they can be one-word answers to questions.

When did he leave? Recently.

And they can be focused on in cleft (see A11) sentences:

It was recently that he left.

Degree adverbs

One type of degree adverbs, namely intensifiers, was first mentioned in A4 in the section on adjectives, since they function very closely with them: *very happy.* Intensifiers also modify adverbs: *very happily.* Many words such as *this* and *that* can be intensifiers:

I swear: it was this big.

However, we need to extend the class to include other words that do not 'intensify', but refer to other types of degree, such as *slightly* (*he's slightly crazy*).

Some adverbs can be degree adverbs as well as central adverbs:

It's awfully cold. It's perfectly horrible. (degree)
She writes awfully/perfectly. (central, manner)

Some degree adverbs can also be used with verbs:

He's completely crazy. He ignored me completely.

Modal adverbs

You may have heard of modal auxiliaries. Modal adverbs cover some of the same ideas, such as certainty, probability and possibility. Examples are *certainly, definitely, probably, possibly*:

I probably won't come.

Maybe and *perhaps* belong to this group but they tend to be placed at the start of the sentence:

Maybe I will come.

The reading in D6 (sections 146c and e) lists a number of other adverbs which are modal in nature in that they are used to weaken (e.g. *generally*) or strengthen (e.g. *obviously*) an argument.

Comment adverbs

Comment adverbs comment on the sentence as a whole, and are often separated from it by a comma, especially if placed at the start of a sentence.

Fortunately, he had another credit card with him. (= it is fortunate that . . .)
They stupidly left it behind. (= it was stupid of them to leave it behind)

They offer a way for the speaker/writer to get their opinion into a sentence without mentioning themselves expressly.

Frankly, it's disgusting. (this is the speaker's opinion)

Such words are often confused with central adverbs, because they are formed by the addition of *-ly* to adjectives, but in the examples above they are not referring to manner, time or place; see Activity B4.1 below. Some, of course, can be central adverbs as well:

> He spoke <u>frankly</u>.
> They behaved <u>stupidly</u>.

They can also consist of a phrase: *personally speaking, curiously enough*.

> <u>Curiously enough</u>, when I got there, everyone had left.

Linking adverbs

These are used to show a particular relationship between the sentence in which they occur and the preceding one. There are different types of linking ideas; here are just a few examples:

❏ concession or contrast: *however, though, nevertheless*:
   This sentence would be an entirely natural utterance if I were at home telling some-one where John was at that moment. <u>However</u>, I would be much less likely to say this if I were actually in the supermarket . . .
❏ result or consequence: *therefore, thus, as a result*:
   Conjunctions make the link between clauses in the same sentence; <u>therefore</u>, the link appears stronger.
❏ addition: *in addition, also.*
   In addition [to a previous point about adverbs], *there are some adverbs that have the same form as adjectives . . .*

Moreover and *furthermore* are often placed in this group, but they have the idea of something which goes beyond what has been said before, not simply something added.

Linking adverbs are similar to some conjunctions in meaning (see A9), but they behave different grammatically. Conjunctions make the link between clauses in the same sentence; therefore, the link appears stronger.

Even though they link a sentence to the previous one, they do not always occur at the beginning; they may also occur in the middle or at the end of the sentence. The use of commas in writing is normal.

B4.1 Distinguishing adverb types

Many adverbs may belong to more than one type, as in these examples:

a) Adverb of time: <u>*Then*</u> *we left.*
b) Linking adverb: *As the table shows, there are several cases which would appear to break the rules quite significantly. First of all,* <u>*then*</u>*, identify the most significant exceptions.*
c) Comment adverb: <u>*Happily*</u>*, she smiled at him.*
d) Adverb of manner: *She smiled at him* <u>*happily*</u>*.*

In b) *then* indicates that the second sentence is a consequence of the first. In c) happily indicates the speaker's feeling (relief) about her smile, while in d) it indicates the manner in which she smiled.

Activity B4.1

It is sometimes said that *hopefully* should not be used as a comment adverb, only as an adverb of manner (meaning 'in a hopeful way'), e.g. 'He travelled hopefully', not 'Hopefully, it won't rain'. However, this use is quite common, and many other *-ly* adverbs are used in this way, e.g. *happily*, as we have seen. See if you can distinguish the two uses in the sentences below.

1. They pressed their noses **hopefully** against the shop window.
2. **Hopefully** we will do well.
3. 'The train won't be late', he said **hopefully**.
4. **Hopefully**, I can take the chance with both hands.
5. These seats will **hopefully** be more comfortable.

Activity B4.2

Look at these sentences for 'however' and distinguish between its two uses. You are probably familiar with one of them, but the other may be unknown; see if you can identify and name it according to the types described above.

1. One thing that was always clear, **however**, was his singing.
2. **However** strange you find it, do not be distracted.
3. You must put up with the pain, **however** terrible.
4. **However**, he is sceptical about its practical value.
5. There was no room in the house for exercise, **however**.

Activity B4.3

Look at the adapted concordance lines for *so* below and work out what types of adverbs each represents. On one line it is not an adverb.

1. That bit doesn't feel **so** bad.
2. But it's softer than it was before. **So** that's good.
3. I'm not **so** young as I used to be.
4. And we have no relatives there, **so** we can't even travel to West Germany.
5. I'm **so** not going to that party.

TERMINOLOGY

One of the problems you face when learning about scientific English grammar is the way in which different terms are used to refer to the same concept, i.e. cases of synonymy. Some that you may be familiar with pedagogically already are:

> *continuous* and *progressive* (for verb forms)
> *reported speech* and *indirect speech*

But in scientific grammar such cases are common. *Agreement* and *concord* (see A8) are one example.

This is particularly true for types of adverb. Here in this section what I have called *comment adverbs* are also known as *sentence adverbs* or *disjuncts*. *Linking adverbs* are also called *conjuncts* by some grammarians (not to be confused with *conjunctions*).

B4.2 Conclusion

The traditional idea of adverbs, as modifying verbs (hence their name) in the same way that adjectives modify nouns, is far from being the full truth. Adverbs do many different jobs and not all are related to verbs. In fact, only the first type, central adverbs, are closely linked to verbs, and then not always.

Comments

Activity B4.1: (1) and (3) are adverbs of manner; the saying and pressing are done in a hopeful way. (2), (4) and (5) are comment adverbs, showing the speakers' position ('they are hoping/hopeful that ...'). Often comment adverbs come at the start of a sentence and there may be commas separating them in writing, as in (4), but not always, as in (5).

Activity B4.2: On lines (1), (4) and (5) *however* is a linking adverb; it contrasts the idea in this sentence with the one in the previous one (which we cannot see). Note the use of commas and the different positions. However, on lines (2) and (3) *however* is a degree adverb, modifying the following adjectives, and meaning 'it does not matter how'. (In (2) it is actually part of a phrasal conjunction.)

Activity B4.3: In lines (1) and (3) *so* is a degree adverb. On line (2) it is a linking adverb, while in line (4) it is a conjunction, though the meaning is still to with a consequence. In (5) there are two possible explanations: either 'not going to that party' is treated as an adjective which can be modified by *so* as a degree adverb; or *so* can be regarded as a modal adverb similar in meaning to 'definitely'.

THE MEANINGS OF TENSE AND ASPECT   B5

While the construction of tense and aspect forms is difficult (see A5 and A6), under-standing their meanings is one of one of the hardest areas of English grammar.

B5.1 The 'meanings' of the tenses

In A5 it was pointed out that there is not a simple one-to-one relationship between tense and time; this was one argument for rejecting the idea of a future tense. And even though there is no dispute about the existence of two tenses for English, the choice of their names, 'present' and 'past' may be somewhat unfortunate, because they reinforce this 'tense = time' fallacy. Indeed, some grammarians do not use these terms. And when we think about it, dividing the whole of human experience into two basic time options, present and past, would be very limiting. What about experiences that cross this division? Since every clause in English must have a verb, and since every verb must have one of these two forms (with limited exceptions), surely we should expect them to be flexible in their relationship to time. This is, in fact, what happens.

What follows is a relatively brief account of the tenses and their relationship to time and other factors.

The present tense

We can assign a number of meanings to the present simple tense ('simple' because it does not involve any 'aspect'). Most of them involve some other time than just the present.

❏ states:
> *The earth is round. I like chocolate.*
This can refer to permanent states as in the first example, or to more specific states, as in the second. The time reference extends from the past through the present to the future.

❏ repeated events or habits:
> *The sun rises in the east. Bill drinks heavily.*
This refers to repeated events or actions that apply to the past, present and (presumably) future.

❏ timeless happenings:
> *At the beginning of the film, the heroine falls in love with . . .*
This is common in the plots of works of arts such as films, novels and plays because they are timeless; they do not relate to real events. Jokes also fall into this category: *A man walks into a pub . . .* as does the use of the present in academic writing: *The results suggest . . .*

❏ declarations of feelings or intentions:
> *That sounds great. I love it! I promise I won't let you down.*

❏ instantaneous events:
> *Rooney shoots . . . and it's a goal.*
This use is common in sport commentaries and descriptions of processes (e.g. cooking: *I take the eggs . . .*) where a series of events is involved. This and the previous use are probably the closest we can get to a 'pure' present, where only present time is involved.

❏ the so-called 'historic' present:
> *'As I sit down, there's a great big noise . . .'*
This attempts to make past events more 'vivid'; it is used for narratives.

❏ schedules:
> *The train leaves at 12. We look at this topic in more detail in the next chapter.*
Here, although the events described are in the future, there is present significance.

❑ in conditionals and other clauses introduced by time conjunctions (see A10) referring to future events:

> *When they <u>come</u> in, don't say a word.*

As can be seen, all of these uses involve the present in some way, even though the state(s) or event(s) referred to may extend into the future (and also from the past). It has been said that the 'present' tense is used whenever the 'past' tense is not appropriate; that the present tense is more 'general', or flexible, than the specific 'past' (and some grammarians have suggested using the term 'non-past' instead of 'present').

The past tense

The past tense has a closer link to past time than the present tense does to present time. It refers to single or repeated events that are distinct from the present:

> *Shakespeare <u>wrote</u> Macbeth.*
> *I <u>walked</u> the dog every day.*

It is typical in stories:

> *Then the wolf <u>jumped</u> out of the bed . . .*

It is associated with specific times so it is the default choice if there is an adverbial (see A8) referring to a completed past time:

> *My sister <u>graduated</u> <u>in 2008</u>.*
> *I <u>hated</u> French <u>when I was at school</u>.*

Other forms can, of course, refer to past time. See below for discussions of the use of the (present) perfect (*I <u>have done</u> it*), and of the difference between simple and progressive forms. The use of the past tense in reported speech is covered in B12.

There are only a few idiomatic exceptions where the past does not refer to past time, but to the present or future:

❑ after expressions such as *would rather*, *it's time* and the verb *wish*:

> *It's time we <u>went</u>.*

❑ Referring to hypothetical events in conditionals:

> *If we <u>left</u> tomorrow, we would still arrive on time.*

There is one more situation where the past tense does not refer to past time.

 Activity B5.1

Think about *wanted* in this example:

> *Excuse me, Professor, do you have a moment? I <u>wanted</u> to ask you a question.*

Is it really past in time? Could the professor say 'Oh, you wanted to ask me a question, but you don't now,' and walk away? What is the difference between *want* and *wanted* here? Can you see any connection between this use of the past tense, and past-time reference of the past tense? What does it have in common with examples where the past tense does indicate past time?

So we may express these relationships in a diagram, adding in the fact that adverbs (*yesterday* etc.) also have past-time reference.

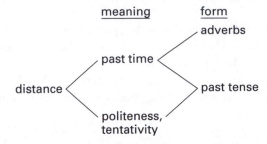

Figure B5.1.1 Expressing past time in English

Identify the time reference of the underlined finite verbs in the following sentences. Use the following possibilities: past, present, future, general time.

1. *May I stay? I'd rather you <u>left</u>.*
2. *Is it true that in the last book Harry Potter <u>dies</u>?*
3. *After you <u>speak</u> to him, call me.*
4. *At that point we <u>decided</u> to leave.*
5. *I <u>hear</u> you <u>are getting</u> married.*

B5.2 Aspect

Aspect is the name given to verb choices which involve the addition of auxiliaries to complete a verb phrase, as opposed to the inflections which indicate tense. The construction of aspectual forms is described in A6. We saw in A5 that in common pedagogic parlance aspect is included in tense, but on a scientific level the two need to be distinguished both formally and semantically.

Aspect involves how events relate to times in addition to their exact timing, i.e.

❑ how an event or state relates to the surrounding time periods
❑ whether an event or state has relevance to another, later, point in time

There are three aspects (excluding the 'simple' forms):

❑ progressive (continuous): *I <u>am singing</u>.* / *They <u>were walking</u>.*
❑ perfect: *I <u>have sung</u>.* / *They <u>had walked</u>.*
❑ perfect progressive: *I <u>have been singing</u>.* / *They <u>had been walking</u>.*

All three can combine with both past and present tenses, as the pairs of examples show. The progressive and perfect aspects are discussed below. It is worth noting that the vast majority of finite verb phrases in English consist of simple forms (i.e. present or past tenses); the perfect and progressive aspects are fairly rare, while the perfect progressive aspect is very rare.

The progressive aspect

Leaving aside the future use (as discussed in A5; see also D5), progressive forms are often said to refer to a lasting or continuous state or activity:

> He's _standing_ outside the door.
>
> I _was talking_ about something else.
>
> She's _been speaking_ for 45 minutes.

However, we need to recognise that simple verb forms can also refer to lasting states. For example

> I _live_ in Paris.

appears to be more 'lasting' than

> I'm _living_ in Paris.

which suggests a temporary state.

There are other problems with the idea of duration or continuity, as with these examples:

> He's _been ringing_ me all day.
>
> You've _been telling_ lies.

Here, rather than a continuous action we are more likely to give an 'iterative' (or 'repeated') interpretation. But this has little to do with the aspect; it is more to do with the semantic nature of the verb; 'ringing' and 'telling lies' are things we do in short bursts, not over long periods, whereas by contrast

> She's _been walking_ all day

could be continuous, because of the nature of walking.

Rather than focusing on a period of time, what the progressive does is focus on a point (the present or past, as specified by the tense) within a period of time. It says 'think about the action at a certain point in time, but don't forget the time before and after'. Thus the progressive aspect often has the idea of dropping the reader or listener into something in <u>progress</u>, bringing an activity to life, making it more 'vivid':

> We jumped into the water and a moment later we _were being_ carried downstream.

It would be perfectly possible to say _we were carried downstream_, as a completed action, but the progressive form tries to make the reader picture the activity in progress. So with the above examples (_I live in Paris / I'm living in Paris_), the latter tries to make the 'living' more an activity than a state, hence its shorter duration.

TERMINOLOGY

You will have noticed that I have used the term 'progressive' instead of 'continuous' to describe these verb forms, even though the latter is more common in some circles. This is because I feel that 'progressive' is a better term, because 'continuous' could be misleading. We have seen a number of situations where an action is not continuous, or where a simple form could be used for something 'continuous'.

The perfect aspect

Perfect forms relate past events and states to the present time (present perfect) or to a subsequent point of time in the past (past perfect). The relationship may involve:

❑ a completed action or state with a relevance to the present (or past): *I've hidden the presents.*
❑ an action or state lasting up to the present (or past): *You've drunk enough.*
❑ an accumulation of experience: *I've met many diplomats.*

Activity B5.3

Consider this joke, told by Groucho Marks, a well-known comedian, in a film. As he is leaving a party, he says to the hostess: 'I've had a wonderful evening'. She is very happy when she hears this, but then he continues 'But this wasn't it!' What two meanings of the present perfect are involved in this 'misunderstanding'?

Activity B5.4a

Match these present perfect forms to their meaning:

a) *I'm afraid you're too late; they've gone.*   1.   past activity, present relevance
b) *I've been to Hong Kong lots of times.*   2.   past action, present relevance
c) *I can see you've been playing football.* 3.   accumulation of experience

Activity B5.4b

We can often make a statement about the present based on a present perfect tense. Take the three sentences in Activity B5.4a and, using the present tense, write a sentence which contains an implication based on the original.

Comparing the present perfect and the past tense

One of the hardest tasks for learners of English is to decide between these two forms, since both commonly refer to past time. However, the past tense, as we saw, refers to specific past times unconnected with the present; the present perfect is more general, referring to a time frame that extends from a point in the past up to the present.

In fact, though, the difference between the two is not absolute; it is not determined objectively by the time and time relationships. The same event can be construed with both the present perfect and past:

Widdowson (1999) claimed that . . .
Widdowson (1999) has claimed that . . .

The choice here depends on whether we think that the claim still 'affects' the present.

VARIATION IN ENGLISH

The adverbs *yet* and *already* are used differently in British and American English when referring to past time:

 American: *Did* you <u>see</u> *the film yet/already?* (past tense)
 British: *Have* you <u>seen</u> *the film yet/already?* (present perfect)

This again suggests that the difference between the past tense and present perfect is not absolute.

B5.3 Stative and non-stative verbs

We need to investigate one more distinction between verbs, that between 'stative' and 'non-stative' (or 'dynamic') verbs. This is closely related to the use of the progressive.

 Stative verbs such as *want, like, need, resemble* and *own* tend not to occur in progressive forms. It would sound strange to say 'He's wanting an ice-cream.' Because they basically refer to states there is no need for an alternative with the progressive to indicate an activity in progress. And they have no imperative (see B9): *Want this!*

 However, there are times when we want to emphasise a state and make it seem like an activity, for example:

 I've been wanting to meet you for ages.
 You'll be needing a haircut soon. ('I can see a point in the future when you will be in need of a haircut.')

And adverts exploit this emphatic interpretation of the progressive with stative verbs: *We're loving it!*

 A number of verbs can be both stative and non-stative, but with different meanings (another example of grammar and meaning being related). Thus *think* is stative when it refers to opinions, but non-stative when it refers to a mental process:

 I think we should go now. (Not 'I am thinking . . .')
 Don't interrupt; I'm thinking.

Similarly, the verb *be* is normally non-stative, but if it is used with adjectives referring to temporary behaviour then it can have progressive forms (and the imperative):

 You're being naughty. Be quiet.

 Activity B5.5

Look at the sentences below containing *have*. One of them is wrong/sounds strange. Which? How can this be explained?

1. *I have three sisters.*
2. *I am having three sisters.*
3. *I have a bath every day.*
4. *I am having a bath.*

> **VARIATION IN ENGLISH**
> In Indian English the use of stative verbs with progressive forms is common, for example:
>> They *are owning* several houses.
>
> And this use is also becoming more common in British and American English:
>> *I'm thinking* we should leave now.

B5.4 Conclusion

Describing the subtle shades of meaning involved in the tenses and aspects is one of the hardest tasks in English grammar. However, much unhelpful information is given out, especially that which encourages the tense = time fallacy, or which suggests that progressive forms are only to do with continuous or lasting events.

The impression is often given that tense and aspect choice relies on objective criteria (such as the timing and nature of the event) which are independent of the speaker or writer. But, as we have seen, the same past event can be described with the present perfect or the past tense according to whether the speaker sees it as relevant or not relevant to the present; or it can be referred to with the past or past progressive according to the impression that the writer/speaker wants to convey. Similarly, stative verbs can be used with the progressive, given the right conditions. Here the concept of construing – the way we perceive the world (or the way we want our listeners to perceive the world) – is crucial, along with the grammatical choices that we have at our disposal. (See the readings in D2 and D4.)

Comments

Activity B5.1: *Wanted* here is referring to a present-time 'want'. The difference between it and the present tense is that the former sounds more polite or tentative, while the latter sounds more 'urgent' and might be inappropriate when addressing one's professor. What unifies this use of the past tense with its normal use for past time is the idea of distance: either distance in time, or personal 'distance' between speaker and hearer.

Activity B5.2: 1, though past tense, is future time; 2 is general time (or timeless, because it is a novel); 3 is future time; 4 is a normal past-time use of the past tense; 5 is referring to the past (*hear*) and future (*are getting*).

Activity B5.3: The hostess thinks he is referring to an up-to-the-present experience, but, as his second sentence makes clear, he is referring to an earlier (accumulated) experience.

Activity B5.4a: The links are a2, b3, c1.

Activity B5.4b: For example:

a)   *She's not here.*
b)   *I know the city well.*
c)   *Your clothes are dirty.*

Activity B5.5: (2) is the one that sounds strange, because when it refers to relationships (or possession) *have* is a stative verb. However, in (3) and (4) it is a non-stative verb, referring to an action (repeated in 3, in progress in 4). In British English *have got* could be substituted for *have* in (1) but not in (3).

MODAL AUXILIARIES   B6

B6.1 Modality

Modality is to do with the way statements are qualified by speakers to show that they are not facts, either because there is some personal element involved in their realisation, or because they are seen as lacking certainty.
   You must do it.
   It might rain.
Sentences without modality are presented as facts:
   I saw him yesterday.
   It's raining.
All four open word classes can express modality. We have already discussed modal adverbs (such as *probably*) in B4; adjectives (*It is probable that . . .*), nouns (*There is a probability that . . .*) and verbs (*It appears that . . .*) can also express modality. However, in this section we are interested in the use of modal auxiliaries to express modality.

B6.2 Modal auxiliaries

There are nine 'central' modals: *can, could, may, might, will, would, shall, should, must.* They are easy to identify as they all possess the following formal features:

❑   they have only one form; unlike verbs (and the primary auxiliaries) there is no infinitive, past tense, third-person *-s* form, *-ed* or *-ing* participle.
❑   they are followed by the bare infinitive of verbs: *I can see.*
❑   they form negatives directly with *not*: *I may not come* (See A7.)
❑   they invert to form questions: *Can I come?* (See A7.)

In these last two respects they are like the primary auxiliaries. But unlike the primary auxiliaries they do not combine with one another; only one modal is possible, as the first element in the verb phrase.

There are a number of other forms which share some of the features of modals, and other verb-like expressions which cover the same meanings as modals. These are discussed below under the headings 'marginal modals' and 'semi-modals'.

Modals and past time

Activity B6.1 ⊕

Look at the following pairs of sentences:

1. a) *Can you come tomorrow?*
    b) *Could you come tomorrow?*
2. a) *I may come.*
    b) *I might come.*

What time reference do they have? What is the difference between them?

In the past it was common to match up the modals in present tense/past tense pairs: *can/could, may/might, will/would, shall/should*. While there is a historical justification for this, such a position is no longer tenable (and what would the past of *must* be anyway?). The relationship between, for example, *can* and *could* is not the same as that between a present/past pair such as *see* and *saw*. All the so-called 'past tense' modals, like *could* and *might* above, can be used for future time, which is not possible for the past tense of main verbs (apart from exceptional cases). For this reason we prefer to talk about the modals one by one.

However, there is something in common between the past tense and *could, might, would* and *should*. This is the idea of tentativity or distance that they can convey. For example, compare the politeness of *might* in
   Might I have a look?
with that expressed by the past tense in
   I wanted to ask you a question.
This distancing effect of modals is particularly true in reported speech: *He can come/I said he could come*). Here the difference is the same as the present/past distinction in main verbs. See B12 for more on reporting.
   There are other past uses of *could* and *would*:
   When I was young I <u>could</u> understand German. (a general past ability)
   After school we <u>would</u> go down to the shopping centre. (for past habits)
In addition, most modals can be combined with the perfect aspect to express past time:
   He <u>must</u>/<u>will</u>/<u>would</u>/<u>could</u>/<u>may</u>/<u>might</u> have finished by now.

B6.3 Meanings of modal verbs

We can distinguish two basic types of modality that apply to all the modals:

❏ intrinsic modality, referring to human control over events, to do with notions such as permission, obligation or volition (e.g. intentions or promises)
❏ extrinsic modality, referring to our perception of the factual nature of events, e.g. possibility, necessity, prediction, deduction.

For example, if you say *he must go*, this is intrinsic modality; you are imposing an obligation. However, if you say *he must be crazy*, this is extrinsic modality; you are making a deduction (there is no obligation to be crazy!). However, if you say

> *You must be crazy to work here*

it could mean two things: 'it is necessary to be crazy to work here' (intrinsic) or 'I think you are crazy to accept a job here'.

We can also group the central modals into three basic groups, according to the general meanings that they indicate. Combining this with the intrinsic/extrinsic distinction, we can arrive at the following table:

Table B6.3.1 Modal auxiliaries: intrinsic and extrinsic meanings

modals	intrinsic meaning	extrinsic meaning
can/could/ may/might	permission you can/may leave (they said) we could/might leave	possibility it can/could/may/might happen any day
must/ should	obligation (strong/weak) you must/should leave	necessity, deduction they must/should be there now
will/would/ shall	volition, insistence, habit I will/shall leave now you will/shall leave now every night we would listen to music	prediction, deduction it will rain today/that will be John

This is a simplification, however, of the meanings of modals, and does not capture all of the nuances and differences. For example, formality is a factor in the use of *may* and *can* for permission: *you may go now* is more formal than *you can go now*. And *would* often has an idea of hypotheticality:

> *I would do it* (*but I don't have the time*).

And we need to mention one very important meaning of *can* that does not fit neatly into the table, namely ability: *I can do it*. Thus a single modal may have a number of different meanings.

The readings in D6 and D10 describe two areas where modals play an important role: in academic and interpersonal communication respectively.

 Activity B6.2

Work out the different meanings of *can* in these sentences.

1. *You can go now.*
2. *She can sing very beautifully.*
3. *It can be done.*
4. *Can you talk to him?*
5. *It can be quite cold at this time of year.*
6. *I can see absolutely nothing.*

B6.4 Marginal and semi-modals

Two groups of words are closely associated with the modals: the marginal modals, *need*, *dare* and *ought to*, and the semi-modals. *Need* and *dare* are said to be marginal as modals because they sometimes behave like modals, i.e. they can form interrogatives and negatives without *do*, have no -*s* for third person singular, and are followed by a bare infinitive (see A7):

<u>Need</u> he <u>do</u> that? No, he <u>needn't</u>.

However, this is rare; they are much more common as (main) verbs:

<u>Does</u> he <u>need</u> <u>to do</u> that? No, he <u>doesn't need to</u>.

And in the positive they are not used without *to*: *He needs <u>to</u> hurry* not 'He need hurry'.

Ought to is quite common as an alternative to *should* for weak obligation. It is included here because it can also behave like a modal, with *to* omitted:

We ought to go, <u>oughtn't</u> we?

The semi-modals are so-called because they cover some of the meanings of the modals, such as futurity, obligation, past habits, permission and ability. And they are all followed by the infinitive (sometimes with *to*, sometimes without):

I am <u>unable to</u> take your call now.

After school we <u>used to</u> go down to the shopping centre.

You'<u>d better</u> apologise.

However, they are structurally different; in fact, they consist of a number of different structures, some of them involving primary auxiliaries. Here is a list of expressions commonly recognised as semi-modals:

be going to (see A5 and D5), used to, have to (have got to)

had better, would rather

be (un)able to, be allowed to, be supposed to

Sometimes they are used when a modal would be impossible:

I would like to <u>be able to</u> come.

'I would like to can come' is wrong because *can* cannot be used as an infinitive. And *have to* can be used as a distancing equivalent of *must* in reported speech:

I <u>must</u> go. He said he <u>had to</u> go.

As function words the finite forms of primary auxiliaries often have weak stress and can have contractions in non-formal writing (e.g. *I am* becomes *I'm*). Of the modal auxiliaries only *will* and *would* have contractions: -*'ll* and -*'d*. See A7 for more on contractions.

NON-STANDARD FORMS

A number of the semi-modals have alternative, non-standard (written) forms, reflecting their pronunciation in casual speech:

I'm gonna, I've gotta, We oughta

as well as the dropping of the auxiliary:

I gotta, You betta/better

B6.5 Conclusion

The meanings and uses of the modal auxiliaries are not easy to capture. This is partly because there is no one-to-one correspondence between form and function (or meaning). One meaning may be expressed by more than one modal (though sometimes with slight differences, such as in formality), and one modal may express several meanings. It is certainly wrong to match one modal with one meaning, e.g. *can* with ability. And it is unhelpful to claim, as some grammars and text-books do, that the modals exhibit present and past tenses in the same way that verbs do.

But the problem is also that the modals are bound up with interpersonal ideas of tentativity and politeness, with functions such as making suggestions and requests (*Can you turn it down?*), directing people to do things (*You will do it*), and so on, in addition to merely moderating the factuality of events. This is particularly true in academic communication, where speakers and writers not only want to express lack of certainty with the use of modality, but also want to be tentative in order not to force their conclusions too strongly on their readers. The reading in D6 covers this aspect of modal verbs.

Comments

Activity B6.1: They all refer to future time. The difference is that 1b) is more polite than 1a), and in 2b) your 'coming' is considered less likely than it is in 2a). In other words, 1b) and 2b) are more tentative.

Activity B6.2:

1. permission
2. ability
3. possibility
4. ability in general, but in fact this functions as a request
5. possibility in general, but the idea is that something sometimes happens
6. ability in general; the use of *can* is common with the senses. Here it would be possible (but less idiomatic) to say *I see . . .*

MULTI-WORD VERBS   B7

In A7 we looked at ways of varying the verb phrase by adding words such as *do* and *not*. But there is another way in which verb phrases can be extended. Many verbs in English get their meaning not only from the verb itself but also from a 'little word' that follows. These combinations of 'little word' plus verb are the topic of this section.

> ### *TERMINOLOGY*
> Some teachers and grammars use 'phrasal verb' as a cover term for all these combinations. In this book, however, 'multi-word verb' is used as the cover term, and 'phrasal verb' is used for just one type, while 'prepositional verb' and 'phrasal-prepositional verb' are two other types. You will see that they are actually quite different.

B7.1 Multi-word and single-word verbs

First of all we need to distinguish multi-words verbs from single-word verbs that are simply followed by a prepositional phrase. An example of the latter would be:

> I *looked* up the chimney

Here we have a single-word verb, *look*, and what follows is a prepositional phrase: *up the chimney*. We can tell this by asking a *wh-* interrogative (see A8) and looking at the answer:

> *Where* did you *look*? *Up* the chimney.

Here *look* and *up* have their usual meanings.

Compare this with an example with a multi-word (phrasal) verb:

> I *looked up* the word

where the corresponding question and answer would be

> *What* did you *look up*? *The word*

and not

> *Where* did you *look*? *Up* the word.

Clearly we have very different grammar at work here. There is also issue of meaning; the meaning of *look up* cannot be guessed from its constituent words. It does not mean to 'look in an upward direction'; it means to 'check something'.

B7.2 Distinguishing phrasal and prepositional verbs

Phrasal verbs and prepositional verbs have a lot in common. If we take a typical prepositional verb, such as *look after*, we can see that, like *look up*, its meaning is idiomatic. If we say

> I *looked after* the cat

there is no idea of looking, nor indeed of 'after'. And if we make a question and answer

> *What* did you *look after*? *The cat*

we get the same structure as for *look up*, where *the cat* appears as the object of the verb.

However, there is one crucial difference.

Activity B7.1 ✪

> Which of these two sentences is incorrect?
>
> 1. I *looked the word up*.
> 2. I *looked the cat after*.

So what is *up* in sentence 1? It is not a preposition according to our definition (because it does not go with a noun phrase). It is usually called a 'particle', or 'adverb particle' (making it another type of adverb to add to the list in B4). Phrasal verbs such as *look up* are combinations of verb + particle. The particle has nothing to do with any following noun phrase; the fact that it can be placed after the object, as in sentence 1 above, shows this. Particle movement is a key technique for distinguishing (transitive) phrasal and prepositional verbs.

★ **Activity B7.2**

Decide whether the verbs in the sentences below are phrasal or prepositional by seeing if the 'little word' can be moved.

1. Don't <u>look at</u> the floor.
2. Who <u>carried out</u> the attack?
3. Let's <u>wait for</u> them a bit longer.
4. I have <u>found out</u> nothing.
5. Everything <u>depends on</u> your answer.
6. Why did you <u>put on</u> those shoes?
7. Cars always <u>break down</u> at inconvenient times.

One reason for confusing phrasal and prepositional verbs is that particles look like prepositions; indeed, their membership overlaps extensively (cf. determiners and pronouns in A3). But some words can only be particles: *out* (in standard English), *away* and *back* are the most common ones. And most prepositions cannot be particles, e.g. *to, at*.

B7.3 Phrasal verbs with a pronoun as object

There is one more restriction on phrasal verbs that we need to consider.

★ **Activity B7.3**

Look at the four sentences below with the phrasal verb *hand in*. Which is wrong?

1. The students have handed their essay in.
2. The students have handed in their essay.
3. The students have handed it in.
4. The students have handed in it.

When the object is a personal pronoun particle movement is obligatory. This is a reflection of the fact that English does not like definite pronouns (such as *it*) at the end of sentences if there is an alternative (see A11). There is also an opposite tendency when the object is a long noun phrase; the particle tends not to move:

   I finally handed <u>in</u> the essay that the lecturer had given me extra time for.
Not 'I finally handed the essay that the lecturer had given me extra time for <u>in</u>.'

Are these sentences correct or incorrect? Can you explain why?

1. *They turned on us.*
2. *They turned us on.*

B7.4 Phrasal-prepositional verbs

It is possible to have a combination of phrasal and prepositional verbs, where there is both a particle and a preposition:

> *We're looking <u>forward</u> <u>to</u> your party.*

Forward is the particle, and *to* the preposition with the object noun phrase *your party*. There may be an object separating the verb from the particle and preposition:

> *Doctors have put <u>his illness</u> <u>down</u> <u>to</u> stress.*

B7.5 Conclusion

Whatever terminology we use, prepositional and phrasal verbs (as labelled here) need to be distinguished – from each other, and from ordinary verb + preposition combinations. We can summarise the different constructions as follows:

MULTI-WORD VERBS	phrasal	V + particle + NP (= object)	I looked <u>up</u> the word. I looked the word <u>up</u>. (*What . . .*)
	prepositional	V + prep + NP (= object)	I looked <u>after</u> the cat. (*What . . .*)
	phrasal-prepositional	V + particle + prep + NP (= object)	I looked <u>forward</u> <u>to</u> it. (*What . . .*)
VERB + PREPOSITION		V + prep + NP (= adverbial)	I looked <u>up</u> the chimney. (*Where . . .*)

Figure B7.5.1 Distinguishing prepositional and phrasal verbs

Multi-word verbs often have single-word alternatives, for example *distribute* alongside *hand out*, or *investigate* alongside *look into*. Learners of English often prefer these since they are simpler grammatically. But they can sound unidiomatic and formal, especially in spoken English: *I got up at eight this morning* is preferable to *I arose . . .*

Comments

Activity B7.1: Sentence 2 is not possible. *After* is a preposition and must be placed in front of the noun phrase.

Activity B7.2:
Phrasal verbs: 2, 4, 6, 7
Prepositional verbs: 1, 3, 5
Break down in sentence 7 is a phrasal verb, even though the particle *down* cannot be moved. This is because it is an intransitive verb with no object (as many phrasal verbs are).

Activity B7.3: Sentence 4 is wrong: the object *it* should not come after the particle *in*. The word order in 3 is correct.

Activity B7.4: Both are correct, but for very different reasons. They have different meanings; in sentence 1 *turn on* is a prepositional verb meaning 'attack', while in sentence 2 it is a phrasal verb meaning 'excite'. In 2 the particle has been obligatorily moved after the object, which is why 1 could only be prepositional. (If we used a noun phrase instead then it would be ambiguous: *They turned on the audience*.)

VERB PATTERNS   B8

As we have seen, it is the verb that determines the structure of clauses: which elements can be included and which cannot. This mainly involves the use of objects, predicatives and (to a small extent) adverbials, but can also be extended to subjects (e.g. to the use of *there* and *it*, as in *It is raining* and *There seems to be a problem*). This is the 'pattern' of the verb. (It is sometimes called 'verb complementation'.)

For example, in addition to a direct object, *say* allows a prepositional object but not an indirect object, which *tell* does allow:

I *said something <u>to her</u>* and not 'I *said <u>her</u> something*'.
I *told <u>her</u> something*.

And *discriminate* requires a prepositional object, not a direct object (in standard English):

They discriminated <u>against</u> him/He was discriminated <u>against</u>.

B8.1 Five patterns

It is common to classify verbs into five types, according to the pattern that they occur in: intransitive, link, link transitive, monotransitive and ditransitive. However, individual verbs, especially the more common ones, occur in more than one pattern (as we saw with verbs that can be both transitive and intransitive in C6), so it is more accurate to specify which patterns verbs are used in. Indeed, we can go further and identify a number of sub-patterns involving the following types of elements:

❑   phrases (noun, adjective, prepositional)
❑   subordinate finite clauses (beginning with *that* or *wh*-words)

❑   non-finite clauses beginning with infinitives and participles
❑   quotes

Below is a list of the most common sub-patterns. In some cases typical verbs are indicated.

Intransitive patterns (i.e. with the clause structure SV)
  I've been walking.
We can also include ergative verbs here (see C7):
  The lesson ended.

Link (copular) patterns (i.e. with the clause structure SVPs)
These verbs have three types of subject predicative:

❑   an adjective phrase: *The girl seemed restless.*
    Typical verbs: *be, appear, feel, look, seem, smell, sound, taste, remain, keep, stay, become, get, go, grow, prove, turn, end up*
❑   a noun phrase: *William is my friend.*
    Typical verbs: *be, appear, feel, seem, remain, become*
❑   a *wh-* word clause: *He is what we need.*

It is usual to include cases where there is an obligatory adverbial in this category (although they are SVA):
  The kitchen is downstairs. She is lying on the grass.

Link transitive patterns (i.e. with the clause structure SVOPo)
These generally have a noun phrase as their object, but there are a number of different elements that can function as the object predicative, depending on the verb:

❑   an adjective phrase: *We painted it red.*
❑   a noun phrase: *They elected him President.*
❑   a *to* infinitive clause: *They forced him to leave.*
❑   a bare infinitive clause: *I saw her leave the room.*
    Typical verbs: *have, let, make, feel, hear, see, watch, help*
❑   an *-ing* participle clause: *I heard someone shouting.*
    Typical verbs: *feel, hear, notice, see, smell, watch, catch, discover, find, have*
❑   an *-ed* participle clause: f) *I got the watch repaired.*
    Typical verbs: *get, have, want, need, like, see, hear, watch*

It is usual to include cases with an object and obligatory adverbial (i.e. SVOA) in this category:
  I put it in the cupboard.
Note how verbs of perception have a choice between infinitive and *-ing* participle, e.g.:
  I saw him run/running.
with a difference in meaning (a complete action vs an activity in progress).

Some link and link transitive verbs are closely associated with their predicatives, in that they may just have a few adjectives that they co-occur with. Complete these sentences with a subject or object predicative chosen from the list on the right. Think of other adjectives that could be used in these patterns.

1. *They're driving me* _____ .   *guilty*
2. *It tastes* _____ .   *responsible*
3. *The judge pronounced him* _____ .   *warmer*
4. *Day by day the weather grew* _____ .   *silent*
5. *We hold you* _____ .   *delicious*
6. *In the end, it proved* _____ .   *alone*
7. *Please leave me* _____ .   *crazy*
8. *They remained* _____ .   *impossible*

Monotransitive patterns (i.e. with the clause structure SVO)

These have a range of direct objects, depending on the particular verb. These include:

❑   a noun phrase: *Tom caught the ball.*
❑   a *that* clause: *I think that we have met.* (*that* can be
                                            omitted)
❑   a *wh-* word clause: *Can you guess what she said?*
❑   a *wh-* word plus *to* infinitive clause: *I learned how to sail a boat.*
❑   a *to* infinitive clause: *We've decided to move house.*
❑   a *to* infinitive clause, with 'subject': *They want us to help.*
❑   an *-ing* clause: *She enjoys playing tennis.*
❑   an *-ing* clause, with 'subject':   *I hate the children quarrelling.*
❑   a quote: *'Leave me alone!' he said.*

As we have seen there can also be a prepositional object (Oi):

> *They laughed at me.*

Ditransitive patterns (i.e. with the clause structure SVOO)

Typically the first element is a noun phrase but there is a variety of second elements. There are four main combinations:

1. An indirect object followed by a direct object which is:
    ❑   a noun phrase: *She gave the girl a doll.*
    ❑   a *wh-* word clause: *I told him what we were doing.*
    ❑   a *to* infinitive clause: *They advised us to leave.*
        Typical verbs: *advise, ask, forbid, invite, order, persuade, remind, teach, tell*
    ❑   a *wh-* word plus *to* infinitive clause: *I told him what to do.*
        Typical verbs: *advise, ask, remind, show, teach, tell*

❏ a *that* clause: You promised us <u>that you would come</u>.
❏ a quote: '<u>I'm used to it</u>', I told him.

2. A prepositional object followed by a direct object which is:
   ❏ a *that* clause: He wrote to me <u>that he was coming</u>.
   ❏ a *wh- word* clause: She described to me <u>what was happening</u>.

3. A direct object followed by a prepositional object:
   He described <u>the situation</u> <u>to everyone</u>.

4. An indirect object followed by a prepositional object: She told <u>him about the secret</u>.

Activity B8.2

You may have noticed that some of the different patterns above appear to be identical in that there is a pronoun and a *to* infinitive following the verb in each case e.g.

1. *They forced <u>him</u> <u>to leave</u>.* (link transitive)
2. *They want <u>us</u> <u>to help</u>.* (monotransitive)
3. *They advised <u>us</u> <u>to leave</u>.* (ditransitive)

However, we can discover the differences by trying to ask questions.

First of all, try to make a *wh-* interrogative by replacing everything after the verb. Then, where it is not possible, try to make a *wh-* interrogative by replacing the two separate parts.

B8.2 Describing verbs

The different patterns and sub-patterns above can be used to establish a picture of the various ways in which a verb is used. It is often assumed that a verb is used in only one pattern; for example, that *run* is only an intransitive verb (meaning a particular way of moving). But in fact it is also common as a monotransitive verb:

She's been running businesses since she was 16.

Note the different meaning here. It is quite common for different patterns to be associated with different meanings. Also, the more common verbs are, the more likely they are to have different patterns.

We also saw with verbs of perception (*see* etc.) under link transitive verbs that the sub-pattern itself may imply a different meaning. Here is another example.

He remembered putting the keys in his pocket.
He remembered to put the keys in his pocket.

Here the first example he put the keys in his pocket and he remembered doing this; in the second he remembered that he was supposed to put the keys in his pocket (so he did).

Activity B8.3

Look at the six sub-patterns above under 'Ditransitive patterns', combination 1 (indirect object followed by direct object). Which apply to the verb *warn*?

Activity B8.4

> Think of which patterns these verbs can be used in; give examples:
>   *look, stand, find, tell*
> Remember that the above examples show single-word verbs, but the patterns
> can also apply to phrasal and prepositional verbs (see B7). You do not always
> need the level of detail in the list above.

B8.3 Conclusion

For learners of English a knowledge of the patterns that each verb can occur in is of
vital importance. However, the most common verbs occur in many sub-patterns, and
it would take a long book to describe all of them. Many can be predicted because of
the semantic nature of the verb, but many cannot.

Learners tend to take one of two extreme positions. Some use a verb in only
one pattern, ignoring all the other possibilities, with the result that their English is
correct but very limited. Others assume that all patterns are available with every verb,
resulting in errors.

A final activity can drive home this point.

 Activity B8.5

> Which of the following verbs can appear in the gap below?
>   *described, told, informed, explained*
>   I _____ her my problem.

Comments

Activity B8.1: 1 crazy; 2 delicious; 3 guilty; 4 warmer; 5 responsible; 6 impossible;
7 alone; 8 silent

Activity B8.2:

1. Not possible: '*What did they force?*' i.e. it is not monotransitive.
2. Possible: *What do they want?* (*Us to help*) i.e. it is monotransitive.
3. Not possible: *What did they advise?* i.e. it is not monotransitive. (This would be a
    feasible question if the answer involved one element e.g. *a bath*, but not *us to leave*.)

When the elements are treated separately, in a) only *him* can be questioned:
    Who did they force to leave?
But this is not possible with *force to leave* ('*What did they force him?*'), showing that
it is a predicative and the pattern is link transitive (see Activity A8.5). On the other
hand, in c) both elements can be questioned:
    What did they advise us? (*to leave*)
    Who did they advise to leave? (*us*)
This shows that there are two objects.

Activity B8.3: These are the possibilities (with the indirect object also underlined):

❑   a *to* infinitive clause: *They warned <u>us</u> <u>to avoid uncooked vegetables</u>.*
❑   a *wh-* word plus *to* infinitive clause: *They warned <u>us</u> <u>what not to eat</u>.*
❑   a *that* clause: *They warned <u>us</u> <u>that a storm was coming</u>.*
❑   a quote: *<u>'Stop messing around!'</u> I warned <u>them</u>.*

There are, of course, other ditransitive patterns, for example, an indirect object followed by prepositional object:

   I warned <u>them</u> <u>against taking me for granted</u>.

Activity B8.4: Here are just some of the more obvious patterns for these verbs; you may have thought of others:

LOOK:	*He looks tired.*	link
	We looked away.	intransitive, phrasal
	He looked at her.	monotransitive, prepositional
	She looked after him.	monotransitive, prepositional
	I looked up the word.	monotransitive, phrasal
	We look up to them.	monotransitive, phrasal-prepositional
STAND:	*I've been standing here for ages.*	intransitive
	The house stands on the corner.	link (with obligatory adverbial)
	I can't stand them. (= 'tolerate')	monotransitive
	I won't stand for such behaviour.	monotransitive, prepositional
	He's standing for re-election.	monotransitive, prepositional
	Let me stand you a drink. (= 'buy')	ditransitive (Oi + Od)
FIND:	*I found your ring.*	monotransitive
	We've found you a job.	ditransitive (Oi + Od)
	We've found a job for you.	ditransitive (Od + Op)
	I find it very amusing.	link transitive
	We found the children watching TV.	link transitive (with *-ing* clause as Po)
	He's found out the truth.	monotransitive, phrasal
TELL:	*The pressure has told on him.*	monotransitive, prepositional
	The book tells of his health problems.	monotransitive, prepositional
	You've been telling lies.	monotransitive
	He told them a long story.	ditransitive (Oi + Od)
	She told the audience about her mother.	ditransitive (Oi + Op)
	We told them to go home/where to go/ where we would be waiting.	ditransitive (Oi + Od, consisting of *to* infinitive clause/*wh-* word + to infinitive clause/*wh-* word clause

Activity B8.5: Only *told* is possible. For the others we would have to use other patterns:

   I described/explained <u>the problem to her</u>. (Od + Op)
   I informed <u>her about the problem</u>. (Oi + Op)

See also Activity B12.2 in B12.

CLAUSE TYPES

After discussing sentences in A9 it may seem strange to revert to the lower unit, 'clause', in this section. In fact, what we are referring to are major, simple sentences, as described in A9, i.e. those involving only one clause (though in one case below two clauses are involved). At the same time there is a relationship with the different clause patterns identified in A8, because clause types can be described partly in terms of clause elements (and partly in terms of other features described elsewhere in this book).

While this section focuses on the form of clause types, it is impossible to ignore their function. The typical function of these clause types is noted briefly in this section (though there is no one-to-one correspondence), while the reading in D9 gives a detailed account of their functions.

Basically there are four types of clause:

❑ declaratives
❑ interrogatives (already described partly in A7)
❑ imperatives
❑ exclamatives

All except the last can have a negative.

B9.1 Declaratives

Declaratives are the basic (and most frequent) clause type. We might call them the 'default' clause type. Throughout this book they are the type that is focused on and exemplified, unless there is a reason to focus on other types.

Their formal characteristics are that

❑ all clause elements are present, i.e. subject and verb, plus whatever further clause elements are required by the verb (see A8, B8)
❑ they have the basic word order of English, namely, subject followed by verb followed by object, predicative or adverbial (commonly called 'SVO word order')

The traditional function of declaratives is as statements, that is, conveying information, feelings, etc. For example:

It's ten o'clock.
I like it.

But there is more to it than this. Take this example:

The door is open?

This has all the characteristics of a declarative and yet the question mark shows that it is a question; that is, rather than an assertion of information, it is an enquiry (or check) about information. This structure is called a declarative question. It is also possible with *wh-* words (see below) to give special emphasis, e.g. to express surprise or ask for repetition:

She said <u>what</u>?   *He sat <u>where</u>?*

B9.2 Interrogatives

The most important formal characteristic of interrogatives is the inversion of the subject with the first auxiliary, as we saw in A7:

Can you spell it for me?

Otherwise they are the same as declaratives in terms of their word order and the presence of elements that are required by the verb. There is one situation, however, where interrogatives do not involve inversion; this is described below. (And we should note that inversion does have other uses; see A11.) In writing, of course, we can usually identify interrogatives by the presence of a question mark, but we have seen one exception to this above (the declarative question), and we will see another below.

We can identify a number of different types of interrogative, all involving inversion. The accepted terminology for them includes the word 'question', so this is how they are referred to below. One other type, indirect questions, is discussed in B12.

Yes/no and alternative questions

Interrogatives beginning with an inverted auxiliary, are called *yes/no* questions, since *yes* and *no* could form the responses to them (but do not have to).

Did you remember to bring the money?

Alternative questions have the same form as *yes/no* questions, beginning with subject/auxiliary inversion, but then continue with *or* so that the responder cannot answer *yes* or *no*:

Will you call or email them?

Requests also have the structure of *yes/no* questions:

Would you mind opening the door?

However, while *yes* and *no* can be responses to them, it is action that is the desired response. So it is debatable whether they are actually questions. Above we saw a case of a question that is not an interrogative, but here we possibly have a case of an interrogative that is not a question.

Tag questions

Tag questions (or question tags) are short interrogatives clauses that follow declaratives and turn them into questions. Tag questions repeat the subject and auxiliary (inserting *do* if there is none) of the declarative, but with inversion and a change from positive to negative or vice versa. For example:

You saw them, didn't you?

You didn't see them, did you?

The tag can either have falling intonation, which indicates that the speaker is merely seeking confirmation of the declarative clause, or rising intonation (like a normal *yes/no* question), which indicates that the speaker is not sure of the answer.

Positive tag questions following positive declaratives are also possible:

So you think you know it, do you?

This can be used to echo a previous statement, or to draw a conclusion based on something said before.

⭐ **Activity B9.1**

Turn the following declaratives into *yes/no* and tag questions.

1. You brought the money.
2. She hasn't brought the money.

NON-STANDARD FORMS AND VARIATION IN ENGLISH

In informal English there are a number of other possibilities, such as *right* and *okay*, which are used as universal tag questions:

You're coming, <u>right</u>?

Innit and *isn't it* are used in the same way in some varieties of English.

Wh- questions

This type of interrogative is introduced by a word beginning with *wh-*:

what, who, whom, whose, which, why, where, when and *how* (plus combinations with *how*, such as *how much*). *How* is an 'honorary' member of this group (since it does not begin with *wh-*).

For example:

What did he say?

How should I know?

The choice of words is firstly a matter of clause elements (see A8):

❑ *why, where, when* and *how* relate to adverbials

<u>Why</u> *did he do it?*

<u>Where</u> *is he living?*

❑ *what, who* and *whom* relate to subjects, objects and predicatives:

<u>What</u> *have you done?*

<u>Who</u> *are you discussing?*

❑ *which* and *whose* are usually determiners (as is *what* sometimes), i.e. part of one element:

<u>Which</u> *route shall we take?*

<u>Whose</u> *money is this?*

But they can occur alone, with the noun implied: <u>Which</u> *shall we take?* <u>Whose</u> *is this?*

The choice between *what, who* and *whom* relates to whether the noun phrase refers to a human (*who, whom*) or non-human (*what*). *Who* can refer to human subjects, objects or predicatives:

<u>Who</u> *is he?*

while *whom* is restricted to objects, and is very formal:

<u>Whom</u> *did you ask?*

The normal question would be *Who did you ask? Whom* is only obligatory with prepositional objects:

<u>At whom</u> *did you laugh?*

but this is not the case if the preposition has been left behind, or 'stranded' (see also relative clauses in B10):

Who did you laugh at?

> What clause elements do the underlined words or phrases represent in these interrogatives (taken from above)?
>
> 1. *Who are you discussing?*
> 2. *Which route shall we take?*
> 3. *Whose money is this?*
> 4. *Who is he?*
> 5. *How should I know?*

Wh- questions do not always have inversion. When *who* or *what* represent the subject of the clause, subject-verb inversion is not allowed, as the question word must come at the start of the sentence. Thus

Who broke the window?

(and not 'Did who break the window?' However, *Who did break the window?* is possible as an emphatic question).

We can suggest the following sequence of operations in the formation of *wh-* interrogatives:

❏ replace the particular unit with an appropriate question word
❏ insert *do* if necessary (transferring the finite element to it) and invert the subject with the first auxiliary (see A7); this will not apply if the subject is the *wh-* word
❏ promote the *wh-* word to the start of the clause (along with the noun if it is *which* or *whose*)

For example, with an object that is 'questioned':

	They criticised me.
Add *wh-* word	*They criticised WHO?* (also a possible question)
Insert DO and invert	*Did they criticise WHO?*
Promote *wh-* word	*Who did they criticise?*

And with a 'questioned' subject:

	I criticised them.
Add *wh-* word	*WHO criticised them?*
Invert	not allowed
Promote *wh-* word	(already done) *Who criticised them?*

And with an auxiliary with a 'questioned' object:

	She is marrying my cousin.
Add *wh-* word	*She is marrying WHO?* (also a possible question)
Invert	*Is she marrying WHO?*
Promote *wh-* word	*Who is she marrying?*

Activity B9.3

Turn the following declaratives into *wh-* questions, focusing on the underlined words and phrases and replacing them with *wh-* words.

1. I've bought <u>a new bike</u>.
2. The concert is <u>in May</u>.
3. I went <u>to the US</u> this summer.
4. <u>Something</u> caused this damage.
5. This is <u>my</u> car.
6. The fire lasted <u>three days</u>.
7. I saw you with <u>a stranger</u>.

B9.3 Exclamatives

Exclamatives are said to be sentences expressing a strong emotion: exclamations, in other words. In writing they are usually signalled by an exclamation mark.

What a nice day it is!

How quickly they reacted!

They may start with either *what* or *how*; in both cases a clause element is fronted (see A11). In the first example a noun phrase containing *what* (a predicative in this case) has been fronted (*It is such a nice day*), and in the second an adverb phrase (functioning as an adverbial) (*They reacted very quickly*).

Exclamatives are rarer than the other clause types, and a negative is not possible: 'What a nice day it isn't!' They are also found in minor sentences: *What a fool!*

B9.4 Imperatives

The formal characteristic of imperatives is that no subject is mentioned; this is the only situation (apart from ellipsis – see B11) where a full clause does not need a subject. The basic form of the verb is used:

<u>Take</u> care.

<u>Be</u> quiet.

There is also an emphatic imperative with *do*:

Oh, <u>do be</u> quiet.

Negative imperatives are formed with *do not* (or *don't*) followed by an infinitive:

<u>Don't laugh</u> at me.

This also applies to *be*:

<u>Don't be</u> scared.

Although there is no subject and auxiliary with imperatives, it can be suggested that the underlying subject is *you* and that there is an underlying auxiliary *will*. This is based on the evidence of tag questions, for example:

Take a seat, won't you?

Close the door, will you? (. . . *can you?* is also possible)

Don't forget my birthday, will you?

Although standard imperatives are addressed to the hearer (i.e. the second person), there is a first person plural equivalent in the shape of *let's* (or formally *let us*), used to make suggestions:

Let's watch a film tonight.

The tag question for this is . . . *shall we?*

B9.5 Form and function

We have seen throughout this section cases where the grammatical form of clause types does not match their function. For example, we saw that interrogatives and questions do not match exactly. The same is true for imperatives. Traditionally their function is said to be as orders or commands, but this is far too limiting. Imperatives can also constitute

- ❏ offers: *Have a seat.*
- ❏ invitations: *Please come tonight.*
- ❏ wishes: *Have a good time.*
- ❏ suggestions: *Try the other door.*

Generally we could characterise them as 'directives', i.e. 'speech acts' that try to direct behaviour (see D9). But there is not a one-to-one correspondence between imperatives and directives. There are other forms of directives which are not imperatives:

The door is open. (a declarative, designed to get someone to close the door)

Can you close the door, please? (an interrogative)

Why don't you close the door? (a negative interrogative)

And there are imperatives that are not directives:

Laugh and the whole world laughs with you; cry and you cry alone.

Activity B9.4

> Which of the two responses to these interrogatives is appropriate in terms of functions (or speech acts)?
>
> 1. *Why don't you sit down?*   A. *Thank you.*
>   B. *Well, my trousers are tight and my bottom hurts.*
>
> 2. *Were you born in a barn?*   A. *Sorry. (Goes to shut a door)*
>   B. *No, I wasn't.*
>
> 3. *Can you tell me the time?*   A. *Yes, it's 10.30.*
>   B. *Yes, I can.*
>
> 4. *How are you?*   A. *Not too bad, thanks.*
>   B. *Well, I've been feeling poorly these last few days and my feet are hurting, not to mention my . . .*

B9.6 Conclusion

Traditional accounts of English assumed that there was a one-to-one relationship between form and function, especially with regard to types of clause. Even nowadays, if you ask students what the function of an imperative is (if they know the term) they will tell you 'an order', ignoring the fact that they regularly use imperatives for other functions. So this assumption is unjustified. This diagram summarises the relationships described above (it should be noted that there are other possibilities):

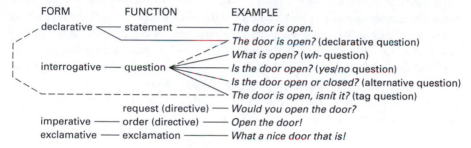

Figure B9.6.1 The relationship between form and function

Comments

Activity B9.1:

1.   Did you bring the money? You brought the money, didn't you?
2.   Hasn't she brought the money? She hasn't brought the money, has she?

Activity B9.2: In 1 and 2 the underlined elements are objects; in 3 and 4 they are predicatives. *How* in 5 represents an adverbial.

Activity B9.3:

1.   *What have you bought?*
2.   *When is the concert?*
3.   *Where did you go this summer?*
4.   *What caused this damage?*
5.   *Whose car is this?*
6.   *How long did the fire last?*
7.   *Who did I see you with?* (or *With whom did I see you?*)

Activity B9.4: In all four cases, A is the normal response. B would only be made if there was a misunderstanding (perhaps deliberate). Question 1 would normally be an offer, to be accepted or declined; 2 is a request for action, i.e. a directive (people who live in barns have no experience of doors); 3 is a request for information, not an enquiry about ability; and 4 is a means of maintaining social relationships, not an enquiry about health.

RELATIVE CLAUSES

Relative clauses are a common type of subordinate clause. They form part of the post-modification of a noun phrase; i.e. they are not a clause element. Their role is to give extra information about the noun:

I have seen the film which won the Oscar.

Here the relative clause *which won the Oscar* is the postmodification of the noun phrase beginning *the film* . . . Overall this noun phrase represents the direct object of the main clause. We can also analyse the structure of the relative clause; in this case it is SVO, with *which* as the subject. Compared to premodification (see A3), postmodification with a relative clause allows quite complicated information to be given (though we could talk about *the Oscar-winning film*).

The construction of relative clauses in English is quite complicated, involving a number of steps and choices.

B10.1 Relative pronouns

Relative clauses are introduced by relative pronouns and determiners:

who, whom, which, that, whose and 'zero'

The choice between them involves several factors:

❏ *who* is used for human subjects and objects:

I know a man who can help us. (subject of the relative clause)

I know a man who we can help. (object of the relative clause)

❏ *whom* is used for human objects:

I know a man whom we can help.

As with questions, it is limited to a very formal style; *who* is normal (as exemplified above) in non-formal situations. There is one situation where *who* cannot be used and where *whom* is obligatory: when there is an accompanying preposition:

I know the woman to whom you spoke.

But this is also very formal and there are non-formal alternatives.

❏ *which* is used for non-human subjects and objects:

This is the book which pleased me most.

This is the book which I liked most.

Which can also be used as a 'sentential' relative pronoun, where it refers back not to one person or thing (e.g. *book* in the above examples) but to the whole of the preceding clause:

They accused him of cheating in the exam, which he denied.

Here, *which* does not refer back to the exam but to the whole of the non-finite clause *cheating in the exam*. It is also possible to use *which* as a relative determiner here:

They said he had cheated in the exam, which accusation he denied.

But this sounds very old-fashioned. More normal (but still formal) would be

> They said _he had cheated in the exam_, _an accusation which_ he denied.

i.e. where _which_ is used as a normal relative pronoun. However, _which_ is commonly used as a relative determiner in certain prepositional phrases such as _in which case_:

> They may be late, _in which case_ we can start the show now.

❏ _that_ is the most common relative pronoun. It can be used for subjects and objects, both human and non-human:

> I know a man _that_ can help us. (subject, human)
> I know a man _that_ we can help. (object, human)
> This is the book _that_ pleased me most. (subject, non-human)
> This is the book _that_ I liked most. (object, non-human)

However, it cannot be used with a preposition: 'I know the woman _to that_ you spoke.'

❏ the 'zero' relative pronoun. When the relative pronoun represents the object in the relative clause it may be omitted in non-formal English:

> This is the book I liked most

These are sometimes called 'contact' relative clauses, because two noun phrases are in contact. However, contact clauses are more common when the second noun phrase is a pronoun, as with _I_ in the above case; if there are two full noun phrases a relative pronoun is often used to separate them:

> This is the book _that_ my mother and father liked most.

NON-STANDARD ENGLISH

In informal spoken English contact relative clauses occur with the subject missing:

> 'There was a great cheer _went up_.' (David Cameron, describing the reaction to his announcement of the royal wedding to his cabinet colleagues)

This is typical with existential _there_ (see A8 and A11); . . . _which_ went up would be normal.

❏ _whose_ is a possessive relative determiner; in other words it is used to link two nouns:

> This is the student _whose essay I was telling you about_.

❏ It shows a relationship between the nouns similar to the genitive (_the student's essay_ – see A2) and the possessive determiners (_her essay_). It is not only used with human reference:

> . . . an idea _whose time has come_.

⭐ **Activity B10.1**

Identify which of the relative clauses below could have the pronoun deleted (i.e. become a contact clause).

1. _Floods are something which we haven't planned for._
2. _Floods are something for which we haven't planned._
3. _She is a woman who everybody respects greatly._
4. _She is a woman who is greatly respected by everybody._

Relative clauses can also be introduced by *when*, *where* and *why*. The antecedents (see below) are basic abstract nouns such as *place, reason* and *time*:

> They've put him in a *place* where he can do no harm.
> The *reason* why she left is still unknown.
> I can still remember a *time* when people left their doors unlocked.

These can be related to sentences with a preposition and *which*:

> They've put him in a *place* in which he can do no harm.

Activity B10.2 ✪

As we have seen, *wh-* words are used in a number of ways: to introduce interrogatives, exclamatives (see B9), nominal clauses and relative clauses. In the first two cases they normally occur at the start of a clause (or at least as part of the first noun phrase in a clause); in the last two cases they typically occur in the middle of a sentence since they are linking two clauses. Distinguish the following sentences according to the above constructions.

1. *I've discovered* where the money is.
2. *He used to work for a bank* which went bankrupt.
3. What a nice day *it is.*
4. Whose woods these are, *I think I know.*
5. *He is a thinker* whose time is yet to come.
6. *I've found a hotel* where we can stay.

B10.2 The position and word order of relative clauses

The relative clause is placed next to the noun which it is postmodifying. This noun is called the 'antecedent':

> I have seen the *film* which won the Oscar.

In all of the examples above the relative clause has been placed at the end of the sentence because the antecedent is the head noun of the predicative or object of the main clause, i.e. it is part of the last noun phrase. However, the antecedent can be the subject of the main clause, in which case the relative clause interrupts the main clause:

> Anybody who passes this point *must show identification.*

Such 'embedded' relative clauses are less common than those at the end. In some cases a long relative clause with a subject antecedent may be placed at the end of a sentence, separated from its antecedent:

> The soldier *is dead* who I thought was in love with me.

But this is not considered correct.

It is not only the position of the relative clause that is important; the relative pronoun must also be placed next to the antecedent (with some exceptions – see below). When the relative pronoun represents the subject, there will be no change to the word order. However, if it represents the object (direct, indirect or prepositional) the word order will be different because the object will come first:

   I saw the teacher that you like.

Here the relative clause structure is OSV; the object relative pronoun *that* has been placed at the start of the relative clause to be next to the antecedent. As we saw above, in such a case the pronoun may be left out:

   I saw the teacher you like.

In this example *the teacher* may be considered both (part of) the direct object (of *saw*) in the main clause and the direct object (of *like*) in the relative clause.

   With a prepositional object, the preposition may either be placed at the start of the relative clause along with the pronoun:

   Is this the text to which you were referring?

or, more normally, be 'stranded' at the end of the clause:

   Is this the text which you were referring to?

The relative pronoun may be part of a phrase, all of which is placed at the start:

   The audience, most of whom were women, were not impressed.

   Police found a large sum of money, the source of which is unknown.

In this second example we could also say *whose source is unknown*.

Analyse the clause structure of both the main and relative clauses in this sentence.

   This is the student whose essay I sent you.

Defining and non-defining relative clauses

One distinction that applies to all relatives is between defining and non-defining relative clauses (also called restrictive and non-restrictive):

   The man who we recognised was a robber. (defining)

   The man, who we recognised, was a robber. (non-defining)

In the first example, the relative clause distinguishes the 'man' from all others; in the second it merely describes him. The use of commas around a non-defining relative clauses is typical in writing, as above. In non-defining relative clauses *that* is not used: 'The man, that we recognised, was the robber.' And object relative pronouns cannot be omitted: 'The man, we recognised, was the robber.'

B10.3 The formation of relative clauses

We can demonstrate how relative clauses are formed – and how the alternatives arise – by taking a finite clause *you were talking to him* and 'adding' it to a noun phrase (the antecedent) as postmodification in a main clause: *The man is a fool.*

   A precondition for relative clauses is that the antecedent refers to the same thing or person as the relative pronoun. Once this has been established (i.e. *the man = him* in this example), there are the following three steps in the process:

❑ place the 'relative clause' next to the antecedent; in this case, because it is the subject of the main clause, the relative clause is embedded:

The man – you were talking to him – is a fool.

❑ move the appropriate pronoun (or noun phrase) in the relative clause next to the antecedent; since we have a prepositional object we can either move the preposition along with the pronoun or leave it behind ('strand it'):

The man – him you were talking to – is a fool.

The man – to him you were talking– is a fool.

❑ choose the appropriate relative pronoun (or determiner). With the second example above there is only one possibility, *whom*:

The man to whom you were talking is a fool.

With the first example (with the preposition stranded) there are four possible pronouns:

The man <u>who</u>/<u>whom</u>/<u>that</u>/<u>---</u> you were talking to is a fool. (--- indicates zero)

Here is another example using two clauses that could be part of the description in this section:

There are three steps. Not all of them are necessary.

❑ place the 'relative clause' next to the antecedent:

There are three steps – not all of them are necessary.

❑ move the appropriate pronoun (or phrase) in the relative clause next to the antecedent:

There are three steps – not all of them are necessary

In this case there is no change since the pronoun (*them*) is already at the start of the relative clause (though it is part of another phrase).

❑ choose the appropriate relative pronoun (or determiner):

There are three steps, not all of <u>which</u> are necessary.

That is not possible since there is a preposition. . . . *of which not all* . . . is an alternative.

Activity B10.4 ✪

Combine these pairs of sentences by turning the second sentence into a relative clause via the three stages as described above (there may be more than one possibility):

EXAMPLE. I know the man. He has been robbed.

    I know the man that/who has been robbed.

1. *This is the answer. We've been looking for it.*
2. *The doctor is a friend of mine. He cured you.*
3. *This is the boy. His mother is a teacher.*
4. *The book belongs to me. You found it.*
5. *I have 50 students. The majority of them are female.*

B10.4 Conclusion

Sentences with relative clauses are difficult to interpret (and produce), especially those that have embedding, objection deletion (i.e. a zero relative pronoun) and preposition stranding:

> The picture <u>*you are talking about*</u> *was painted by my brother.*

Learners (and some native speakers) have trouble with their construction, producing such errors as 'The picture you are talking about <u>it</u> was painted by my brother'.

Comments

Activity B10.1: 1 yes; 2 no; 3 yes; 4 no (though *who is* can be deleted to form a non-finite clause).

Activity B10.2:

1. nominal
2. relative
3. exclamative
4. nominal: the clause beginning *whose* is an object that has been fronted. (This is the first line of the poem 'Stopping by woods on a snowy evening' by Robert Frost.)
5. relative
6. relative

Activity B10.3:

> main clause: SVPs (the relative clause is part of the predicative)
> relative clause: Op (*whose essay*), S (*I*), V (*sent*), Oi (*you*)

Activity B10.4:

1. *This is the answer that/which/--- we've been looking for. (or . . . for which . . .)*
2. *The doctor who cured you is a friend of mine.*
3. *This is the boy whose mother is a teacher.*
4. *The book that/which/--- you found belongs to me.*
5. *I have 50 students, the majority of whom are female.*

BEYOND AND BENEATH THE SENTENCE   B11

B11.1 Grammar beyond the sentence

The sentence is usually regarded as the upper limit of grammar. But we have already seen a number of ways in which a sentence can influence the grammatical make-up of a following one:

❏   personal pronouns (see B2)
    His wife is sick. However, she will try to come.
❏   the definite article (see B3)
    I found some old coins and a painting. The painting seemed valuable.

This referring back is called 'anaphora'.

The grammatical links between sentences are called 'cohesion'. In fact, such links may occur between clauses as well as between sentences.

Two further techniques in creating cohesion are the use of proforms and ellipsis.

Proforms

Proforms are words that are used to replace or refer to a longer construction in a sentence. The most typical proforms are pronouns:

I've got a new car and John's got one too. (= 'John's got a car')
John and Mary hurt themselves in the accident. ('... hurt John and Mary ...')

However, there are other words which have this function, for example *so*:

Are they coming? – I hope so.

Here *so* represents a subordinate clause 'that they are coming'. *Not* can be used for the equivalent negative:

I hope not. ('... that they are not coming.')

This should not be confused with the archaic use of *not* for forming negative verb phrases (as in *I know not ...*) discussed in A7.

Do is another proform:

Who knows how to do it? – I do. (= 'know how to do it')

Here *do* replaces not just the verb but the object as well.

Ellipsis

Ellipsis involves leaving out elements; it is common in answers:

Would you like to go to the cinema? – I'm afraid I can't.

Here 'go to the cinema' has been 'left out'. We also find ellipsis in coordination:

He finished his drink and then (he) walked home.

The difference between this and proforms is that ellipsis replaces something with nothing. But in both cases the missing text can be recovered from the context.

The purpose of such proforms and ellipsis is not only to make sentences shorter and avoid being repetitive, but also to create 'cohesion' within a text – to show readers or listeners that the sentences belong together. There are other ways of showing cohesion: linking adverbs (across sentences – see B4) and conjunctions (within sentences – see A9), for example:

Most of the audience didn't like the film, but I enjoyed it.

There are also lexical links which may reinforce grammatical ones, as in this case of anaphora:

I bought a BMW last week and the next day the stupid car wouldn't start.

And we will see extensive use of another type of ellipsis in A12 regarding spoken English.

> ★ **Activity B11.1**
>
> Identify the cohesive links in these short passages taken from the text in C11.
>
> 1. For a brief moment I understood what Betty and Barney Hill went through. It was today in 1961 that something extraordinary happened to this rather ordinary American couple – they were abducted by aliens.
> 2. Ötzi lived about 5,300 years ago, yet we know quite a lot about him.

B11.2 Grammar beneath the sentence

The idea that there is grammar 'hidden' beneath sentences may seem strange, but we have already seen lots of evidence to suggest that what we see or hear on the surface of language is not 'the real thing'. First of all, we have recognised that sentences are not made up of strings of words; rather, words are grouped together into phrases, and phrases into clauses, and clauses into sentences. In other words language is not linear; it is two-dimensional (at least). Furthermore, the ways in which units can be grouped into larger units are governed by the rules of grammar.

To take an example, compare these two major, simple sentences:

a) *She ran over the road.*
b) *She ran over a pedestrian.*

On the surface these sentences seem to have a similar structure; the only apparent difference is in the noun phrases at the end. Yet in fact they are quite different. Using clause elements (see A8) we would analyse them as

a) *She* (S) *ran* (V) *over the road* (A).
b) *She* (S) *ran over* (V) *a pedestrian* (Od).

The central difference is that *over* in b) goes with the verb *ran*, while in a) it goes with *the road* in a prepositional phrase. In a) it is a preposition, in b) a particle as part of a phrasal verb; as we saw in B7, this particle could be placed at the end, while the preposition could not. Of course, there is also the difference between the adverbial in a) and the object in b).

Deep and surface structure

But when we talk of grammar being hidden, we are not simply referring to links between words that cannot be seen on the surface. There are other aspects that may be hidden. For example, in this sentence

I want him to tell me the truth.

while *him* is in the objective case (representing the object of *want*), it also represents the 'hidden' subject of the non-finite verb *tell* (see A10).

We can explain this and other phenomena by making a distinction between 'surface structure' and 'deep structure'. In the above example there is no surface structure subject of *tell*, but there is in deep structure.

The distinction between surface and deep structure can account for a number of problems:

❑   cases of ambiguity: *I saw the man <u>with the telescope</u>*.
    Here *with the telescope* can either go with ('postmodify') *the man* (the man had
    a telescope), or be a separate adverbial element, indicating that the telescope was
    used to see the man.
❑   why sentences which look alike really are not, for example:
    She is eager to please.
    She is easy to please.
    On the surface these two sentences appear to be have the same structure: SVP,
    with the predicative consisting of an adjective with an infinitive complement.
    However, in the first sentence *she* is the deep structure subject of *please*, which
    is intransitive, whereas in the second *she* is the deep surface object of *please*
    ('something pleases her'), which is of course transitive.
❑   why sentences which do not look alike really are, e.g. actives and passives:
    I wrote it vs *it was written by me*
❑   why elements which are present really are not, i.e. meaningless 'dummy' elements
    which are introduced to make a sentence grammatically acceptable:
    e.g. the dummy auxiliary *do*: *<u>Do</u> you believe her?*
    e.g. dummy subjects: *<u>It</u>'s raining.*
    Here we can suggest that there is no subject in deep structure and that it is
    introduced in surface structure to satisfy the rule that English clauses must have
    a subject.
❑   why units which are not present on the surface really are: see proforms and
    ellipsis above
❑   why words which go together are not always next to each other; one unit may
    be split up into two, separated by another unit:
    e.g. phrasal verbs: *He <u>picked</u> the ball <u>up</u>*.
    e.g. verb phrases in interrogatives: *<u>Can</u> you <u>come</u>?*
    e.g. stranded prepositions in interrogatives, passives and relative and nominal
    clauses
    <u>Who</u> you were speaking <u>to</u>?

Activity B11.2 ✪

Explain this joke (told by Groucho Marx) using the concept of ambiguity.
Yesterday I shot an elephant in my pyjamas. How he got into my pyjamas
I'll never know.

Activity B11.3 ✪

Explain the deep structure difference between this pair of sentences, using
the concepts of clause elements and transitivity.

1.   *She has an ability to perform.*
2.   *She has a function to perform.*

B11.3 Conclusion

Grammar is a complex and multi-dimensional mechanism, not the simple random collection of rules that is presented to learners of language. But we should not expect anything less of a system that is the basis of the subtleties of human communication and the expression of human thought.

Comments

Activity B11.1:

1. The links are anaphoric: 'Betty and Barney Hill' – 'this rather ordinary American couple' – 'they'.
2. The links are: 'Ötzi' – 'him', and the use of *yet* to show the relationship between the ideas in the two clauses.

Activity B11.2: We logically think first of all that he was wearing his pyjamas, that *in my pyjamas* is an adverbial, and that is how he shot the elephant. But from the second sentence we understand the elephant was wearing them and that *in my pyjamas* is part of a noun phrase *an elephant in my pyjamas*.

Activity B11.3: If we only looked at the clause structure here we would get the same analysis: SVO. However, in 2 *function* is the deep-surface object of *perform* (as well as the object of *has*), whereas in 1 *perform* is intransitive, and *ability* is only the object of *has*. If we paraphrase with a relative clause we can see the difference:
> She has an ability that she has to perform. This makes no sense.
> She has a function that she has to perform.

If we choose another noun such as *duty* the sentence becomes ambiguous:
> She has a duty to perform.

REPORTING   B12

B12.1 Direct and reported speech

An important feature of speech is reporting to others what someone has said to us. There are two ways of doing this:

❑ direct speech, i.e. to repeat what the person said:
> '*I will not stand for re-election,*' he said.
❑ reported speech (or 'indirect speech'):
> *He said that he will not stand for re-election.*

Both involve a reporting clause (functioning as the main clause – introduced by *he said* above), plus a reported clause in the case of reported speech (*that he . . .*), or a quote in direct speech ('*I will . . .*'); both the reported clause and the quote function as the object of the reporting verb (*said*). However, the reported clause is integrated more closely into clause structure; above it is a subordinate clause, but non-finite clauses are also possible (*He said <u>to come</u>.*)

Backshift

Learners of English are commonly presented with a list of rules for 'transforming' direct speech into reported speech when the reporting verb is in the past (as it usually is). These involve shifting tenses 'backwards' in time:

'change the present simple into the past simple'

'change the present continuous into the past continuous'

'change the present perfect into the past perfect'.

'change the past into the past perfect', etc.

plus changes for pronouns (e.g. *I* to *you*) and adverbials of place and time (e.g. *here* to *there*), etc. ('deixis', as described in B2). For example, this sentence in direct speech:

'*I am coming to the party tomorrow*'.

would 'become', using the above rules:

She said she <u>was</u> coming to the party <u>the next day</u>.

However, these rules are very problematic. The first problem is that any 'changes' that might be made depend on the context. So if the party has not yet taken place we might say:

She said she <u>is</u> coming to the party <u>tonight</u>.

In other words, the adverbial may have numerous realisations, and the tense need not change. Here are two examples (from Thomson 1994) where there is no change in tense (the original text is in brackets):

('*I <u>am</u> willing . . .*') *Yeltsin, for his part, said he <u>is</u> willing to try.*

('*We <u>carried</u> out the attack.*') *An opposition group said it <u>carried</u> out the attack.*

Such 'exceptions' are usually explained in terms of recency and continued validity (especially if the reporting verb is in the present), but this is not a complete explanation. For one thing, the past tense rarely 'changes' into the past perfect.

The second problem is that the way speech is reported is also dependent on the (new) speaker's attitude to what he or she has heard. This is only to be expected; reporting someone else's words as if they are yours could get you into trouble if the original speaker is unreliable or uses swear words. So how does A report to B what C said? How can A distance himself or herself from commitment to the original statement? The answer is to use the past tense, for example:

('*I <u>am</u> very unhappy.*') *She said she <u>was</u> very unhappy.*

We have already seen in B5 situations where the past is used for distancing. Its use here in reported speech is similar. This explains why the past rarely 'changes' to past perfect, unlike the present perfect; the distance is already there in the past tense. But such a change may imply a change of state:

('*We <u>were</u> intending . . .*') *They said they <u>had been</u> intending to carry out the attack.*

(but they are not now)

This is the only situation where modals (*can*, etc.) can be said to have 'past' tense forms (*could*, etc.), which can be used to achieve the same distancing as the past tense, for example:

('*I can come.*') *She said she could come.* (but *can* would also be possible)

Another problem with the notion of transforming direct speech into reported speech is that we normally base what we say on the meaning that we remember, not on the words. If the exact words are important – and we remember them – then we will use direct speech. If not, we will construct the sentences using the same rules for tense usage as apply elsewhere. There is a story by Agatha Christie in which a dying man's last words are remembered as 'heap of fish', which mystifies everyone. What he actually said was 'pilocarpine' (the name of the poison used in his murder); however, this was heard as 'pile o' carp' and then wrongly remembered.

⭐ **Activity B12.1**

If you are going through this section in class, try to recall what your teacher/ lecturer said at the start and represent it in reported speech. Compare your version with those of your colleagues. How similar are they? What tenses have you chosen?

The unwarranted focus on rules for tense backshift can obscure a number of areas which are important for reporting:

❑ the status of the reported clause. It functions as the direct object of the reporting verb, most commonly as a nominal *that* clause:

   He said that he is coming.

But other non-finite structures, such as *to* infinitive, are possible.

❑ the use of reporting verbs in the correct pattern (see B8). Thus

   He told me that you are lazy. (and not 'He told that you are lazy.')

An indirect object is required for *tell*. See Activity B12.2 below.

❑ the ordering of elements when direct speech is used in reporting. The reporting clause may come before or after the quote:

   She said 'come here'. / '*Come here', she said*

or in the middle:

   '*Come on,*' *he said,* '*let's try to get there first*'.

❑ the choice of reporting verb. There is a wide range of such verbs (see those used in the text in C11). *Say* is by far the most frequent; *tell* and *ask* are also common:

   He said that you are lazy.

Not all verbs referring to the act of speaking can be reporting verbs. *Scold* and *talk* are two such exceptions. You cannot say 'He talked that you are lazy.'

❑ reported thought, which follows the same patterns as reported speech, and can even involve direct reporting with a quote:

   I thought he was crazy.

   '*You must be crazy*', *I thought.*

Activity B12.2 ✪

Fill in the gaps with a suitable reporting verb from the list below.

a) He _____ to her for causing the accident.
b) She _____ that she caused the accident.
c) He _____ her of causing the accident.
d) He _____ her for causing the accident.
e) She _____ that I caused the accident.

blamed, accused, claimed, apologised, admitted

A final issue is the reporting of questions. Here the word order is important (there is no inversion), as is the use of *if* or *whether* to introduce the reported clause (rather than *that*):

('*Can I come?*') He asked *if he can/could* come.

B12.2 Conclusion

The rules for 'backshift' in reported speech are one of the great 'deceptions' in English teaching, for the following reasons:

❏ when we report what someone else said using reported speech, we normally base it on the meaning that we remember, not on the exact words that we heard. If the exact wording is important, then we will use direct speech. Exercises that present the direct speech and ask learners to transform it into reported speech are artificial and misleading.
❏ the choice of tense (and of other features, such as personal pronouns) in reported speech is subject to the same rules of usage that apply elsewhere in English. In the case of tense 'change' the deciding factor is whether we wish to distance ourselves from what the speaker said or not.
❏ other factors, such as the choice of appropriate reporting verbs and the ordering of elements should receive more focus. This is why the heading of this section is 'Reporting' and not 'Reported Speech'.

Activity B12.2: a) apologised, b) admitted, c) accused, d) blamed, e) claimed
Note that in b) and e) the past tense is used in the reported *that* clause. A past perfect
(. . . *had caused*) would be unlikely, even though the original statement would have
been in the past tense: *I/you caused* . . .)

Section C
EXPLORATION

WORDS WITH MULTIPLE WORD-CLASS MEMBERSHIP

The first eight exploration sections involve the study of concordance lines. You may already be familiar with them; there are a number of websites where you can obtain your own concordance lines. Basically they are taken from an electronic 'corpus' (or collection of texts) which can be searched for examples of any word of interest (among other things). The lines used here come from the British National Corpus, 'a 100 million word snapshot of British English', made up of 4000 spoken and written texts from the 1990s. More information can be found at www.natcorp@oucs.ox.ac.uk

The lines do not always make up complete sentences; sometimes they are too long for the page. But there is always enough information to analyse the word we are interested in – the keyword, which is in bold. In order to make the lines understandable, some selection has been carried out; in other words, they are not entirely random. But an attempt has been made to make them as representative as possible (e.g. to make the lines reflect the major uses proportionately), while also showing as wide a range of uses as possible. And the text of the lines is authentic – there has been no editing to simplify them (apart from the occasional addition of a bracketed subject).

Here are some techniques which you might find useful when analysing concordance lines (and when you are trying to understand texts in general):

❏ Look at the words around the keyword. Which words does it 'go with'? For example, a word preceded by *a* and followed by *of* is almost certainly a noun. However, the important words may not be directly before or after. For example, *a* may occur several words ahead of the noun it goes with.

❏ Try replacing the keyword with a similar word which you are sure about.

❏ Change the form of the keyword. For example, add *-s* to a noun to make it plural to find out if it is count or not.

❏ Try moving words around. Does it make a difference? For instance, is there a difference between *they turned us on* and *they turned on us*?

❏ Work out the meaning and relate this to the grammar.

❏ Take away or add some 'little' words. What effect does this have? For instance, you can test for adjectives by putting a word such as *too* in front of them.

❏ Do not be distracted by unknown words. It is possible to understand the grammar of concordance lines without understanding all of the meaning.

Now look at the activities below, which involve keywords which belong to more than one word class.

⭐ **Activity C1.1**

Look at the concordance lines below for *round*. Work out on which line it is

a)   an adjective
b)   an adverb
c)   a noun
d)   a preposition
e)   a verb

Check the meanings associated with each word class in a dictionary if necessary.

> Example: Why don't you come **round** for dinner? (Answer: adverb.)

1.   . . . [he], to the surprise of the gallery, turned the match **round** by winning a second set . . .
2.   It was supposed to work the other way **round**.
3.   The next step will be a **round** of preliminary talks. . . .
4.   This is a Perspex tube that runs **round** the outside rim of the table . . .
5.   . . . she paused briefly to hand **round** the plates and a bowl of crisp salad . . .
6.   It was agreed to hold the sixth **round** of talks in January 1982.
7.   . . . a man's mates might collect for him by passing **round** a hat.
8.   We told him weeks ago that we were writing **round** trying to get a mortgage.
9.   . . . [he] had been stung by the nettles that grew thickly **round** the boathouse.
10. . . . the post of Director was advertised but first time **round** was not filled . . .
11. . . . [she] could be out of the second **round** of the Four Nations tennis championship . . .
12. Woil stared **round** at him and seemed to be in a state of shock . . .
13. . . . relaxation techniques I had learned in drama, sending **round** my mental supervisor . . .
14. . . . [they managed] to **round** up stragglers and ensure no one got lost.
15. He strode **round** the room, shouting: 'I am number one . . .

⭐ **Activity C1.2**

A possible synonym for *round* is *around*. Try replacing *round* with *around* in the above lines. Where is it possible? Do you notice anything about these lines?

Look at the concordance lines below. First of all think of the word classes which are possible for *back* and then work out which class is shown in each line. Which word class do you think will be most common?

1.   All he owned were the clothes on his **back** and a few cassettes . . .
2.   They walked **back** into the main bar . . .
3.   . . . governments have been considering action to cut **back** on emissions of greenhouse gases . . .
4.   **Back** at the office you said something about a secret . . .
5.   . . . [he] walked past her up the narrow passage and into the **back** kitchen.
6.   You stopped being angry with them and held **back** your furious rage.
7.   Dolly was wedging the doorhandle with the **back** of a chair . . .
8.   . . . I'll be **back** for dinner . . .
9.   . . . and now he thumped George on the **back** with great bonhomie . . .
10. . . . she managed to bring them both **back** to earth again.
11. What they often get instead is a pat on the **back**, a stack of reading matter . . .
12. She hurried **back** down the stairs . . .
13. . . . through the lounge into the kitchen at the **back**.
14. . . . as one goes further **back** through the geological record . . .
15. Fold **back** the ear flap, and briskly pull out one or two hairs . . .

Comments

Activity C1.1: Although we generally think of *round* as an adjective, its absence from the lines reflects how rare it is. Adverbs (lines 1, 2, 5, 7, 8, 10, 12, 13), nouns (3, 6, 11) and prepositions (4, 9, 15) are in fact more common. It can also be a verb, usually a phrasal one, as is the case with line 14 (*round up*). If you had trouble with 5, 7 and 13, see B7 on phrasal verbs/multi-word verbs.

Note how the difference in word class is generally associated with a difference in meaning. However, it can be argued that there is little, perhaps no, difference between the adverb and preposition meanings, apart from the absence or presence of the noun phrase following the preposition. For example, if we remove the noun phrase from line 15, there is very little difference:

he strode round / he strode round the room

but the same is not possible for line 9:

nettles that grew thickly round (?) / nettles that grew thickly round the boathouse

Activity C1.2: The answer is lines 1, 2, 4, 5, 7, 8, 9, 10, 12, 13, 15. These correspond exactly to the instances of adverbs and prepositions. This could be seen as another reason for grouping them.

Activity C1.3: We tend to think of *back* as a noun meaning a part of the body (just like we think of *round* as an adjective), but again adverbs are more common, as the lines reflect:

adverb: 2, 3, 4, 6, 8, 10, 12, 14, 15

noun: 1, 7, 9, 11, 13 (Note that 13 does not refer to part of a body.)

adjective: 5

Back can also be a verb: *Will you <u>back</u> me?*

NOUNS WHICH CAN BE BOTH COUNT AND NONCOUNT C2

Many nouns in English can be both count and noncount. Sometimes there is little difference in meaning except between a general idea and a particular example of it:

cake/a cake, difference/a difference, divorce/a divorce, string/a string

See the Website Reference C2.1 for more examples.

In other cases there is a difference of meaning that goes with the difference in grammar. Sometimes this difference is predictable, in which case we say that a noun is basically count or noncount and that the other version is derived from the original by a process of conversion. Two cases where there is a systematic and predictable difference occur when a noncount noun is converted to count, as in the next activity.

Activity C2.1

Consider these two examples where the noncount *beer* is used as a count noun. What two meanings are expressed?

1. *They serve 12 beers in that bar.*
2. *He drank 12 beers in that bar.*

Another more 'literary' type of noncount to count conversion is when abstract nouns are modified: *<u>a</u> strong <u>hatred</u> of communism*

Activity C2.2

Consider this sentence:

They played <u>a little football</u> with <u>a little football</u>.

Does this make any sense? How is it possible to repeat the underlined noun phrase exactly?

Conversion also turns count into noncount nouns. One regular situation where it occurs is when an animal's meat is being referred to: *I don't like <u>chicken</u>.*

Look at the text below. It is a short passage from a recent historical novel by Bernard Cornwell called *Azincourt*. Two English soldiers, part of an army besieging a French town, are talking. Look at the different ways the noun *dog* is treated in the text (underlined) in terms of number and count status. Why is there a difference?

1. 'Is that a dead <u>dog</u>?' the man asked, nodding towards a furry corpse lying
2. halfway between the English forward trench and the French barbican.
3. *Three ravens were pecking at the dead beast.*
4. 'The French shoot them,' Hook said. 'The <u>dogs</u> run out of our lines and
5. the crossbowmen shoot them. Then they vanish in the night.'
6. 'The <u>dogs</u>?'
7. 'They're food for the French,' Hook explained curtly. 'Fresh meat.'
8. 'Ah, of course,' the man said. He watched the ravens for a while. 'I've
9. never eaten <u>dog</u>.'
10. 'Tastes a bit like hare,' Hook said, 'but stringier.'

Then there are cases where the count/noncount difference is associated with different meanings which are not predictable:

reason/a reason, paper/a paper, room/a room

A room is a particular part of a building; *room* means 'space'. The difference here is that these meanings cannot be explained by a predictable process of conversion. See the Website Reference C2.4 for more such cases.

What is the difference in meaning between these count/noncount pairs?

1. *I've been invited to a <u>dinner</u> to celebrate the occasion.* / *My favourite meal is <u>dinner</u>.*
2. *She gave an interesting <u>speech</u>.* / *<u>Speech</u> is the most essential human ability.*
3. *I see you've had quite an <u>experience</u>.* / *<u>Experience</u> is what young people lack most.*
4. *It was found in <u>a wood</u>.* / *It's made of <u>wood</u>.*

✪ Activity C2.5

Look at the concordance lines below and work out whether *paper* is count or noncount. What are the different meanings associated with the difference?

1. They consist of two layers of **paper** with wood chips sandwiched between them . . .
2. In 1903 he launched a **paper**, West African Mail . . .
3. . . . [it] has issued a consultation **paper** . . .
4. What they normally do is they get some **paper**, they light it, they'll drop it . . .
5. Lo Gazzetto dello Sporto, Italy's leading sports **paper**, gave him 5 out of 10 . . .
6. . . . it may have looked good on **paper**, but in practice it was another thing entirely . . .
7. . . . a separate piece of **paper** packed into the box.
8. . . . [he] has recently suggested, in an as yet unpublished **paper**, that . . .
9. . . . an account of the cost of software (**paper**, film, video-tape, slides) must also be included . . .
10. . . . [they] submitted a **paper** based on the analysis . . .
11. . . . IPC moved the **paper** from its cheerful Covent Garden hovel . . .
12. . . . just far enough to dimple but not fracture the **paper** surface.
13. Yes, it's a page of Government **paper** in Summerchild's judicious hand . . .
14. Peeping out of tissue **paper** was a small red shoulder bag.
15. . . . dismissed by the Institute in its consultative **paper**.

✪ Activity C2.6

Look at the concordance lines and decide whether *glass* or *glasses* is

a) a noncount singular noun referring to the substance
b) a count noun (singular or plural) referring to the thing we drink out of
c) a plural noun (see A2) referring to the thing we wear for eyesight.

1. And it's made of fibre **glass**, is it?
2. Many, like steel, **glass** and paper can be re-used . . .
3. . . . he was trying to read the leg bands through his **glass**.
4. . . . [it] gives the beer a natural sparkle in the **glass**.
5. In particularly sunny locations, tinted **glass** may be desirable . . .
6. . . . [they] presented her with a specially engraved **glass** candle-holder . . .
7. . . . smashing dozens of windows and bombarding police with bottles and **glasses**.
8. [He] hit him on the side of the head and sent his **glasses** flying . . .
9. Leave both **glasses** in the same place . . .
10. . . . they could scarcely see their car from 25 metres without **glasses** . . .

C2

Comments

Activity C2.1: (1) refers to types of beer, while (2) refers to units (bottles or glasses). There are a number of other nouns referring to food and drinks that behave like this. See C2.2 and C2.3 for more nouns which can behave in these ways.

Activity C2.2: The answer is: it is perfectly possible – because the two noun phrases refer to two different things – one count and one noncount (and also because *a little* has two interpretations). This is how the two interpretations work:

a) GRAMMAR: DETERMINER   NONCOUNT NOUN
   (*They played*) *a little*   *football* . . .
   MEANING: **a small amount** **of the game**

b) GRAMMAR: DETERMINER   ADJECTIVE   COUNT NOUN
   (. . . *with*) *a*   *little*   *football.*
   MEANING: **a**   **small**   **round thing**

In a) *a little football* is the object of *play*, referring to the type of game they played (noncount), whereas in b) it refers to the thing they used (a ball, which is count). (See C3 for an explanation of *a little*.)

Activity C2.3: On line 1 *dog* is a singular, count noun; on lines 4 and 6 it is plural, count; on line 9 it is (singular) noncount. The reason why *dog*, normally a count noun, is noncount on line 9, is that the speaker is referring to its meat.

There is another noun which is usually count but is noncount here, referring to the meat. Can you find it?

Activity C2.4: Check the meanings in a good dictionary.

Activity C2.5:

❏ on lines 2, 5 and 11 *paper* is count, referring to a newspaper
❏ on lines 3, 8, 10 and 15 it also count, but referring to an official document
❏ on lines 1, 4, 6, 7, 9, 12, 13 and 14, it is noncount, referring to the substance.

Note the following points:

❏ on line 6 *paper* is noncount; it is *piece* that is count
❏ on line 12 *paper* acts as a premodifying noun; *surface* is the head noun
❏ on line 8 *an* is separated from its noun by three words.

Activity C2.6:

a) 1, 2, 5, 6 (used as a premodifier; *a* determines *candle-holder*)
b) 3, 4 (with generic reference – see B4), 7, 9
c) 8, 10

USAGE PROBLEMS WITH DETERMINERS

There are a number of problems with the usage of determiners, concerning how to use them, or which one to use. Some of them are discussed elsewhere in the book:

- ❏ the difference between *all*, *every* and *each* (A3)
- ❏ the difference between *some* and *any* (A1)
- ❏ alternative structures for *all*, *both*, and *half*: *both men*, *both the men*, *both of the men* (D3)
- ❏ the formal nature of some determiners such as *much* and *many* (D3).

This section focuses on just three issues:

1. The difference in meaning between a few and a little vs few and little

We saw in A3 that *a few* and *a little* need to be regarded as single determiners, not a combination of two. But this brings them into 'conflict' with their single-word counterparts, *few* and *little*. So what is the difference?

★ **Activity C3.1**

Consider these two sentences. What is the difference in meaning?

1. *We invited 100 people; in spite of the rain <u>a few</u> turned up.*
2. *We invited 100 people; in spite of the good weather <u>few</u> turned up.*

---

2. The acceptability of less with plural nouns

★ **Activity C3.2**

What do your intuitions tell you about these two sentences with *less*?

1. *I expected more food and <u>less</u> people.*
2. *He is suffering from a form of leukemia that affects <u>less</u> than 70 children a year.*

---

3. Distinguishing determiners from other word classes

As we saw in A3, most determiners can be pronouns as well, when they are used alone without a noun: *I found <u>some</u>*. But this is not all; there are several determiners which can also be adverbs:

I feel <u>all</u> itchy. He is <u>all</u>-powerful. (= completely)
There are <u>some</u> 150 irregular verbs in English. (= approximately)
Is she <u>that</u> good? (= to that extent)

Activity C3.3

Work out the word class of *little* on the lines below. In addition to being a determiner, pronoun or adverb, it can also be an adjective with the meaning of 'small'. In this case it goes with singular or plural count nouns, and if the noun is singular it must have a determiner (such as *a*); if it is a determiner it means 'a small amount' and precedes non-count nouns. If you are not sure, try replacing *little* with *small*. If this is possible, then it is an adjective.

1. They have **little** to look forward to . . .
2. . . . to leave school and grow up in a world with **little** work.
3. . . . this is a decent **little** time-wasting package . . .
4. . . . as you can see I returned a **little** early.
5. . . . many homeless families receive **little** or no health care.
6. I will tell you a **little** about the story line .
7. . . . but you had very **little** eye contact with Maggie.
8. . . . she found herself following him to the dark **little** bar . . .
9. . . . if things go ill, it is goodbye, but at **little** personal cost.
10. That was mainly because of a lot of niggly **little** injuries . . .
11. . . . [they] increasingly, as I grew older, understood very **little** of what I read.
12. . . . this is often **little** understood.
13. . . . too much to do in too **little** time . . .
14. . . . I always thought she looked a **little** bit like Blues official Dessie Moore . . .
15. . . . in order to make as **little** contact as possible with the soft oozing mud . . .
16. . . . whose talents have been all too **little** met by the emphasis on . . .

Activity C3.4a

Work out whether *less* is a determiner, adverb or pronoun on these lines:

1. The quicker you get to your opponent's goal the **less** obstacles you find . . .
2. For the **less** wealthy, there were silver bracelets . . .
3. . . . a helicopter requires **less** power to maintain height . . .
4. Ban all bands with names of one syllable or **less**.
5. . . . some of this more recent legislation has been **less** effective in securing convictions.
6. . . . other conductors with a **less** complete control find it hard . . .
7. If she spoke **less** and listened more . . .
8. . . . this did not mean necessarily there was **less** literacy.
9. They want to use **less** fuel and cause **less** pollution . . .
10. In Britain this trend has been **less** marked . . .
11. . . . failure to provide adequate services means **less** is being achieved . . .
12. . . . and is therefore due to expire in **less** than ten years from now . . .

★ Activity C3.4b

Now look at the same lines again and find where *less* is a determiner being used with a count noun, where it could be replaced by *fewer*.

★ Activity C3.5

Look at these concordance lines and decide whether *some* is

a)   a determiner with a singular noncount noun
b)   a determiner with a count noun in the plural
c)   a pronoun
d)   an adverb

1.   We did **some** blood tests . . .
2.   . . . we'll just have **some** music now.
3.   More than 12,000 people . . . have been treated, and **some** have complained of glare . . .
4.   [He] farms **some** 230 acres north of Chatteris . . .
5.   . . . and in **some** cases this has caused a chafing . . .
6.   We will carry out **some** work on this . . .
7.   We hope soon to introduce paper banks at **some** of our larger stores . . .
8.   **Some** publishers are making heavy weather of 1992.
9.   They will inevitably replace humans in **some** medical tasks.
10. I'm writing to you with **some** good news . . .
11. Keep **some** of these in the house.
12. There's **some** programme on tonight about it.

Comments

Activity C3.1: In 1 *a few* has a positive idea; it implies that more than expected turned up, given the conditions. In 2 *few* suggests a disappointing result; more should have because of the good weather. It has the same idea as 'not many'. There is a similar positive/negative distinction between *a little* and *little*.

Activity C3.2: In both cases *fewer* could be used: *fewer people* and *fewer than*. And some people would insist that it must be used, especially in 1. They cite a 'rule' that says that *fewer* (and *few* and *fewest*) should be used with count nouns (and *little*, *less* and *least* with noncount nouns). But concordance lines show that this usage is common (and it has been for a long time). And even people who object to 1 do not notice a problem with 2. Also, when we think about it, there is no similar distinction with *more* and *most* (though there is with *much* and *many*).

Activity C3.3: Here are the answers:
    Determiner: 2, 5, 7, 9, 13 and 15.
    Pronoun: 1, 6 and 11.

Adverb: 4, 12 and 16.
Adjective: 3, 8, 10 and 14.
In 14 *little* is modifying *bit* (i.e. it is an adjective); but *a little bit* functions as an adverb. If we simply said *a little like* then it would be an adverb too. Note modification of the determiner with *very*, *too* and *as* on lines 7, 13 and 15. Note also the lines where *a little* (determiner, pronoun or adverb) expresses a positive idea.

Activity C3.4a: Here are the answers:
    Determiner: 1, 3, 8, 9
    Pronoun: 4, 7, 11,
    Adverb: 2, 5, 6, 10, 12

Activity C3.4b: There are three lines where *less* is used with, or is referring to, a count noun. In two (5 and 9) it could possibly be replaced by *fewer*, though the text does not sound strange. Only in one (1) does *less* sound informal (or perhaps incorrect to some people). In 12 it would sound strange to use *fewer*, because *ten years*, although technically plural, is considered as a single period. See A3 for more on this.

Activity C3.5:

a) a determiner with a singular noncount noun: 2, 6, 10
b) a determiner with a count noun in the plural: 1, 5, 7, 8, 9
c) a pronoun: 3, 11
d) an adverb: 4

12 does not involve any of the above cases; it shows *some* used with a singular count noun, meaning something unspecified or vague.

C4   THE COMPARISON OF ADJECTIVES

This section explores two problems to do with the comparison of adjectives as described in A4.

C4.1 Identifying phrasal comparison

Section A4 discussed the two ways of making comparative and superlative adjectives: phrasal and inflectional. Identifying inflectional comparison is relatively easy; all you need to do is to see if an adjective has an *-er* or *-est* inflection. However, it is not so easy with *more* and *most*, because they have a number of different functions. First of all, they can be determiners (*more/most people*) or pronouns, as well as adverbs (*I like him more/most*).

There are other cases we need to distinguish where *more* and *most* can precede adjectives but are not part of comparatives or superlatives:

❏ *most* as a formal intensifier, especially with *a*, where it has the idea of 'very' or 'extremely': *That's most interesting / That's a most interesting idea.*
❏ *more* and *most* as determiners when they have an adjective intervening between them and their head noun: *more happy people* means 'more people who are happy' (not 'happier people')
❏ cases where two adjectives are being compared (rather than two degrees of the same adjective): *He was more <u>happy</u> than <u>sad</u>.*

⭐ **Activity C4.1**

Identifying superlatives with *most*.
   Look at the following concordance lines for *most* and identify when it is part of a superlative.

1. For **most** mothers, the experience of poverty is one which . . .
2. Airships offer the **most** rewarding and comfortable way of travelling . . .
3. . . . this is what you can get **most** easily.
4. Calling for his **most** precious stones . . .
5. And **most** of those who do will only try it once . . .
6. . . . which forms of design and layout were **most** associated with 'lapses in civilised behaviour'.
7. . . . both parents spoke to him in Punjabi for **most** of the time . . .
8. His entry was **most** dramatic . . .
9. Certainly this is the single **most** crucial event . . .
10. **Most** adults said the story was just a story . . .
11. The **most** convenient system in which to exploit these effects . . .
12. . . . is an express condition in **most** legal leases . . .
13. . . . including one of the **most** popular of all . . .
14. I'd always made **most** of my own clothes . . .
15. That's what I dislike **most** about you . . .

C4.2 Examining the rules for comparison

The 'rules' for the comparison of adjectives in A4 – i.e. whether to use inflectional or phrasal forms – were rather vague and extensive at the same time. What happens in actual usage?

   Martin Hilpert (2008) counted the occurrence of comparative forms in the British National Corpus (see the start of the C section for a description of this). He found a total of 245 adjectives which alternated between phrasal and inflectional comparison.

The table below shows selected results for some of the more noteworthy cases. It is organised in six groups:

❏ one-syllable adjectives
❏ two-syllables adjectives ending in –*er*
❏ two-syllables adjectives ending in syllabic /l/
❏ two-syllables adjectives ending in –*ow*
❏ two- (and three-) syllable adjectives ending in a consonant + *y*
❏ some other two-syllable adjectives that are often mentioned in reference grammars

Activity C4.2

As the table below shows, there are several cases which would appear to break the rules quite significantly. Identify the most significant exceptions and see if you can spot any tendencies in the groups.

Table C4.2.1 Frequencies of phrasal and inflectional comparison

adjective	more	-er	adjective	more	-er
dead	19	4	easy	28	4031
free	21	270	happy	10	1007
real	109	4	healthy	26	500
			likely	3724	17
clever	21	101	lively	19	46
slender	15	44	sorry	12	18
tender	15	6	unhappy	18	15
			unlikely	27	1
humble	25	77	wealthy	15	148
simple	60	1115	worthy	38	17
subtle	339	114			
			common	594	73
narrow	14	550	handsome	24	10
shallow	6	125	pleasant	90	50
yellow	8	9	remote	179	87
			polite	23	7

Overall the rules that were stated in A4 seem to be quite useless. Rather than the length of adjectives (in terms of syllables) being the decisive factor, it seems in real life that there are a number of other factors which affect the choice between phrasal and inflectional comparison:

❏ morphological relationships between adjectives
❏ phonological features other than the number of syllables
❏ postmodification

In addition, planning is obviously a factor in the use of *more* in places where it might not be expected: the idea of comparison may arise before an adjective has been selected (as in the one case of *more big*). And reduplication may also be an influence: *more and more handsome* rather than *handsomer and handsomer*.

Another plausible explanation offered by Hilpert is frequency: it seems that rare adjectives are more likely to form the comparative phrasally. This could explain apparently exceptional cases such as *real*, *dead*, *yellow*, and *tender*.

The fact that there are alternatives for 245 adjectives, not to mention the multiplicity of factors apparently at work, suggests that we should be cautious about presenting simple rules for this complicated area; we should rather be talking about tendencies. If some advice for learners is needed, we might say that they should not worry so much about 'mistakes', and that if they are in doubt phrasal comparison is acceptable with most two-syllable adjectives.

Comments

Activity C4.1:

Most forms the superlative of adjectives on lines 2, 4, 6, 9, 11, and 13; on line 3 it forms the superlative of an adverb. On line 8 it is an intensifier (meaning 'extremely') and on lines 1, 10 and 12 it is a determiner, meaning 'the majority of'. It has the same meaning on lines 5, 7 and 14, where it is a pronoun (with postmodification beginning with *of*). Finally, on line 15 it is an adverb.

Activity C4.2:

Comments are made according to the six groups.

1) one-syllable adjectives

There are two things to be said here. The first point to note is that *dead* and *real* have comparison with *more* rather than with *-er*. This contradicts the most basic rule about one-syllable adjectives.

But perhaps what is most surprising is that they have comparison at all. All three are supposedly non-gradable adjectives. You are either dead or alive, there is no in-between; 'deadness' is absolute. And yet creative writers may tell us that someone was 'very dead', and of course *dead* can have a metaphorical meaning: *I'm feeling dead*, and so presumably *I'm feeling more dead than I ever have*. Other supposedly non-gradable adjectives like *perfect* and *unique* often occur with comparison and intensifying adverbs. (See Activity A4.2 in A4.)

2) two-syllables adjectives ending in *-er*

There is a difference here between *clever* and *slender* on the one hand, and *tender* on the other. A possible reason for this is that, as suggested above, *tender* is less frequent than the other two and so is more likely to take phrasal comparison.

3) two-syllables adjectives ending in syllabic /l/

There is a big difference between *subtle* on the one hand and *humble/simple* on the other. There may be phonological influence here in that /bl-/ and /pl-/ are possible consonant clusters but /tl-/ is not.

4) two-syllables adjectives ending in *-ow*

Inflectional comparison is much more common here (though not significantly so for *yellow*)

5) two- (and three-) syllables adjectives ending in a consonant + *y*
There are startling differences here: *easy* and *happy* took inflectional comparison by a vast majority while *likely* was the reverse. Postmodification may be a factor with the latter, since it is so commonly part of an adjective phrase. Compare
    We are more likely to . . . and *We are likelier to . . .*?
Which of these two sounds better?

    The comparison of *unhappy* and *unlikely* is probably influenced by their unmarked counterparts. The occurrence of *unhappier* breaks the 'rule' that three-syllable adjectives cannot take *-er*, influenced no doubt by the frequency of *happier*.

    6) some other two-syllable adjectives. At least there is a clear conclusion here. In all of these cases phrasal comparison was more common (commoner?) than inflectional.

C5 DISTINGUISHING *-ING* AND *-ED* FORMS

We saw in A4 that two important groups of adjectives end in *-ed* and *-ing*. But these are also the participle forms of verbs, and the *-ed* ending can form the past tense of verbs as well, while the *-ing* ending can also be a marker of action nouns. How then do we distinguish them?

C5.1 Distinguishing the word class of *-ing* forms

-ing forms can belong to three word classes:

nouns:	*I don't like that <u>painting</u>.*
verbs (as *-ing* participle):	*You're <u>hurting</u> me.*
adjective:	*That's an <u>interesting</u> conclusion.*

Usually we can apply the normal criteria to decide a word's class. Thus *painting* above is preceded by a determiner, *that*; *hurting* is preceded by an auxiliary and followed by an object; and *interesting* is used attributively and could be preceded by *very*.

    However, there are situations where the distinction is not entirely clear:
1) noun vs verb, as in this example:
    This house needs <u>heating</u>.
Are we talking about a heating system which needs to be installed (in which case it is a noun), or about the need to turn on the heating and warm the house (a verb)? If we add *up* (. . . *needs heating up*) then it is a verb; if we add *new* (. . . *new heating*) then it is a noun.
2) noun vs adjective, as in these two phrases:
    living standards vs *living creatures*

These have the same structure consisting of premodifier plus noun, but there is a difference. In the first *living* is a noun; in the second an adjective (see A3). The first can be turned into postmodification with a preposition: *standards of living*, whereas the adjective can be derived from a verb form: *creatures which are living*. The converse forms do not make sense ('standards which are living' / 'creatures of living').

3) verb vs adjective. *-ing* adjectives can be used predicatively (after *be* etc.) and so they may look like a progressive form:

The story is amusing. (*be* + *-ing* adjective)

The story is developing. (*-ing* participle, part of present progressive)

Usually *-ing* adjectives are related to transitive verbs (see A6 and C6) and so the corresponding verb form would need an object:

The story is amusing me.

and so no ambiguity would be possible. However, there are some *-ing* adjectives which are not related in meaning to a transitive verb, and so we can find ambiguous sentences, for example:

The students are appealing.

This could mean that the students are making an appeal (participle) or that they have the quality of affecting people positively (adjective).

Activity C5.1

Another well-known example of ambiguity is

Flying planes can be dangerous.

What are the two meanings here?

Activity C5.2

Look at the following sets of concordance lines and decide whether the *-ing* form represents a verb or adjective (in the case of *promising*), or verb, adjective or noun (in the case of *entertaining*).

A. *Promising*

1. Fashion designers are **promising** a return to the austere clothing of the 1950s.
2. The company is also **promising** data compression.
3. If the site is **promising** enough, compared with all others . . .
4. The Centre has had a very **promising** first year . . .
5. . . . the bill may be **promising** more than it can deliver.
6. . . . several times **promising** movements failed for want of a penetrative final pass . . .
7. . . . its credentials look **promising** on paper.
8. He's taken them away, **promising** to get back to me in a couple of days.

B. *Entertaining*

1. We try to create an **entertaining** and constructive atmosphere.
2. They preferred **entertaining** at home.

3. Any match of nine tries . . . is bound to be **entertaining**.
4. Franker discussion about the nature and value of conventional **entertaining** could improve matters even more.
5. . . . there are two function rooms overlooking Princes Street for **entertaining** customers.
6. **Entertaining**, in this context, seems an unnecessary luxury.
7. A public relations company is **entertaining** its clients.
8. Not really successful but **entertaining** on the whole.
9. Flag officers have considerable **entertaining** responsibilities.
10. There was, however, a more significant side to Surrealism, as this **entertaining** show documents.
11. . . . it is **entertaining** to look at some of the blind alleys of the past.
12. . . . we're **entertaining** there for a weekend's golf.

C5.2 Distinguishing the word class of -*ed* forms

The -*ed* ending is found with two verb forms: the past tense and the -*ed* participle, as well as with -*ed* adjectives, i.e.:

❏ past tense: *This answer <u>satisfied</u> them.*
❏ -*ed* participle: *This has <u>satisfied</u> them.* (perfect) / *They were <u>satisfied</u> by this.* (passive). The -*ed* participle has two functions: in perfect verb forms and passives (see A6), as shown.
❏ adjective: *I am <u>satisfied</u>.* (predicative) / *They are <u>satisfied</u> customers* (attributive).

The past tense and the -*ed* participle are identical for all regular verbs (e.g. *liked*) and for some irregular verbs (e.g. *brought*), as described in A5. (Remember that we use the term '-*ed* participle' even where the form does not end in -*ed*.) The basic difference between them is that the past tense is finite (can stand alone), whereas the -*ed* participle is non-finite. So for example, though it seems that

I tried and *I have tried*

are only distinguished by the addition of *have*, in fact they are quite different; the first has the finite past tense -*ed*, while the second has the non-finite participle -*ed* (and it is *have* that is the finite verb). With some irregular verbs this distinction is obvious:

I <u>saw</u> it / I have <u>seen</u> it.

When considering -*ed* adjectives, it is important to distinguish them from the passive use of the -*ed* participle (rather than from the perfect use or the past tense). This is because -*ed* adjectives can be used predicatively and so may look like passives (and there is a historical connection). Thus

The door was <u>closed</u>.

is ambiguous. It could refer to a state (adjective) or to a passive action (participle). The addition of different types of adverb may clarify:

The door was <u>probably</u> <u>closed</u>. (adjective)
The door was <u>quickly</u> <u>closed</u>. (participle, part of a passive)

Interestingly, if we change the meaning there is no confusion:

The door was (probably) open.

The door was (quickly) opened.

This is because there is no adjective 'opened'.

Activity C5.3

Look at these concordance lines for *bored* and work out whether it is an adjective or -*ed* participle (in either a passive or perfect construction).

1. So after a while the wolf became **bored** and decided to go and catch a little pig . . .
2. Mary looked out of the window in a **bored** way . . .
3. It's quite a while since I've **bored** you with my observations . . .
4. I began to get **bored** with my walk-on roles . . .
5. It's like being lectured to and **bored** at the same time.
6. I suppose I was **bored**.
7. . . . they had to be carefully marked out so that . . . they would be **bored** in the right place.
8. The devil always started whispering to him when he was especially **bored**.

See also Activity C7.4 in C7 on *closed*.

Another problem occurs with verbs whose three main forms are identical, such as *put* or *set*. Here it is not only the past tense and -*ed* participle that can be confused.

Activity C5.4

Set is a highly irregular verb in that its three forms for memorising are all the same: *set-set-set*. Look at the concordance lines below and decide whether *set* represents

a)   the present tense   b)   the infinitive

c)   the past tense   d)   the -*ed* participle

1. The firm said . . . the bionauts **set** a new world record . . .
2. Some villas had several rooms **set** aside just for sleeping . . .
3. . . . we will **set** and communicate targets in these areas . . .
4. . . . it could be **set** against your salary . . .
5. I haven't **set** any essays on Napoleon, have I?
6. Although we **set** ourselves high standards, if we do not meet your expectations . . .
7. One sunny morning recently I **set** about painting the house
8. . . . something which if **set** in a contemporary context . . .
9. From a crest above the hut we watched the sun **set** on a line of peaks . . .
10. The science-fiction thriller topped the record **set** nearly a year ago . . .

C6

Comments

Activity C5.1: One meaning is that it is dangerous to fly planes (verb), the other that planes which are flying – but not those on the ground – are dangerous (adjective). Possible paraphrases would be *Flying planes is dangerous* and *Flying planes are dangerous.*

Activity C5.2:
A
Verb (*-ing* participle): 1, 2, 5, 8
Adjective: 3, 4, 6, 7,
B
Adjective: 1, 3, 8 (a minor sentence; see A9), 10, 11 (a case of extraposition; see A11)
Noun: 4, 6, 9 (a premodifier; see A3)
Verb: 5, 7, 12 (intransitive; see C6)
Line 2 could be interpreted as a noun or a verb.

Activity C5.3:
Adjective: 1, 2, 4, 6, 8
-ed participle: 3, 5 (a passive), 7 (a passive, = 'drill a hole')

Activity C5.4:

a)   the present tense: 6
b)   the infinitive: 3, 9
c)   the past tense: 1, 7
d)   the *-ed* participle: 2, 4, 5, 8, 10. Lines 2, 8 and 10 contain 'reduced passives' (see A6) which can be expanded: . . . *rooms which were* . . . ; . . . *if it is/was* . . . ; . . . *record which was* . . .

C6 VERBS WHICH CAN BE TRANSITIVE AND INTRANSITIVE

Transitivity was introduced in A6 as a determining factor in the formation of passives. It is discussed in more detail in A8 as a fundamental feature in different types of clauses. In this section it is investigated as a characteristic of verbs. The main question is: to what extent can verbs be characterised as transitive or intransitive?

It is impossible to divide verbs neatly into two sub-classes: transitive and intransitive. There are a number of reasons for this:

- many frequent verbs occur in a number of patterns (see B8), some transitive and some not, usually with a difference in meaning:

    He _runs_ every day.

    He _runs_ a multi-million-dollar corporation.

    And in fact many frequent verbs that are typically regarded as transitive have less common intransitive uses:

    That will _do_! (= 'is enough')

    We pulled hard but it wouldn't _give_. (= 'move')

- some verbs seem neutral to the idea of transitivity, appearing with or without an object with the same meaning, e.g. _drive, drink, eat, read_:

    I can _drive_ / I can _drive a car_.

    Some are very limited in their range of objects, having a 'cognate' object when transitive, e.g. _sing_ with _song_ and similar nouns:

    He was _singing_ in the bath.

    He was _singing_ his favourite _song_ in the bath.

- verbs that involve a reflexive or reciprocal action verbs can omit their object

    He _washed_ and _dressed_ before going out.

    They've been _fighting_ ever since they got married.

    Compare these with the transitive versions with the appropriate object pronouns inserted:

    washed and dressed _himself_ (reflexive), fighting _each other_ (reciprocal)

    In many European languages an object pronoun would be obligatory in this situation.

- many verbs seem basically transitive but have missing (ellipted) objects, which are already known:

    Can you _re-send_? (talking about an email message)

    To _repeat_, . . . (cf. To repeat _what I said before_ . . .)

    If we _paraphrase_ we can see the hidden passives. (from A6)

    Are you going to _buy_ or not?

    In fact many of so-called transitive verbs in English seem to have the ability to appear without an object, given the right circumstances.

Another phenomenon involving a relationship between transitive and intransitive verbs, ergativity, is investigated in C7.

The following activities examine some of this variation.

⭐ **Activity C6.1**

Look at the sets of concordance lines below. In each case identify the lines where the verb is used transitively and where it is intransitive. There may be cases where this is not clear, or where other factors are involved.

Then say what the relationship is between the transitive and intransitive forms according to the above bullet points. Is it possible to say whether each verb is mainly transitive or intransitive?

A. RUN

(Note that the form *run* can represent the infinitive, present tense or *-ed* participle.)

1. You can still **run** a storage heater for less than 70p per week!
2. She used to **run** a playschool . . .
3. The pair reckon the story will **run** and **run** until conclusive proof is provided . . .
4. A course in cancer counselling is to be **run** at Magee College . . .
5. There's ditches where the water has **run** away all the boulder clay . . .
6. . . . they're timid creatures who will **run** away at the slightest sound . . .
7. Peak-hour trams will **run** every six minutes . . .
8. I don't want one of them to **run** her fingers through my hair . . .
9. There's a couple of ideas I'd like to **run** in front of you . . .
10. If I had been able to **run** my own theatre . . .
11. . . . all new cars will have to be able to **run** on unleaded petrol . . .
12. . . . what happens when the wine has **run** out.
13. . . . ensuring that all phases of the programme **run** smoothly . . .
14. We may need to have another look at him and **run** some tests . . .
15. The measures will **run** to the end of 1990.
16. We've **run** up a cost of two hundred and fifty quid . . .

B. DRIVE

(The form *drive* can represent the infinitive or the present tense.)

1. . . . I happen to **drive** a very small car . . .
2. It was fast, fun to **drive**, and, despite a high price, had an enthusiastic following.
3. He had the mobility and authority to **drive** around the reserve after dark . . .
4. People may smoke, **drive** at 80 miles an hour in fog on a motorway . . .
5. Unless you **drive** everywhere at less than 40mph . . .
6. Others . . . scheduled business calls first thing so that they could **drive** in later.
7. The doctor would not test his fitness to **drive**.
8. I'll let you **drive** me all the way round . . .
9. That's guaranteed to **drive** me to despair.
10. What are you going to do next? **Drive** my taxi into the river?
11. . . . I'm learning how to **drive** now . . .
12. Can you **drive** over with Christina or Edward?
13. But the plan is not just an ideal for those who do not **drive**.
14. . . . a build-up of stress which can **drive** people to rely on drink . . .
15. Who will **drive** the publication?
16. You have a car, so one way is to **drive** there . . .

C. MET

(The form *met* can represent the past tense or *-ed* participle.)

1. The club has **met** four times in SDCI's office . . .
2. I have never **met** a more beautiful woman.

3.   ... and there we **met** a group of people ...
4.   ... people only obey his decisions if certain conditions are **met** ...
5.   ... the poverty and injustices which he daily **met** around him ...
6.   We all **met** at a pre-luncheon reception ...
7.   Five criteria must be **met** before merger accounting can be used.
8.   Give me a line-up of blokes I've never **met** before ...
9.   Such arguments were **met** by an unwillingness ...
10. I seem to remember that when we **met** earlier in the year ...
11. [This] pitched the Cabinet into more controversy as it **met** for the first time since the summer break ...
12. I've never **met** his wife ...
13. Your committee **met** on 2 December ...
14. Each time we **met** we just felt closer ...

Comments

Activity C6.1:

A

Transitive: 1, 2, 4 (passive), 5 (phrasal), 8, 9 (a relative clause), 10, 14, 16 (phrasal)
Intransitive: 3, 6 (phrasal), 7, 12 (phrasal), 13, 15

11 could be either transitive or intransitive. In other words, *on unleaded petrol* can be interpreted as a prepositional object (*What will they run on?*) or an adverbial (*How will they run?*). See A8 for an explanation of the use of *wh-* words in identifying objects or other clause elements. See also C8 ('Hidden verb patterns') for cases such as relative clauses where the object may not be obvious.

Note that *run* is quite commonly used as a phrasal verb (both transitive and intransitive): *run away / out (of) / up.*

Overall, it is impossible to characterise *run* as principally a transitive or intransitive verb. It has a whole range of meanings linked either to the transitive use ('manage', 'operate') or to the intransitive ('last'). Note that, of the intransitive uses, none actually represents the 'basic' meaning of moving quickly using one's legs.

B

Transitive: 1, 2*, 8, 9, 10, 14, 15
Intransitive: 3, 4, 5, 6, 7, 11, 12, 13, 16

*: *It* refers to 'a car', the object of *drive*. If the sentence was *It was fun to drive along the beach in our car* then *it* would not refer to a car; this would be a case of extraposition (see A11) and the verb would be intransitive.

In all the intransitive lines 'a car/vehicle' could be inserted. This suggests that there is little difference between the transitive and intransitive forms. But the metaphorical transitive uses (lines 9, 14 and 15) do not correspond to any intransitive use.

C

Transitive: 2, 3, 4, 5, 7, 8, 9, 12
Intransitive: 1, 6, 10, 11, 13, 14

All the intransitive lines could be characterised as reciprocal (*we all met each other*).

C7 ERGATIVITY

Section C6 investigated the concept of transitivity in some detail, finding that the distinction between transitive and intransitive verbs is not a simple one. A number of relationships were identified, for example

❑ verbs which can be both transitive and intransitive, but with a difference (or differences) in meaning
❑ verbs which include or do without an object 'at the drop of a hat'

This section looks at one more relationship.

Activity C7.1

Look at these two extracts.
  a)   A master and servant are talking.
       'I have . . . ruined my clothes'.
       'They will clean, sir.'
  (from a historical novel, *Dissolution*, by C.J. Sansom)
  b)   Some men are discussing a ship.
       The fuss that was made while that ship was building.
  (from a short story by Joseph Conrad, 'The Brute')
How can you explain the use of *clean* and *build* here? Are they intransitive verbs? What do 'they' and 'the ship' refer to?

Verbs such as *clean* and *build*, where the 'object' replaces the subject without any other change, are called 'ergative'. Ergative verbs are both transitive and intransitive (though the term is usually applied to the latter use). In the transitive/intransitive verbs that we have seen so far it is the object that is left out when a transitive verb becomes intransitive:

  I sang <u>a song</u>. / I sang.
  I'm learning to drive <u>a car</u>. / I'm learning to drive.

But with ergative verbs it is the subject that is omitted, to be replaced by the object.

  <u>They</u> started the game. / <u>The game</u> started.
  <u>He</u> moved his head. / <u>His head</u> moved.

Ergativity is common with verbs involving movement and change of state where the thing affected may be more important than the agent or doer, for example

  The glass suddenly <u>shattered</u>.
  Prices <u>have doubled</u> in the last month.

Ergatives look very similar to passives without a *by* phrase:

The door <u>was</u> slowly <u>opened</u>.

And the meaning is similar, in that both avoid mentioning the agent, but there is a difference. The passive implies an action with an 'agent' (the person or thing that causes an action – see A8) even if not mentioned, while the ergative suggests a spontaneous event without an agent:

The door slowly <u>opened</u>.

In many European languages the equivalent sentence would be constructed with a reflexive pronoun ('The door opened <u>itself</u>.').

Sometimes a verb is used ergatively only if there is an adverbial:

This car <u>drives</u> <u>beautifully</u>.

The book <u>is selling</u> <u>like hot cakes</u>.

Your essay <u>reads</u> <u>well</u> until the conclusion.

And some ergative verbs have a restricted range of subjects:

Then the <u>bell/alarm</u> <u>rang/sounded</u>.

⭐ **Activity C7.2**

Decide what patterns (intransitive, transitive, transitive/intransitive, ergative) these verbs have:

    fall, bounce, show, die, boil, dance

Think of examples of each use. (NB: By calling a verb 'ergative' we are saying that it is both transitive and intransitive, but in the way described above.)

⭐ **Activity C7.3**

Look at the concordance lines for various forms of the verb *improve*. Identify those which are transitive, and those which, while intransitive, are in an ergative relationship to the transitive form. What do you notice about the subjects in each case?

1. . . . it's done very well indeed to **improve** its profits . . .
2. So people tried to set up unions to **improve** living and working conditions . . .
3. . . . many head injured patients will fail to **improve** and could even get worse.
4. But it has to be applied properly or it will not **improve** the quality of education.
5. . . . we will continue to look for ways to **improve** the nutritional properties of our products.
6. . . . only when government took action did situations **improve** at all.
7. Some have received large capital grants to **improve** their buildings . . .
8. Until recently most pundits expected the market to **improve** in the spring . . .
9. What do we want to **improve** most of all?
10. Current video printers . . . are **improving** all the time.

11.   ... with a clear objective of increasing sales and **improving** customer service.
12.   Their health **improved** and a cure was claimed in many cases.
13.   Imaging quality has now been vastly **improved** ...
14.   Gradually agricultural tools **improved** as well.
15.   ... we've marginally **improved** our market share.

Activity C7.4

Look at the concordance lines for *closed* below. Identify those which are transitive, and those which, while intransitive, are in an ergative relationship to the transitive form. Note also that some instances of *closed* are adjectives.

1.   ... he worked at the Admiralty ... until it **closed** 10 years ago.
2.   ... it's been **closed** for a couple of years now ...
3.   ... when the whistle went for nine o'clock that door was **closed** ...
4.   ... even more Midlands pits could be **closed** down.
5.   The nitric acid plant has **closed** down ...
6.   ... I heard that the house would be **closed** for renovation.
7.   The house is currently **closed** for extensive conservation works ...
8.   ... a silent Locomotive Shed with its doors **closed** for the last time ...
9.   The Opera House **closed** for two weeks.
10.   ... US markets were largely **closed** for a holiday.
11.   On Wednesday night the main runway was **closed** for maintenance ...
12.   On 1 May 1956 this branch finally **closed**, having been opened to passenger and freight traffic in 1856.
13.   ... it has not yet **closed** its books for the first quarter ...
14.   ... the line has been **closed** only thirty-five years.
15.   No, we're **closed** Saturday.
16.   One of the girls ran and **closed** the door ...
17.   ... the chairman **closed** the meeting at ten past ten.
18.   Its cavernous classrooms became silent in 1977 when the school **closed**.
19.   It remained **closed** until the idea of a union was forgotten.
20.   The evening **closed** with questions to the Speaker ...

And finally a story:

The broken window, or how grammar can get you out of trouble
Four boys were playing football in their school playground – where it was not allowed. One of them mis-kicked the ball and it smashed a window in one of the schoolrooms.

Now they were honest lads and, instead of running away and hiding, they decided to report the broken window to the principal. But first they discussed how to describe the breakage.

The first one, who was a little naïve linguistically, suggested *I'm sorry; we have broken the window*. But the other three said that it was much too obvious; it would get them into lots of trouble.

The second student, who had taken a basic course in English grammar and knew something about the passive, suggested *The window has been broken by us.* 'It focuses more on the thing affected than on those responsible for the action', he said. But the other two said it was still too obvious who was responsible.

The third student, more advanced, knew that the actor could be omitted in the passive. So he suggested *The window has been broken.* The first two nodded their agreement, but the fourth said 'But the principal will still know that someone did it and will ask "Who by?"'

Now this fourth student had read this book and so he knew all about the ergative, and how it could be used to present an action as a happening without any 'actors'. So he suggested *The window has broken.* The other three looked at him in awe, and agreed. So that is what they said when they went to see the principal; and the principal just nodded and thanked them for telling him.

MORAL: grammar is good for you. (© Roger Berry 2012)

Comments

Activity C7.1: In a) *They* refers to the clothes. We would normally expect clothes to be the object of *clean*, but here they are the subject and there is no object. Similarly, in b) *the ship* would normally be the object of *build*, or the subject of a passive (. . . *was being built*), but here it is the subject.

So although *clean* and *build* are normally transitive verbs, they are intransitive here, but intransitive in a different way from other verbs that we have already seen.

Activity C7.2:

fall	intransitive	*Prices have fallen.*
bounce	ergative	*He bounced the ball. / The ball bounced.*
show	ergative	*He showed his anger. / His anger showed.*
die	intransitive	*Those flowers are dying.*
	(It can also be transitive with a cognate object: *He died a painful death.*)	
boil	ergative	*She boiled the water. / The water boiled.*
dance	transitive/intransitive	*They danced. / They danced a samba.*

Activity C7.3:
Transitive: 1, 2, 4, 5, 7, 9 (interrogative), 11, 13 (passive), 15
Ergative (intransitive): 3, 6, 8, 10, 12, 14

With the transitive sentences the subjects are basically agents (as discussed in A8 and D8), though in 11 and 13 the agent is not stated. With the ergatives, the subjects are basically people or things affected by the process of improvement.

Activity C7.4:
Transitive: 3 (passive), 4 (passive), 13, 16, 17
Ergative (intransitive): 1, 5, 9, 12, 18, 20
On lines 2, 7, 8, 10, 14, 15, 19 *closed* is an adjective; see C5.
Lines 6 and 11 are ambiguous; they could be transitive (passive) or adjective.

Note the phrasal verb *closed down* (which can be ergative, just like *close*)

Note that *close* can also be intransitive with an object omitted: *She closed (her talk) by saying* . . . Here it is not ergative.

ANALYSING CLAUSES

The clause patterns and verb patterns discussed in sections A8 and B8 are in many ways two sides of the same coin. If we have worked out the clause pattern then we generally know the verb pattern. Thus if there is an SVOO pattern this indicates that the verb is ditransitive; if SVOP, then link transitive.

There are some differences, however. The analysis of a passive such as *It has been finished* in terms of clause pattern – SV – would not correspond to the verb pattern: transitive. And sometimes the classification of the verb is not sensitive enough to distinguish two different underlying structures e.g. to label a verb link transitive would not describe the patterns of a verb fully; see the activity with *make* below.

Moreover, their purposes are different. Clause pattern analysis is more appropriate for the analysis of texts, i.e. of already-existing language, whereas a knowledge of verb patterns is more useful in constructing texts correctly (though it can also explain cases of ambiguity).

C8.1 Analysing clause patterns

When analysing clauses, we need to be able to distinguish cases where a unit is an element in its own right and where it is only part of an element. This can be particularly tricky when clauses are involved inside the clause we are interested in. Thus in

He's a man <u>that we can trust</u>.

the underlined clause is a relative clause that postmodifies *man*; in other words, it is part of a noun phrase which is a predicative: *a man that we can trust*; it is not a clause element. In

I'm happy <u>that you are here</u>.

that you are here is part of an adjective phrase (again functioning as a predicative) beginning *happy* . . . However, in

I said <u>that he could go</u>

the underlined clause is a nominal clause that functions as the object of *said*, i.e. it is a clause element. Clauses beginning with *that* are described in some detail in A10 and B10.

One way to establish whether something is a clause element or not is to try replacing it with a pronoun or something similar. Thus in the first two examples above it is not possible to replace the underlined clauses ('He's a man it', 'I'm happy it') but in the third it is: *I said it*.

Identify the clause pattern in these simple sentences. Distinguish between subject and object predicatives, and between direct, indirect and prepositional objects. If there is an adverbial element, indicate if it is obligatory or optional using brackets. Remember that one element may consist of several words. Use the substitution test if you are unsure.

> EXAMPLE: *My uncle knows the President.* → *My uncle | knows | the President.* SVOd

1. *I'll see you soon.*
2. *The girl standing over there is my sister.*
3. *I find it very amusing.*
4. *The children have been swimming.*
5. *The train arrives in Guangzhou at night.*
6. *He told her all his problems.*
7. *I bought the ring for her.*
8. *Suddenly, the room felt very cold.*
9. *I'll put it on top of the cupboard.*
10. *They made him emperor.*
11. *He seems incapable of laughter.*
12. *The man in the bank was arrested.*
13. *Her grandmother made her a cake which had 18 candles.*
14. *Share prices are falling to new levels.*
15. *She depends on me.*

C8.2 Analysing verb patterns

Make is a very versatile verb. You are probably familiar with its use as a transitive verb, but there are several refinements of this, and it can also be a link verb.

Look at the following sentences and distinguish the verb and object and predicative clause elements. You may find some clause patterns that you have not met before.

1. *She'll make a cake.*
2. *She'll make him a cake.*
3. *She'll make a cake for him.*
4. *She'll make a good wife.*
5. *She'll make him a good husband.*
6. *She'll make him a good wife.*

Hidden verb patterns

There are a number of situations where the pattern of a verb may be 'hidden' in some way, especially if an object has been moved from its typical position after the verb:

a) passive constructions. Passive sentences should be converted into their active equivalents to find which pattern the verb has. So

> *The ball was caught by Tom*

is the passive equivalent of *Tom caught the ball* (i.e. it is SVOd).

b) reduced passives. In

> *A man called Jones telephoned.*

call is link transitive. It has a predicative (*Jones*) and an object which is hidden but is equivalent to *a man* (compare with *A man who is called Jones . . .*)

c) relative clauses (see B10). In

> *The girl that he likes . . .*

that is the object of *likes* and so *like* is transitive here.

d) *wh-* interrogatives representing the object, as in

> *Who does he like?*

e) infinitives following adjectives and nouns, as in:

> *She's difficult to please.*

Please is transitive here; its (deep structure) object is *she* (compare *It is difficult to please her*). See also 'fronting' in A11.

Activity C8.3

Now look at the concordance lines for *make* and identify the verb pattern. The two main choices are monotransitive and link transitive.

1. *Billy was too close to the policeman to **make** any suggestion . . .*
2. *Perhaps an illustration can **make** this difference clear . . .*
3. *. . . use these to **make** even more profit.*
4. *Do not learn your lines as this can **make** the talk rather stilted . . .*
5. *. . . the diverse interests that **make** up one profession.*
6. *. . . if you . . . have any comments to **make** on this briefing.*
7. *. . . the Magistrate Sahib had tried to **make** them strengthen the embankments.*
8. *The point I'm trying to **make** is . . .*
9. *. . . it is a good idea to **make** it the destination of an excursion from there.*
10. *When you were little I used to **make** up stories for him . . .*
11. *Does it **make** any sense to put in the same numbers . . .?*
12. ***Make** your sandwiches look as attractive as you can . . .*
13. *If so, did it **make** the rest of the winter any warmer?*
14. *Not to **make** eye contact with anyone in the audience.*

Comments

Activity C8.1: The vertical lines show the divisions between clause elements.

1.	I |'ll see | you | soon.	SVOd(A)
2.	The girl standing over there | is | my sister.	SVCs
3.	I | find | it | very amusing.	SVOdPo
4.	The children | have been swimming.	SV
5.	The train | arrived | in Guangzhou | at night.	SV(A)(A)
6.	He | told | her | all his problems.	SVOiOd
7.	I | bought | the ring | for her.	SVOdOp
8.	Suddenly, | the room | felt | very cold.	(A)SVCs
9.	I |'ll put | it | in the cupboard.	SVOdA
10.	They | made | him | emperor.	SVOdPo
11.	He | seems | incapable of laughter.	SVCs
12.	The man in the bank | was arrested.	SV
13.	Her grandmother | made | her | a cake.	SVOiOd
14.	Share prices | are falling | to new levels.	SV(A)
15.	She | depends on | me.	SVOp

Activity C8.2: The first three are relatively straightforward to analyse:

1. monotransitive verb with a direct object
2. ditransitive verb with indirect and direct objects
3. ditransitive verb with direct and prepositional objects

The next three are perhaps unexpected:

4. link verb with subject predicative (*a good wife*). Here *make* could be replaced by a link verb such as *be*.
5. link transitive verb with direct object and object predicative
6. link transitive verb with indirect object and subject predicative

Sentences 5 and 6 seem to be identical structurally, but obviously are contradictory in terms of meaning. 5 means she will turn him into a good husband, but in 6 *him* represents an indirect object while *a good wife* is a subject predicative; a paraphrase would be *She will be a good wife for him*. The use of a subject predicative after an object is rare; another example would be *She left the room angry* (i.e. 'she' was 'angry'), which is not to be confused with *She left the room angrily*, where *angrily* is an adverbial. *She left him angry* could also have the same structure but is more likely to mean that 'he' was 'angry', i.e. *angry* is an object predicative.

There are other patterns involving *make*, for instance 'make someone do something'.

Activity C8.3:
Monotransitive: 1, 3, 5 (a phrasal verb), 6 (*make comments*), 8 (*make a point*), 11 (see extraposition in A11), 14

Link transitive: 2, 4, 7, 9, 12, 13
Ditransitive phrasal-prepositional: 10

Note that in 6 *on this briefing* belongs with *comments* as part of the object, as does *with anyone in the audience* with *eye contact* in 8.

EXPLORING TEXTS (1)

From now on in the exploration sections we will be looking at authentic texts rather than concordances or made-up sentences. Studying texts can be somewhat problematic because the grammarian has no control over them; they can involve many features that are not part of the current focus, and include structures that have not been discussed so far. And sometimes the structure can become very complicated, but you must be prepared to analyse such texts.

The text below is from the novel, *The Joy Luck Club*, by Amy Tan, first published in 1989 and made into a film in 1993. In it the narrator, a young Chinese girl, is watching her mother at the death-bed of her grandmother ('Popo'). We have already seen paragraph B in section A9, and you will need to check this section for most of the concepts in the activities, in particular the different sentence types.

Note the American spelling: *honors. Shou* in paragraph H is a rendering of a dialect word meaning filial piety, or respect for one's parents and grandparents.

(Paragraph letters and sentence numbers have been added for ease of reference.)

A (1) I worshipped this mother from my dream. (2) But the woman standing by Popo's bed was not the mother of my memory. (3) Yet I came to love this mother as well. (4) Not because she came to me and begged me to forgive her. (5) She did not. (6) She did not need to explain that Popo chased her out of the house when I was dying. (7) This I knew. (8) She did not need to tell me she married Wu Tsing to exchange one unhappiness for another. (9) I knew this as well.

B (1) Here is how I came to love my mother. (2) How I saw in her my own true nature. (3) What was beneath my skin. (4) Inside my bones.

C (1) It was late at night when I went to Popo's room. (2) My auntie said it was Popo's dying time and I must show respect. (3) I put on a clean dress and stood between my auntie and uncle at the foot of Popo's bed. (4) I cried a little, not too loud.

D (1) I saw my mother on the other side of the room. (2) Quiet and sad. (3) She was cooking a soup, pouring herbs and medicines into the steaming pot. (4) And then I saw her pull up her sleeve and pull out a sharp knife. (5) She put this knife on the softest part of her arm. (6) I tried to close my eyes, but could not.

E (1) And then my mother cut a piece of meat from her arm. (2) Tears poured from her face and blood spilled to the floor.

F (1) My mother took her flesh and put it in the soup. (2) She cooked magic in the ancient tradition to try to cure her mother this one last time. (3) She opened

Popo's mouth, already too tight from trying to keep her spirit in. (4) She fed her this soup, but that night Popo flew away with her illness.

G (1) Even though I was young, I could see the pain of the flesh and the worth of the pain.

H (1) This is how a daughter honors her mother. (2) It is *shou* so deep it is in your bones. (3) The pain of the flesh is nothing. (4) The pain you must forget. (5) Because sometimes that is the only way to remember what is in your bones. (6) You must peel off your skin, and that of your mother, and her mother before her. (7) Until there is nothing. (8) No scar, no skin, no flesh.

⭐ **Activity C9.1**

Look at paragraph D and identify the minor sentence in it. How could you include it in the previous sentence?

⭐ **Activity C9.2**

Look at paragraph A and identify the conjunctions. How do they relate their clause to the main clause?

⭐ **Activity C9.3**

Look at paragraph H and study the sentences in it.

a) How many finite verb phrases (see A6) are there, i.e. how many clauses? Which sentence does not have a finite verb phrase?
b) Which other sentences are also incomplete (minor), although they have a finite verb phrase?
c) Analyse the major sentences according to whether they are simple or multiple, compound or complex.)
d) Analyse the main clause elements in these sentences. Which one has an unusual word order?
e) How many grammatical (as opposed to graphological) sentences are there? How could you rewrite the whole paragraph in 'grammatical' sentences?

⭐ **Activity C9.4**

In sentence (4) of the above activity the object has been 'fronted'. Why is this so? Can you find another sentence in the text where this has taken place?

⭐ **Activity C9.5**

Another feature of the text is ellipsis (see B11). Look at sentence (A5) and the second clause in (D6) and rewrite them in full.

Comments

Activity C9.1: (2) is a minor sentence. It could be added to (1) as follows:

    I saw my mother, quiet and sad, on the other side of the room.

Technically, (4) is also a minor sentence (a clause fragment) that could be added to sentence (3).

Activity C9.2: There are four conjunctions: *but* (2), *because* (4), *and* (4), and *when* (6). Both *but* and *because* are used to initiate their graphological sentences (and so are part of minor sentences), while *and* and *when* are used 'properly', to join their clause to the previous one.

Activity C9.3:

a)   In total there are 10 finite verb phrases – and therefore 10 clauses. (The verbs are underlined in the version below.) Sentence (8) has no finite verb phrase – in fact it has no verb at all.

b)   (5) and (7) are minor sentences – clause fragments, in fact. (5) contains another (subordinate) clause.

c)   (1) and (2) are multiple (complex) sentences; (3), (4) and (6) are simple sentences.

d)   (1)   SVPs. There is also a subordinate clause introduced by *how*.

       (2)   SVPs. There is also a subordinate clause introduced by *so . . . that*.

       (3)   SVPs. Note the repetition of this basic clause pattern in the first three sentences.

       (4)   OSV. This is an unusual word order; the object has been 'fronted' (see A11).

       (6)   SVO. Note the co-ordinated object, with *and* repeated.

e)   overall there are five grammatical sentences. The graphological sentence (5) would be joined to (4), and (7) and (8) would be joined to (6).

This is how the paragraph would be if written using only grammatical sentence divisions (the original 'sentence' numbers have been left in place):

    (1) This <u>is</u> how a daughter <u>honors</u> her mother. (2) It <u>is</u> shou so deep it <u>is</u> in your bones. (3) The pain of the flesh <u>is</u> nothing. (4) The pain you <u>must forget</u>, (5) because sometimes that <u>is</u> the only way to remember what <u>is</u> in your bones. (6) You <u>must peel</u> off your skin, and that of your mother, and her mother before her, (7) until there <u>is</u> nothing: (8) no scar, no skin, no flesh.

This separation of 'grammatical' sentences into smaller graphological sentences is typical of a certain 'literary', creative style of writing.

Activity C9.4: The reason for fronting *The pain* is so that it parallels sentence (3). The other sentence with a fronted object is A(7).

Activity C9.5:

(A5) *She did not come to me and beg me to forgive her.*

(D6) *. . . but could not close my eyes.*

EXPLORING TEXTS (2)

In this exploration section we will analyse complex sentences, involving several subordinate clauses. You will need to identify both clause elements and different types of phrase, e.g. a noun phrase acting as a subject, or a prepositional phrase acting as an adverbial.

The text below is part of a description of British cultural peculiarities. It is quite dense in terms of information and the clause structure of the sentences is quite complicated. There are two sentences and both are multiple and complex. Read the text and then answer the questions below.

> No other nation can produce a book collector on quite the heroic scale of Sir Thomas Philips (1792–1872), who in 50 years amassed the greatest private library the world has ever seen, spending on it some £250,000 (add two noughts for inflation). Few other nations can produce such dedicated book loonies as Bernard Levin, who has been advised that should he ever be rash enough to display on shelves the tons of books he has amassed so far, he would assuredly bring the walls of his London apartment crashing about his ears.

Identify all the finite and non-finite verb forms. (Remember modals and imperatives count as finite.) How many clauses are there?

⭐ Activity C10.1

Some small points.

1. Find two contact relative clauses (i.e. where there is no relative pronoun).
2. The object of *produce* in the second sentence begins *such* . . . Where does it end?
3. What clause type is *add two noughts for inflation*?

⭐ Activity C10.2

Analyse the structure of the second sentence according to its finite clauses; name each type of subordinate clause and show how they relate to each other.

⭐ Activity C10.3

Explain the role of *his ears* in the second sentence. Each time it becomes part of a larger unit, explain that unit's role, and so on till you reach the sentence level. Ignore the text from . . . *should he* . . . to . . . *so far* . . .

⭐ Activity C10.4

Comments

Activity C10.1:

There are nine finite and eleven non-finite verb forms. There are therefore nine finite clauses. There are also three non-finite clauses (starting with *spending, to display* and *crashing*). In the copy of the text below the verb phrases (both finite and non-finite) are underlined; the finite verb forms are also italicised. Note the different roles of the two cases of *amassed*.

> No other nation *can* produce a book collector on quite the heroic scale of Sir Thomas Philips (1792–1872), who in 50 years *amassed* the greatest private library the world *has* ever seen, spending on it some £250,000 (*add* two noughts for inflation). Few other nations *can* produce such dedicated book loonies as Bernard Levin, who *has* been advised that *should* he ever *be* rash enough to display on shelves the tons of books he *has* amassed so far, he *would* assuredly bring the walls of his London apartment crashing about his ears.

Activity C10.2:

1. The two contact clauses are (with their antecedents and with the relative pronoun *that* inserted):

    the greatest private library *that* the world has ever seen . . .

    the tons of books *that* he has amassed so far . . .

    One way to work this out is to note that although there are finite clauses there is no subordinator connecting them to the previous clauses. Another clue is the presence of two nouns phrases together (. . . *the greatest private library the world* . . .).

2. It ends with *ears* at the end of the sentence. This is all one long object noun phrase.

3. An imperative.

Activity C10.3: Here is a diagram of the analysis:

(1) Few other nations can produce such dedicated book loonies as Bernard Levin,
    THE START OF THE MAIN CLAUSE . . .

          (2) who has been advised
          A RELATIVE CLAUSE,
          POSTMODIFYING *BERNARD LEVIN*

(3) that he would assuredly bring the walls of his London apartment crashing about his ears.
    A NOMINAL CLAUSE ACTING AS THE OBJECT OF *ADVISED*

(4) should he ever be rash enough to display on shelves the tons of books
    A CONDITIONAL CLAUSE (USING INVERSION) ACTING AS AN ADVERBIAL IN (3)

          (5) he has amassed so far,
          A (CONTACT) RELATIVE CLAUSE

Figure C10.1.1 Analysis of a complex sentence

And this is without dealing with the non-finite clauses.

Activity C10.4

His ears is a noun phrase which is part of a prepositional phrase (*about his ears*)
... which is an adverbial in the non-finite clause (*crashing* ...)
... which is an object predicative of the verb *bring* (*bring something crashing* ...)
... which is the verb in a nominal clause (*that he would assuredly bring* ...)
... which is the direct object of *advise*
... which is the main verb in a relative clause (*who has been advised* ...)
... which is the postmodifcation of *Bernard Levin*
... which is part of a prepositional phrase (*as Bernard Levin*)
... which in itself is the postmodification of a noun phrase (*such dedicated book loonies* ...)
... which is the object of *produce*
... which is the main verb of the main clause (*Few other nations can* ...)

The figure below represents the same information in visual form.

Activity C10.4: A tree diagram of the grammatical structure

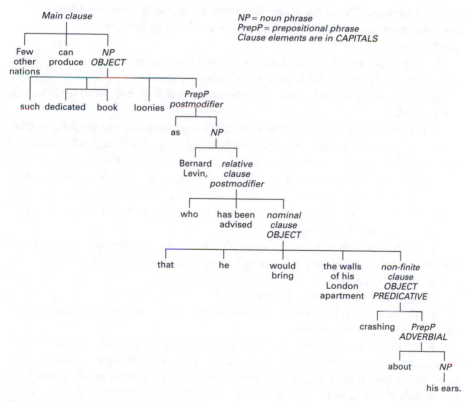

Figure C10.1.2 A tree diagram of grammatical structure

Sentences are like the Russian dolls called 'babushkas' – you unpack one and find another inside, and so on. A noun phrase may contain another noun phrase or even a clause. This concept is called 'recursion'.

EXPLORING TEXTS (3): PUTTING IT ALL TOGETHER

In this section we will try to analyse a fairly long text from many different angles, not just according to sentence type (C9) or subordinate clause type (C10), as was the case with the texts in those sections. You will need to refer back to many previous sections; these are indicated in the activities. In this way, this section serves as a summary and revision of much of the book.

The text is an article taken from a magazine accompanying an English Sunday newspaper. It is written in a humorous style, and the use of grammar in it is part of that style. Read it and then do the activities afterwards.

Sandi Toksvig, 'Proving your identity to a bank can be like proving you were abducted by aliens', Sunday Telegraph, *September 19, 2010*

A (1) The other day I phoned my bank, which, in essence, sounds a simple operation. (2) Yet even the least cynical among you will sniff the beginning of a saga. (3) The bank had made a slight error and I wished to assist them in correcting it.

B (1) After making many numeric choices I was asked to input the long number across the front of my debit card on my telephone keypad. (2) This takes time as I have to find the card, then my glasses, then juggle the phone, the card, the glasses. (3) I found, I juggled, I inputted and finally spoke to someone whose first question was: 'What is the long number across the front of your debit card?' (4) I know better than to reply: 'It's the one that I just inputted' so the glasses went back on, I juggled the phone, I repeated the number.

C (1) The operator was not satisfied. (2) Perhaps she thought that she could hear the washing machines quietly laundering money in the background. (3) 'What is your date of birth?' she asked.

D (1) 'Third of May 1958', I replied.

E (1) There was a long pause. (2) 'That's not what I have here,' she intoned with an unexpected hint of menace.

F (1) 'I don't know what to tell you,' I stammered, 'that is my birthday. (2) Has been since, well since, since 1958. (3) I'm 52,' I added, even though she worked for a bank and so presumably had some basic arithmetic skills. (4) 'What do you have as my birthday?' I inquired.

G (1) 'I can't tell you that,' she said, 'it's a security question.'

H (1) 'Right. (2) So I can't pass security because I don't know when you think my birthday might be which isn't when I thought it was?'

I (1) I have reached a stage where I have so many different passwords in varying formats for such a range of activities that I began to wonder if I had in fact forgotten my birthday. (2) The upshot is that, having been with the same bank since I was 14, I now find myself having to prove to them who I am. (3) How absurd. (4) They must know who I am. (5) I spend quite a lot of time in a property that strictly speaking belongs to them.

J (1) Proving who you are is a curious notion and should be reserved for people like Ötzi the Iceman. (2) It was today in 1991 that two German tourists (Helmut and Erika Simon, if you must know), were sauntering about a glacier on the Austrian–Italian border when they came across what they thought was someone who had recently spoiled a nice day out by dying.

K (1) In fact, they had discovered Europe's oldest natural human mummy. (2) Ötzi lived about 5,300 years ago, yet we know quite a lot about him. (3) He was roughly 5ft 5in, 107 pounds when he popped his bear skin, grass lined shoes.

L (1) It's remarkable really, but by poking around his tooth enamel archaeologists have worked out what village he came from, that his last venison supper was eaten in a 'mid-altitude conifer forest', he probably worked in copper-smelting, often went for long walks and was poorly three times in the months before he died, for which he may well have had acupuncture. (2) All of this information gathered without him saying a thing or having a password.

M (1) I don't feel I need such rigorous analysis and think it would be nice if the bank could just believe me when I declare I know when I was born. (2) They weren't even interested when I offered to get my mother to call and say she was there at the time.

N (1) For a brief moment I understood what Betty and Barney Hill went through. (2) It was today in 1961 that something extraordinary happened to this rather ordinary American couple – they were abducted by aliens. (3) Not for long. (4) They were home the next day. Betty and Barney lived in Portsmouth, New Hampshire, where he worked for the Post Office and she was a social worker.

O (1) Driving home from holiday they saw a bright light in the sky. (2) Soon an object with multicoloured lights was flashing above the place. (3) Naturally the road was entirely deserted as everyone knows there is nothing extraterrestrials hate more than a crowd. (4) When the thing began hovering over their 1957 Chevy, Barney did the only sensible thing – he got a gun which, like any self-respecting American, he kept in the boot for bears, and went to have a closer look.

P (1) He could see 'about 8 to 11 humanoid figures' looking at him through the space craft windows and decided now was a good time to depart. (2) The aliens, though, proved faster than a Chevy and nabbed them.

Q (1) By the time the Hills got home they had torn clothing and a slight ringing in the ears. (2) They phoned the Air Force who helpfully decided the whole matter was clearly a misidentification of the planet Jupiter. (3) This failed to explain the Hills' recollection of being aboard a disc-shaped craft where small men with big eyes poked at their teeth and genitals in a clumsy alien attempt at making intergalactic friends. (4) Needless to say no one believed the poor couple.

R (1) Bankers seem like aliens to me. (2) Maybe I should let them have a poke at my teeth. (3) Of course, if they decide to have a go at my nether parts as well, I shan't be the least bit surprised.

Some difficult vocabulary

laundering (*money*)	turning money obtained through crime into 'respectable' money
mummy	a preserved dead body
popped his . . . shoes	'died'
poorly	ill
acupuncture	a form of treatment for illness using needles
extraterrestrials	aliens, creatures from another planet
1957 Chevy	a Chevrolet car built in 1957
humanoid	resembling humans but not the same
nabbed	caught
intergalactic	from different galaxies
nether parts	genitals

Activity C11.1

Tense (B6)

Most of the article uses the past tense. However, there are places where the present tense (including present perfect) is used as well – paragraphs A, B and I, for example. Why is this so? (Ignore the tenses in direct speech.)

Activity C11.2

Identifying and using the passive (A6, A11)

There are six places in the text where an *-ed* word is preceded by a form of *be*; they are shown below. Some of these represent passives but others are combinations of the verb *be* (as opposed to auxiliary *be*) and an *-ed* adjective. Distinguish them and say why the passive is used in each case.

B(1) *I was asked . . .*
C(1) *The operator was not satisfied . . .*
M(2) *They weren't even interested . . .*
L(1) *his last venison supper was eaten . . .*
N(2) *they were abducted . . .*
O(3) *the road was entirely deserted . . .*

Activity C11.3

Complex sentences and subordinate clauses (A9, A10)

a) Look at sentences H(2) and M(1). How many finite verb phrases (and therefore finite clauses) are there in each?
b) How are they joined (i.e. what conjunction or subordinator is used)?
c) How can we explain that some of the subordinate clauses have no explicit link? How could we make the links explicit?

Activity C11.4

Reporting speech (B12)

In paragraphs A to I speech is normally represented directly, using the exact words of the speakers. A number of different reporting verbs are used in the first part (paragraphs A to I): *reply* B(4), *asked* C(3), *replied* D(1), *intoned* E(2), *stammered* F(1), *inquired* F(2), and *said* (G1). However, one piece of direct speech in this part is introduced not by a verb but by another word class. What is it? And there is one piece of reported speech. What is it, and what might the exact words have been?

Activity C11.5

Clause elements (A8)

Analyse sentence J(1): *Proving who you are is a curious notion.* Analyse the subordinate clause and non-finite clause as well as the main clause.

Activity C11.6

Adverbs and conjunctions. (A9 and B4)

Look at the use of *so* in B(4), F(3), H(2), I(1) and *yet* in A(2) and K(2). What word classes and sub-classes do they belong to?

Activity C11.7

Verb forms (A5, A6, C5)

Look at sentence L(2): *All of this information gathered without him saying a thing or having a password.* What verb form is *gathered* here? Past tense or *-ed* participle?

Activity C11.8

Some more questions.

a) What is the clause element represented by *on my telephone keypad* in B(1)?
b) Look at paragraph B and find some verbs which are normally transitive being used intransitively. Why is this so? (A8)
c) Look at B(1). Identify the premodifiers and decide whether they are adjectives or nouns. (A3)
d) What is missing from F(2)?
e) What kind of word is *which* in L(1)?
f) Can you find two cleft sentences in the second part (paragraphs J to R)? (A11)
g) Find a contact relative clause in paragraph O. (B10)
h) Describe sentence I(3): *How absurd.* (A9, B9)

Comments

Activity C11.1:

The past tense is used because the writer is talking about the experiences of herself and other people. However, at times she departs from the narrative to make a generalisation, for example

A(1) *which . . . sounds a simple operation.*

B(2) *This takes time as I have to . . .* (She could equally have written *This took time as I had to . . .* if she had wanted to refer to that specific moment.)

or to refer to the current state of affairs

I(1) *I have reached a stage where I have . . .*

I(2) *The upshot is . . . I now find myself having to prove to them who I am.*

Activity C11.2:

C(1), M(2) and O(3) contain *-ed* adjectives, not participles as part of passives. The passive is used in:

B(1) to avoid mentioning the agent. She was talking to an automatic answering machine; so the passive shows how impersonal the process was.

L(1) because the agent is already known.

N(2) to satisfy the information principle: *they* represents given information, while *abducted by aliens* is new.

Activity C11.3:

a) There are seven finite verb phrases in H(2) and eight in M(1), underlined below:

H(2) *So I can't pass security because I don't know when you think my birthday might be which isn't when I thought it was?*

M(1) *I don't feel I need such rigorous analysis and think it would be nice if the bank could just believe me when I declare I know when I was born.*

Both have a highly complex clause structure; the subordination is very dense, especially in H(2), where the writer is trying to show the stupidity of the situation.

b) The links are:

H(2) *because, when, which* and *when*

M(1) *and, if, when* and *when*

c) Some of the subordinate clauses are nominal contact clauses (see A10); they have no subordinator to introduce them and separate them from the preceding clause (in which they function as objects). This is why there are only four explicit links in H(2) (when there should be six), and four in M(1) (when there should be seven). We can make the links explicit by inserting *that*, as follows:

H(2) *So I can't pass security because I don't know when you think that my birthday might be which isn't when I thought that it was?*

M(1) *I don't feel that I need such rigorous analysis and think that it would be nice if the bank could just believe me when I declare that I know when I was born.*

Activity C11.4: In B(3) the direct speech is introduced by a noun: *whose first question was* . . . The reported speech is in B(1): *asked to input* . . . (from possibly 'Could you please input . . .')

Activity C11.5:
The clause structure is S (*Proving who you are*) V (*is*) Ps (*a curious notion*). The subject is itself a non-finite clause consisting of the verb (*proving*) and its object (*who you are*), which is itself a nominal subordinate clause consisting of a predicative (*who*) that has been fronted, a subject (*you*) and verb (*are*). Note that *Proving who you are* acts as a link to the previous text, which is why this information is placed first.

Activity C11.6: *So* in B(4) is a conjunction, while in F(3) and H(2) it is a linking adverb. In I(1) it is, of course, an intensifier, or degree adverb. As regards *yet*, it is a linking adverb in A(2), but a conjunction in K(2).

Perhaps the hardest one is F3 (for *so*) because it seems to be joining two clauses. But *and* is the conjunction here, and *so* has the meaning of *as a result*. This could replace *so* in F(3) but not in B(4).

Activity C11.7: At first sight this sentence appears to have the structure of a major sentence: *All of this information* (S) *gathered* (V) . . . ; in other words, *gathered* seems to be the (finite) past tense. However, there are three arguments against this analysis. First, *All of this information* is an unlikely subject for an action verb such as *gather*. Second, *gather* is normally a transitive verb, but there is no object. Third, the time period for 'gathering' appears to be up to the present, so a past tense sounds inappropriate.

The answer, of course, is that *gathered* is an *-ed* participle and that the rest of the verb phrase has been omitted (for stylistic reasons). The full phrase would be *has been gathered*, indicating a passive meaning. The sentence as it stands is therefore a minor one.

Activity C11.8:

a) It is an adverbial clause element in the non-finite clause beginning *to input* . . . Note that it could be placed directly after *input*.
b) The verbs are *found, juggled* and *inputted* in B(3). Their objects have been omitted because they have already been mentioned in B(2).
c) *Numeric* and *long* are adjectives; *debit* and *telephone* are nouns.
d) Two clause elements are missing: the subject *It*, which is a case of informal 'contextual' ellipsis (see A12), and the predicative (*my birthday*), which is a case of 'textual' ellipsis because it can be reconstructed from the previous text (see B11).
e) It is a sentential relative pronoun (see B10); it refers back to the previous clauses.
f) The two cleft sentences are in J(2) and N(2): *It was today in 1991/1961 that* . . . Note how each introduces a story.
g) The contact relative clause is in O(2). It begins *extraterrestrials* . . . We could insert *which* or *that* as a relative pronoun before it to make the relative clause more explicit.
h) It is a minor sentence and exclamative clause type.

C12 ANALYSING SPOKEN TEXTS

A) Study this transcript of an unplanned monologue by a woman recalling a high-school experience.

The recording can be listened to on the website. The speaker is from the American Midwest and displays some of the accent features of that region.
 Note the lack of punctuation other than the use of dashes (to indicate pauses).

1. *well – being a semi-geek – in high school – I – was also in the marching band –*
2. *and – basically – we had to – perform at football games – at the 4th of July parade*
3. *of course – and we had to wear these horrible uniforms – that were – in our*
4. *school colours of course – red white and blue – made of 120 per cent polyester –*
5. *and we had to march in formation out on the football field – before the games and*
6. *during half time – and one time we were marching – doing our little – kind of –*
7. *sequence of movements on – the field – right before a game and the football*
8. *players were – warming up – and I played the flute – and – at one point some guy*
9. *from the opposing team – kicked the ball – out of control – and – the ball came*
10. *flying towards me and hit me in – the mouth – which – hit my flute as well –*
11. *luckily I didn't have any broken teeth but I had a broken flute – and – a bloody lip*
12. *– anyway – there was mass panic – the whole formation kind of fell apart – and*
13. *all these – you know – panicking women were running out onto the field to see*
14. *what was wrong – and I was holding my – hand to my mouth – and – some women*
15. *from the – I don't know – what do you call it – the – what is it called – it's kind of*
16. *sports – this group of people who raise money for sports and kind of you know*
17. *distribute the money and stuff for school activities – came over and started yelling*
18. *at me to not get blood on my white gloves – that those white gloves cost ten*
19. *dollars a pair or something – here I am – blood streaming from my mouth – my*
20. *thousand dollar flute in pieces – and lucky to be alive – and she's screaming at*
21. *me about getting blood on my – gloves – anyway I quit marching band after that*

Vocabulary: *geek* – a person who is not very sociable

Activity C12.1 ⊗
Do the dashes indicating pauses correspond to any grammatical divisions?

Activity C12.2 ⊗
Would it be possible to add more punctuation, for example commas, and if so where? Could the text even be divided into grammatical sentences (as was done in C9)? For example, how about *anyway* on line 12; does it go with the preceding or following text?

> Take the section starting with *luckily* on line 11 and ending with *mouth* on line (14) and transform it into 'written' English. What needs to be changed apart from punctuation? Does the result seem like normal written English?

★ Activity C12.3

> Look at the use of conjunctions and subordinators in the first ten lines of the passage (up to *as well*). How complex are the noun phrases in terms of postmodification?

★ Activity C12.4

> Is there any contextual ellipsis (see A12)?

★ Activity C12.5

> Are there any interruptions to the flow of her story?

★ Activity C12.6

> Listen to the recording of this passage. How careful do you think the speaker is being? What does this suggest?

★ Activity C12.7

B) Study these two extracts from conversations between housemates at a UK university and answer the questions underneath. The second can be listened to on the website.

B1. Two of them are sitting in the living-room.
    A.   Lecture earlier?
    B.   Yeh – had a fire alarm in it.

> What grammatical feature typical of speech does this demonstrate? How would the lines appear without it?

★ Activity C12.8

B2. In this extract several of the students are talking about golf.

1   A. it's gotta be the best professional sport
2   B. racing driver
3   C. footballer
4   A. think how much effort you have to put in to play football
5   D. yeh think about the danger involved in racing driving
6   B. yeh but that – it makes you feel alive=

7   D. =you can smoke – you can drink – anything you wanna do playing golf – you get to go to some amazing locations=

8   E. =you can get smashed

9   A. all over the world

(= indicates overlapping utterances)

Activity C12.9 ✪

In general, how much 'grammar' in terms of grammatical structure is there in this conversation? How easy is it to identify sentences, i.e. to insert full stops?

Activity C12.10 ✪

a)   Is there any cohesion, i.e. explicit links between utterances (see B11), in the text?

b)   How could you make utterances 2 and 3 more explicitly related to 1?

Activity C12.11 ✪

Are there any non-standard written forms indicating informal speech?

Activity C12.12 ✪

Who does *you* in utterances 4, 6, 7 and 8 refer to?

Activity C12.13 ✪

Compare the second conversation with the monologue above in (A) in terms of grammatical structure.

Comments

Activity C12.1: Generally the dashes do not correspond to anything grammatical. However, they do not split phrases (except for *in – the mouth* on line 10)

Activity C12.2: Yes, the text could be divided into four sentences on lines 9 and 10, 16, 18 and 19. *Anyway* clearly goes with the following text: *Anyway, there was mass panic . . .*

Activity C12.3:
The 'written' version would look something like this:

> *Luckily, I didn't have any broken teeth, but I had a broken flute and a bloody lip. The whole formation kind of fell apart, and all these panicking women were running out onto the field to see what was wrong and I was holding my hand to my mouth . . .*

The text seems to run on more than it would if it was a written description, especially with the double use of *and* in the second sentence. *Kind of* also seems inappropriate or unnecessary. In other words, it still sounds like speech.

Activity C12.4: There are several uses of *and* to link clauses; this is the only conjunction used. There are two relative pronouns: *that* on line 3 and *which* on line 10. With the aid of these relative clauses and other postmodification there are some complex noun phrases, for example:

> *these horrible uniforms – that were – in our school colours of course – red white and blue – made of 120 per cent polyester*
> *our little – kind of – sequence of movements*

Activity C12.5: There is none.

Activity C12.6:
The only place where there is a major interruption is on lines 15–17, from *I don't know* to *school activities* where the speaker is lost for a word or phrase and fills in with appeals to the listener (*what do you call it?*) and hesitations (*kind of you know*). The result is that the subject of *came* on line 17 is *some women from the . . .* on line 14.

There are other minor 'insertions', for example *at the 4th of July parade of course* on line 2.

Activity C12.7: The speaker appears very careful. This is borne out by the large number of hesitations, where she is planning what to say, and by the lack of any grammatical 'errors' or restarts. This suggests that the description should be considered quite formal, even though it is spoken and unplanned. The absence of ellipsis supports this view.

Activity C12.8: Both lines have contextual ellipsis. In full the first one would be something like
> *<u>Did you have a</u> lecture earlier?*
and the second would be
> *Yeh – <u>it</u> had a fire alarm in it.*

Activity C12.9: The amount of 'grammar' is rather limited; for example, several utterances, e.g. 2, 3 and 9, consist only of phrases. Overall it would be impossible to make this text look like writing; only utterances 1, 4 and 5 could be said to be 'complete' sentences.

Activity C12.10:

a)   The only obvious link is *but* in utterance 6, showing an inconsistency between it and utterance 5. Otherwise the utterances have little obvious connection, though utterance 9 is clearly a continuation of 7. This is not to say that the conversation does not hold together; however, much has to be inferred from the context (this kind of 'connection' is sometimes called 'coherence').

b) Adding for example *What about . . . ?* would show that they are making alternative suggestions.

Activity C12.11: *Yeh* instead of *yes*, as well as *gotta* and *wanna* (instead of *got to* and *want to*).

Activity C12.12: It is generic *you*, referring to people in general (though with an appeal in particular to the listeners); see B2.

Activity C12.13: There are a number of differences between A and B2:

❑ B2 has a number of short utterances; this is a reflection of the nature of a multi-sided conversation, where participants may only have a moment to make their contribution (note also the overlapping); the fact that the conversation is rather 'competitive' may be to do with the all-male cast.
❑ A could be rendered using full punctuation and complete grammatical sentences (though it would still sound like speech); this would not be possible for B2.
❑ in A links are made explicit, although in a simple way (e.g. via the use of *and*); in B2 they have to be guessed.

These differences reflect the difference in the situations: in A someone is trying quite carefully to make a coherent narrative, while in B2 the participants are performing spontaneously and casually as they know each other well; other conversations, e.g. between strangers, might not sound so informal. From this we can see how much difference there is within spoken language.

Section D
EXTENSION

D1   WHAT IS GRAMMAR?

Michael Swan (2005) reprinted from Chapter 1 of *Grammar*. Oxford: Oxford University Press, pp. 4–7.

In this paper Michael Swan attempts to get to the very fundamentals of grammar. He believes that at the deepest level grammar is the same for all languages, with the same function and the same basic options.

Most of the paper consists of a 'thought experiment' — an exercise designed to get readers thinking about how language evolved. We have no way of knowing if anything like this actually occurred, of course, but it does throw light on what we actually do with language, and what language (and life) would be like without grammar.

What is grammar for?

To understand what grammar is, we really need to know what it is for. Why do we need 'rules for combining words into sentences' anyway? Couldn't we manage well enough just by saying the words? This is a perfectly sensible question, and an excellent starting point for our enquiry. The best way to understand what grammar is, what it does, and why it is necessary, is in fact to try to imagine language without it.

Language without grammar

Nobody knows how language originated, but let us carry out a thought experiment. Suppose that you are an intelligent primate that would like to invent a rich communication system. There are various possible ways to signal information, some of which you already use to a limited extent: cries and grunts, facial expressions, gestures. For your new system, you decide that cries and grunts are the most effective option: you can get more variety into vocal signs, and they are not dependent on visibility (so they will work round corners and in the dark).

At first sight, it might look as if the obvious thing to do would be for you and your companions to devise a distinctive vocal sign – let's call it a 'word' – for each of the things in your world. (For this to work, you would also need to create a phonological system, but that is not relevant to the present discussion.) So you invent words for your mother, the other mothers in the tribe, the cave mouth, the chief of the tribe, the big tree by the river, the river, the rain that is falling just now, your best stone axe, your second-best stone axe, and so on. However, it quickly becomes clear that this will not work. First of all, there are too many things around for a communication system constructed on this basis to be learnable. And second, the system only enables you to talk about particular things that you have already paid attention to. You cannot talk, for example, about another tree, a new river that you have discovered, a stranger, or the axe you intend to make.

A more promising approach is to use words to designate classes of things instead of individuals, so that your words for 'tree', 'rain', 'mother', 'axe', 'baby', 'bear', and so on can refer to any tree, any instance of rain, etc. (This is anyway an extension of your existing signalling system, which already consists of a few calls indicating recurrent elements in your world like 'danger', 'panther', 'food', 'enemy'.)

And with an important mental leap, you realise that words can refer not only to people and things, but also to their shared characteristics, like 'big', 'good to eat', 'red', or 'cold'; and to the events, situations, and changes that regularly occur in your world, like 'eat', 'fall', 'run', 'die', 'coming', 'gone'. (Strictly speaking, it probably does not make sense to separate your consciousness of categories from your labelling of them, as if one came before the other; but it simplifies the discussion to look at things in this way.)

Now you are ready to use your new tool. There are three things you and your companions can do with it. First of all, you can draw each other's attention to the existence of something in your environment, or to the fact that you want something, by simply using the appropriate class word ('Bear!', 'Axe!', 'Eat!'). Second, when necessary, you can combine words to pin down individual members of classes and make it clear which one you are talking about: if you want to ask for a particular axe, you can produce the equivalent of, for instance, 'axe big'. This is an enormously powerful device–think how the four English words 'your', 'big', 'blue', and 'mug', each of which refers to a class with vast numbers of members, can be put together to immediately identify one particular item. And thirdly, you can combine words to indicate events or states of affairs: 'Fall baby'; 'Rain cold'; 'Bear die'; 'Axe big break'; 'Eat baby acorn'.

You have invented language! Up to a point.

Problems

Your language is, however, rather different from the human languages we are familiar with. For one thing, the order of words has no significance: 'Fall baby' and 'Baby fall' are alternative forms of the same message. And for another, there is only one kind of word ('bear', 'die', and 'cold' are not respectively a noun, a verb, and an adjective – they are just words).

Does this matter? Well, you can certainly do a lot with the language you have, and it is a remarkable advance on your earlier, very limited communication system. However, it has some limitations. There are three in particular:

1. It can be difficult to specify exact meanings in situations involving more than one element. Putting together your words for 'big', 'bear', and 'cave', for example, will not make it clear whether there is a big bear in the cave or a bear in the big cave. Context will often remove the ambiguity, but this will not always be the case.

2. Your language will enable you to identify and talk about things in the world as separate elements, but not to clarify the causal, spatial, and other relationships

between them, and these may need to be spelt out. For instance, in a situation where A is doing something to B, you cannot easily make it clear, just by saying the words, who or what is the 'doer' (or 'agent'), and who or what is the 'doee' (or **'patient'**). Again, context or common sense will often make this clear ('Eat baby acorn' can only be sensibly understood in one way), but confusion can easily arise, as in 'Kill brother bear' (remember that as things stand the order of words communicates nothing).

3. And finally, with this system you cannot get beyond requests and affirmative statements – 'Bear cave' can convey the fact that there is a bear in the cave, but you have no way of asking whether there is a bear in the cave, or suggesting that there may be, or saying that there is not a bear in the cave.

So you need:

(i)   a way of saying what word goes with what – of indicating how general concepts need to be grouped in order to represent particular elements in the world

(ii)   a way of expressing agency and other relationships

(iii)   a way of indicating the communicative status of your utterances – statement, question, suggestion, negation, or whatever.

You have discovered the need for grammar.

Solving the problems

There are quite a number of ways in which you might meet this need. One approach would be to signal the necessary extra meanings by the way you arrange words. To show what goes with what, for example, you could have a rule that you always put words for connected ideas together, perhaps with pauses between phrases: 'bear big – small cave'. You could refine this – and avoid the need for pauses – by always putting the word for a quality immediately before or immediately after the word for the thing that has the quality: 'bear big'; 'cave small'. Another way of using word order would be to consistently put the expression for an agent or 'doer' earlier or later than other expressions, so that 'brother kill bear' and 'bear kill brother' would have distinct meanings. And again, you could use a different order of phrases for statements and questions: 'Brother kill big bear' versus 'Kill brother big bear?'

A second strategy would be to alter words in some way to signal their functions. Latin did this: *ursus* and *frater* meant 'bear' and 'brother' as agents; as patients they became *ursum* and *fratrem*. Russian does much the same. This trick – **inflection** – could also be exploited to show what goes with what: related words could all be changed or extended identically. In Latin you could talk about a big bear without needing to put the two words next to each other: if 'bear' was *ursus*, 'big' was *magnus*; if it was *ursum*, 'big' was *magnum*, so the relationship was clear. Pronunciation, too, could indicate the functions of words. To show that a word referred to an agent, for example, you could pronounce the first sound differently; or you could say the word more slowly, or on a higher pitch: *Kill* ^{bear} *brother*. You could also use **intonation** to mark the status of a whole utterance, as we often do in English to indicate that we are asking questions.

Yet another possibility would be to invent new non-referential words that do not label anything in the world, but that are used to show the function of other words. English 'may' is a word of this kind: it indicates that your sentence refers not to a definite fact, but to a possibility. Japanese puts small words – **particles** – after nouns to mean such things as 'topic', 'agent', 'patient', and 'possessor'.

These strategies are all variants on three basic options: ordering, inflection, and the use of **function words**. Once you have selected from these three options the devices you want to use for your language, you have devised a grammar. You now have a human language.

So, to answer the question we started with: grammar is essentially a limited set of devices for expressing certain kinds of necessary meaning that cannot be conveyed by referential vocabulary alone.

Questions, suggestions and issues to consider

1. Compare Swan's 'thought experiment' with the illustration in A1 (where we imagined a learner memorising all the words of a language and then trying to communicate). Are they similar?
2. Compare Swan's definition of grammar in the final paragraph with the three in A1. How are they similar/different?
3. Consider the three strategies mentioned above by Swan. English makes use of all three to some extent, for example:
    - ❏   arranging words (word order): adjectives generally come before the noun they modify, for example *blue cheese*
    - ❏   altering the shape of words ('inflections' and 'derivations'): for example, the plural and genitive endings for nouns (*dog, dogs, dog's, dogs'*)
    - ❏   using little function words such as *of* (see B1)

    Think of other examples in English.
4. Think of another language you know well and compare it with English according to these three strategies. (For example, most European languages make much more use of inflections.)

COUNT AND MASS NOUNS

David Lee (2001) reprinted from Chapter 8 of *Cognitive Linguistics*, South Melbourne: Oxford University Press, pp. 137–145.

David Lee

We have assumed so far that nouns come with their count status already established. Dictionaries tell us that a certain word is count or noncount, or, in certain cases, both. In the paper below, David Lee tries to account for count status using an approach called Cognitive Linguistics, which seeks to find a semantic (i.e. meaning-based) rationale for grammatical phenomena. We have already seen in C2 that the count status of a noun can change if a specific meaning is needed (e.g. 'beer' can become 'a beer'). But Lee goes much further, arguing that count status is principally determined by meaning.

While this approach is not free from criticism, the paper certainly provides some interesting insights into the way the count status of a noun may have arisen, historically at least. And it serves as a useful reminder that we should not blindly accept simplified, pedagogic rules based on form without looking for deeper, scientific rules based on meaning (as we saw in A1 regarding the difference between 'some' and 'any').

A few words about the text. Lee uses the term 'mass' rather than 'noncount', as some other grammarians do. A central concept in the paper is that of 'construal' (from the verb 'construe'). This refers to how we perceive or make sense of the world. Another important concept (which Lee is disagreeing with) is arbitrariness: the idea that connections (between meaning and grammar in this case) are random or accidental. Finally, note the use of asterisks to indicate unacceptable forms.

8.1 Introduction

It was noted in earlier chapters that one of the defining features of Cognitive Linguistics is its view of the nature of the relationship between form and meaning. The traditional view, firmly asserted by Saussure ([1915] 1974) is that this relationship is characterised by arbitrariness – the forms of language bear no direct relationship to their meaning.

This view is undoubtedly correct in certain respects. For example, there is nothing about the form of words in a particular language that bears any relationship to their meaning – with the minor exception of onomatopoeic words such as *crack, crunch, creak,* and so on. This does not mean that the form–meaning relationship is always totally arbitrary. In general, the cognitive claim is that grammatical structure is more strongly motivated than has traditionally been thought to be the case. In this chapter, we explore this issue with respect to various types of noun in English.

Nouns can be divided into a number of different subclasses with respect to their inflectional properties.

❏ Class A These are prototypical nouns, having both a singular form and a plural form: *cat ~ cats.*
❏ Class B These nouns have only a singular form: *equipment ~ *equipments; furniture ~ *furnitures; crockery ~ *crockeries.*
❏ Class C These nouns have only a plural form: **scissor ~ scissors; *trouser ~ trousers; *clothe ~ clothes.*
❏ Class D These nouns have both a singular and a plural form but they are identical: *sheep ~ sheep; deer ~ deer; salmon ~ salmon.*
❏ The distinction between class A nouns and class B nouns has a number of other grammatical reflexes.
❏ The singular form of class B nouns occurs without a determiner in positions typically occupied by noun phrases (*Furniture is useful, I bought furniture,*

I'm looking for furniture), but this is not generally true of class A nouns (*Cat is useful, *I bought cat, *I'm looking for cat*).

❑ The indefinite determiner *a* occurs with class A nouns (*a cat*) but not with class B nouns (*a furniture*).

❑ The determiner *much* occurs with class B nouns (*much furniture*) but not with class A nouns (*much cat*).

❑ Expressions such as *a lot of* occur with the singular form of class B nouns (*a lot of furniture*) but not with the singular form of class A nouns (*a lot of cat*).

These observations have led linguists to make a terminological distinction between 'count' nouns (class A) and 'mass' nouns (class B). The question on which I will focus in this chapter is whether this distinction is motivated or arbitrary.

Certain examples seem to support the view that it is arbitrary. For example, there seems to be no obvious reason why *vegetable* is a count noun but *fruit* is (normally) a mass noun. Ware (1979: 22) makes this point in the following terms:

> Turning now to why it is that words sometimes have count occurrences and sometimes mass occurrences, we are immediately faced with the problem of a tremendous amount of variation that appears unnecessary and inexplicable (. . .) There is a count-mass difference between *fruit* and *vegetable* but they apply to things that for all accounts and purposes seem to be alike. Nor can I see anything that would explain the count-mass difference between *footwear* and *shoe, clothing* and *clothes, shit* and *turd* or *fuzz* and *cop*.

Other contrasts that could be taken to support the arbitrariness view involve examples such as *noodle* (count) and *rice* (mass), *bean* (count) and *spaghetti* (mass). For example, why do we refer to lots of noodles in a bowl as *these noodles* (using the plural form of a count noun) but to lots of grains of rice in a bowl as *this rice* (using the singular form of a mass noun)?

In many cases, however, there is an obvious basis for the distinction between count nouns and mass nouns. There is a strong tendency for count nouns to refer to 'objects' and for mass nouns to refer to 'substances'. For example, the fact that *cup, cat,* and *table* are count nouns whereas *custard, water,* and *sand* are mass nouns seems far from arbitrary. What then is the distinction between 'objects' and 'substances', and can it be used to motivate the count/mass distinction in general?

8.2 Count and mass phenomena

Let us take as the starting point the fact that solid physical objects such as bicycles and cats are typically designated by count nouns, whereas liquids such as water and oil are typically designated by mass nouns. One salient difference between solid objects such as bicycles and cats on the one hand and liquids such as water and oil on the other is that the former have a characteristic shape and well-defined boundaries, whereas the latter lack such a characteristic profile, moulding themselves to the shape of their container. And whereas solid objects have an internal structure typically consisting of discrete components (a bicycle has a frame, wheels, handlebars, pedals, and so on), liquids tend to be internally homogeneous. One consequence of this is that any particular 'segment' of a liquid counts as equivalent to any other segment. For example, if I dip a cup into a pond and remove some water, then this particular segment of 'water' is, for all practical purposes, identical to any other segment of water that I might have scooped up. But most parts of a bicycle are different from the other parts.

Consider now such phenomena as slime, mud, and silt. In terms of their texture, these are intermediate between solids and liquids but they resemble liquids more than solids with respect to their external boundaries (they lack a characteristic shape) and internal structure (they tend to be homogeneous). It is therefore not surprising that the corresponding nouns belong to the mass category (*several slimes, *these muds).

The same applies to internally homogeneous solids such as earth, clay, and cement. Chemically speaking, of course, all these substances consist of particles (as indeed does water), so that in this sense they are made up of large numbers of elements. But this is irrelevant to practical human concerns – and therefore to language.

When we come to consider phenomena such as sand, sugar, rice, soot, dust, and so on, we begin to approach the point where there is a potential motivation for construal in terms of a collection of individuated objects rather than a substance. The particles of which sugar and sand are composed are at least discernible to the human eye. In principle, therefore, there is no intrinsic reason why English should not have a word that refers to a single grain of sugar (for example, *flig*), in which case I might point to a pile of sugar and say *Here are some fligs*. But there are obvious reasons why there is no such word. Whenever sugar manifests itself to us, it always does so in the form of a conglomerate of thousands of 'fligs', tightly packed together, so that the word *flig* would serve little practical purpose. Moreover, sugar in this form behaves just like water. It moulds itself to the shape of a container and is internally homogeneous.

Some of these points also apply to noodles, but grammatically speaking we have now crossed the mass/count frontier, since *noodle* is a count noun. Individual noodles are bigger than individual grains of rice, which provides some motivation for the grammatical distinction. (It is easier to eat a single noodle than a single grain of rice.) It has to be said, however, that a single noodle is unlikely to be of great interest to anyone. To take a similar example, there is very little difference between the size of the particles that make up a pile of gravel and those that make up a pile of pebbles, but *gravel* is a mass noun, whereas *pebble* is a count noun.

Although there is undoubtedly a certain degree of arbitrariness in these cases, located as they are at the boundary between objects and substances, this does not mean that there is no semantic motivation for the count/mass distinction in general. In fact, the indeterminacy that we find in cases such as *gravel* and *pebbles* is precisely what one would expect in a theory in which the objective properties of entities are subject to processes of perception and construal. Time and again in language, we come across situations where the distinction between two categories is semantically motivated, but where the behaviour of phenomena located at or near the boundary is not wholly predictable. Just as a pile of gravel is not a prototypical mass phenomenon (since it is composed of a number of perceptually distinguishable particles), so pebbles and noodles are not prototypical count phenomena, given that individual pebbles and noodles are generally not as perceptually salient as individual cats and bicycles and are of much less interest to human beings.

One strong argument for the claim that there is a semantic basis for the count/mass distinction is the fact that some nouns have both count and mass uses, associated with a clear difference in meaning. Consider:

1. (a) *Could I have a potato?* (count)
   (b) *Could I have some potato?* (mass)
2. (a) *I'll have an egg.* (count)
   (b) *I'll have some egg.* (mass)
3. (a) *I'd like a pumpkin.* (count)
   (b) *I'd like some pumpkin.* (mass)
4. (a) *There were a lot of newspapers in the box.* (count)
   (b) *There was a lot of newspaper in the box.* (mass)
5. (a) *There's a glass on the table.* (count)
   (b) *It's made of glass.* (mass)

Potatoes, eggs, and pumpkins normally manifest themselves as unitary, individuated, countable objects and they may retain this character in cooking and serving. However, if a potato or pumpkin is mashed or an egg scrambled, its character changes. It becomes a homogeneous substance from which portions can be removed or further portions added without changing its character. These examples show that, strictly speaking, the terms 'count' and 'mass' do not refer to types of noun but to particular uses of nouns, though it is true that many nouns normally appear only in one or the other use-type, given the nature of the entity that they designate.

It would be a mistake, however, to attempt to motivate the count/mass distinction purely in terms of the physical properties of phenomena. Consider, for example, the case of liquid substances. I began this discussion by observing that liquids are typically designated by mass nouns (*I'll have some water, There's beer in the fridge, He drank a glass of wine*). However, count uses of these nouns are by no means unusual.

6. *There were several wines on show.*
7. *He drank a few beers.*
8. *The waters were rising.*

These uses have a variety of motivations. As far as wine is concerned, human beings find it highly relevant to their everyday concerns to divide the phenomenon into various subtypes. Since each such subtype is an individuated entity, it is designated by a count noun, as in (6). Example (7) can also be interpreted in this way (that is, as meaning that he drank a few types of beer), but it is more likely to be used to refer to a rather different kind of countable phenomenon such as the contents of a container (*He drank several wines, Two sugars please*). In (8) floods are typically fed by water from different sources (for example, different rivers), so that even after they have merged, they can still be conceptualised as different entities. (This usage may also be motivated by the fact that flood water manifests itself in different places.) In objective terms the nature of the phenomenon in (8) is of course no different from any other manifestation of water as a mass. If the claim were that objective criteria determined linguistic form, then this usage would constitute a powerful counter-example. But if language reflects conceptualisation, it is not difficult to identify a cognitive basis for the example.

So far, it has been argued that mass phenomena are characterised by internal homogeneity. Let me now consider nouns such as *cutlery*, *furniture*, and *crockery*. These phenomena seem to constitute a counterexample to the argument, since they refer to collections of discrete, countable entities. The motivation for their assimilation to the mass category has to do with the level at which the concept applies. A set of knives, forks, and spoons can either be construed as a collection of separate objects performing different functions (cutting food, picking up food, stirring liquids) or as a collection of objects which manifest themselves contiguously and which all perform the same function (facilitating the consumption of food). At this level, any part of the phenomenon counts as equivalent to any other part. Similarly, a collection of chairs, tables, and cupboards is subject to alternative construals. We can think of them either as a group of separate objects or as a unitary entity with a single function – that is, as 'furniture'.

Note, however, that more general levels of categorisation do not always produce a mass noun in English. The concept 'tool', for example, constitutes a superordinate category with respect to hammers, screwdrivers, drills, and so on, but *tool* is never-theless a count noun. As in the case of 'cutlery', we are dealing here with an experien-tially related set of entities that perform different functions at one level and a single function at a more abstract level. But the grammatical character of the form *tools* continues to foreground the essentially plural nature of the phenomenon. On the other hand, the same set of entities could be designated by the mass noun *equipment*, which foregrounds their functional unity.

This observation helps to explain the contrast between *fruit* and *vegetables*. Like *cutlery*, *furniture*, *crockery*, and *equipment* the word *fruit* is a manifestation of a general pattern in the language, such that the grammatical character of the word foregrounds the pragmatic contiguity and functional similarity of the entities that constitute the category. *Vegetables* is a manifestation of a different pattern, whereby the abstraction to a superordinate level is realised lexically but where the grammatical character of the word continues to highlight the essentially plural and diverse nature of the phenomenon, as in the case of the word *tools*. Again, there is nothing in reality that requires the language to work in this way (that is, nothing that requires a grammatical distinction between *fruit* and *vegetables*), but there is no difficulty in identifying characteristics of the phenomenon that motivate the distinction.

The contrast between *clothing* and *clothes* constitutes a similar case. Whereas the unitary nature of the phenomenon is captured by the fact that the word *clothing* has only a singular form, the diverse nature of the objects that constitute the category and the fact that different items normally occur together are reflected in the fact that *clothes* has only a plural form.

8.3 Nouns lacking a singular form

So far, we have focused on the distinction between class A nouns (count) and class B nouns (mass). However, it was noted at the beginning of the chapter that there is also a subcategory of nouns (class C) that lacks a singular form, *clothes* being a member thereof. Nouns of this type can be further divided into a number of subclasses according to the nature of the motivation.

As far as ailments such as measles, mumps, shingles, hives, and haemorrhoids are concerned, the motivation for the inherently plural character of the corresponding nouns is obvious. This is also true of words such as *pants, braces, scissors, shears, binoculars, tweezers, clippers, tongs, goggles, spectacles, glasses,* and so on, though the motivation for the inherent plurality of these forms has not always been recognised. Gleason (1961: 224), for example, writes:

> . . . by a convention of English, *pants* is plural. Interestingly enough, this is not an isolated case; compare *trousers, breeches, shorts, slacks,* etc. This whole group of words are grammatically plural with no evident semantic justification.

It is interesting to speculate about the factors that led Gleason to make this surprising observation, since it cannot have escaped his notice that a prominent feature of these objects is that they consist of two identical parts. Gleason's comment presumably derives from the fact that a pair of trousers is a unitary object, so that in one sense there is no obvious reason why the language should treat such a garment differently from any other unitary object, particularly when other items of clothing such as coats and shirts, which also possess two identical parts, are designated by count nouns. Certainly there are many languages that use ordinary count nouns to refer to a pair of trousers (*pantalon* in French, *Hose* in German). Again, however, this clearly does not mean that the use of a plural noun is unmotivated, nor that the distinction between *trousers* on the one hand and *coat* or *shirt* on the other is arbitrary. After all, the sleeves of coats and shirts do not constitute as great a proportion of the whole garment as do the legs of a pair of trousers. What is missing, then, from Gleason's way of thinking about these examples are the notions of foregrounding, construal, and motivation.

8.4 Nouns with identical singular and plural forms

The class D words identified at the beginning of this chapter (*salmon, cod, sheep, pheasant, mackerel,* and so on) differ from other noun classes in that they have identical singular and plural forms (compare *this salmon ~ these salmon, one cod ~ several cod,* and so on). The fact that most of the phenomena in question belong to the same conceptual domain suggests that there is some underlying rationale here – that the class of nouns with this unusual grammatical property do not constitute an arbitrary set.

The semantic property shared by most of these nouns is that they traditionally belong to the domain of hunting and fishing. In other words, the phenomena in question constitute a food resource. When someone catches a fish, it is both an individual entity and a representative of the species to which it belongs. This latter property is salient in this context because it involves characteristics that are crucial to the general fishing scenario – whether the catch is edible, how it will taste, how many will be needed to make it a viable meal, and so on. To put it slightly differently, when you are fishing for 'salmon' (or indeed simply buying 'salmon' at the fishmonger's), it is relatively immaterial which particular individual you acquire. What is important is that it is 'salmon' rather than 'cod' or 'mackerel'. This property relates entities of this kind to mass phenomena. Just as any arbitrary portion of water is equivalent to any other portion, so any individual salmon is as good a representative of its species as any other from the point of view of the consumer. The grammatical character of these nouns, therefore, seems to be a reflex of a general ambivalence concerning the individuated and mass aspects of the phenomenon. Their individuated character is often highly salient (the difference between catching one salmon and several can be important), so that it is useful to have a singular ~ plural contrast, but the absence of explicit plural marking seems to be a reflex of the fact that the individual is an arbitrary manifestation of a general resource.

[. . .]

8.5 Conclusion

The discussion in this chapter supports the general claim of cognitive linguists that grammar is a much less arbitrary phenomenon than has traditionally been thought to be the case. It is important not to overstate this claim. Cognitivists do not argue that grammatical properties are invariably explicable in terms of underlying cognitive or pragmatic factors – that is, that grammar is wholly determined by such factors. As has been noted, the fact that *vegetable* is a count noun whereas *fruit* is normally used as a mass noun is an arbitrary fact to some extent. Given that both terms involve a generalisation across a somewhat disparate set of phenomena, the option is available for the concept to be treated either as a collection of individuated entities or as a mass. This does not mean, however, that the grammatical count/mass distinction is entirely arbitrary. The crucial concept that allows a degree of arbitrariness to be reconciled with the notion of motivation is construal. Since this concept specifically allows for alternative ways of conceptualising a situation, it allows for phenomena that are perceptually similar to be treated either as grammatically similar or as grammatically different.

Certainly we sacrifice here some of the determinacy that linguists have often hankered after in their search for linguistic generalisations, but given the fact that language is a social phenomenon subject to the constraints of convention and cultural variability, total determinacy may prove to be an unrealistic goal in linguistic description and theory. In the next chapter we pursue this theme with respect to certain grammatical characteristics of verbs, taking up the count/mass distinction in a more abstract form.

Questions, suggestions and issues to consider

1. To what extent do you agree with Lee's hypothesis? Do you feel that the way you 'construe' nouns conditions the way you use them grammatically? Or do you simply follow usage: what other people say, or what teachers and grammars tell you to say?

2. Take some of the nouns he discusses and think about how you construe them. For example, do you feel that the noncount status of words like *furniture* and *information* is illogical? In other words, do you construe them as individual, divisible entities? If so, would this allow you to use them as count nouns, in contravention of the 'rules' of English grammar?

3. Lee does not discuss collective nouns such as *government* or *team* (see A2). How would they fit into his four classes at the start? Do they provide evidence for or against his theory?

4. Could this approach account for the nouns described in C2, such as *reason* or *paper*, where the count/noncount difference is associated with an unpredictable difference in meaning?

5. Lee claims that the perception of meaning (construal) conditions the grammar of nouns. But is it not also possible that the grammar conditions the meaning, i.e. there is a two-way relationship? What if we encounter a word first, before we have any idea of what it is referring to? Might the fact that it is noncount lead us to think of it as a mass, regardless of its true nature?

6. One of the criticisms of this approach to nouns is that equivalent words in two languages may have different count status. For example, *information* is noncount in English but count in French (where it is spelt exactly the same), and the French word for *furniture* (noncount) is *meubles* (count). Does this mean that French and English people regard 'information' and 'furniture' differently? What about when bilingual speakers switch from English to French? Do they suddenly change their perception of the world? Or is this a grammatical accident that is conditioned by the language? To what extent do you feel grammatical phenomena are as they are because of convention, or repetition, rather than creativity?

DETERMINERS: A CLASS APART   **D3**

Roger Berry (1998) reprinted from *English Today*, 14/1, pp. 27–34.   **Roger Berry**

This article is based on a book I wrote in 1997: Collins COBUILD English Guides 10: Determiners and Quantifiers. It describes the problems encountered during the writing process, including the main one: are determiners a distinct word class? It provides some more evidence on topics which are mentioned elsewhere, such as 'some' vs 'any' (A1) and the use of 'less' with count nouns (C3).

The article has been shortened quite significantly.

[. . .]

Troubles

Determiners are a very problematic group of words in a number of different ways. I have divided these various troubles into three levels: for linguists, for applied linguists, and for learners/teachers. One might characterise these as being analysis, (pedagogic) description, and application respectively. The borderline between them is arbitrary to some extent, and a problem may apply to more than one of them. However, generally they represent stages in what may be called 'the process of pedagogic grammar'.

Troubles for linguists

Are determiners a valid word-class?

The first issue is whether determiners are distinguishable as a class from e.g. pronouns (with which they were conflated in earlier treatments of English). According to Hudson (1990) the answer is no: there is a generalisation that will be missed if we follow the normal practice and treat determiners and pronouns as two unrelated word-classes' (1990:269). This generalisation is that most words that are determiners can also function as pronouns, for example *that*:

> I don't like <u>that</u> idea much.
>
> <u>That</u> was many years ago.

The exceptions to this are *a/an*, *the*, *no*, *every*, plus *my*, *your*, *her*, *our* and *their*, which cannot be used as pronouns. Of these the possessives can easily be excluded since they have readily available pronoun counterparts (*mine*, etc). Likewise, *no* has a counterpart in *none*. *Every* is more problematic, unless one accepts that *every one* (not *everyone*, of course, which can only refer to humans) is a pronominal counterpart. This would then only leave the articles; these can be accounted for by saying that they are the basic determiners in that they add nothing to the meaning of a noun phrase apart from the basic idea of definiteness or indefiniteness.

After the above prestidigitation, the case for establishing determiners as a distinct class would seem to be rather thin. Similarly, in terms of meaning, there are few reasons for a distinction. In certain cases the use of a word as a pronoun implies human reference, as in the examples below, whereas there would be no such restriction of interpretation for a determiner.

> He returned home a global figure, an almost godlike figure for <u>some</u>.
>
> <u>Those</u> determined to kill can always find suitable opportunities.

In addition, there is often a degree of formality associated with certain pronominal uses, as the two examples show, which is absent from the determiner. (This is discussed further below.) But in the vast majority of cases the meaning of the determiner and the pronoun are the same.

What, then, is the reason for all the attention given to determiners? The answer would seem to lie in an increasing trend (in this structuralist-oriented century) to rely on syntagmatic criteria for establishing word-classes.

Membership problems

Even if one does accept the existence of determiners as a distinct class of words, there are several problems with delineating its membership. Beyond what may be called the 'prototypical' determiners alluded to above, there are cases of a more borderline nature. I will only mention a few briefly below:

❑ open classes, e.g. cardinal and ordinal numbers and multipliers (*twice, three times,* etc.). Semantically, all that distinguishes them from the quantifiers is that they refer to specific amounts. However, they come later in the noun phrase, after postdeterminers (see below)

❑ words like *same, next, latter* etc., which semantically would seem to be more like adjectives but which syntactically have something in common with postdeterminers (see below) in that they can precede numerals. There is an (unwritten) assumption in the analysis of determiners that they cannot be discontinuous; thus, if numerals are determiners, so is anything that can precede them.

    They lived together for the <u>next three</u> years.

❑ the Saxon genitive, which structurally and referentially does the same job as possessive determiners.

    Mother's cooking was horrible.

Zero determiner

One particular problem of membership concerns the so-called 'zero article', which is said to 'occur' in positions when neither definite or indefinite article nor other determiner is present. The concept of 'the presence of nothing' as opposed to 'the absence of anything' is a common one in linguistics, and in this case it allows linguists to say that all nouns have a determiner (if they do not have one, how can they be said to refer to anything?).

Most scholarly grammarians have advocated the acceptance of this as a third article (strictly speaking, it should be called 'zero determiner'). However, there is some disagreement about where it operates. For Christophersen (1939), for example, it operates in all situations where a noun phrase lacks a determiner. Quirk *et al.* (1985:246), on the other hand, make a distinction between the zero article, as in:

    I like music.

and no article with proper nouns, which can be said to incorporate their own determiner:

    I like Sid.

Another way of looking at proper nouns is to say that they do not need determiners to refer.

Ordering problems

A noun phrase can have more than one determiner, up to an (intuitive) maximum of four: 'all the many such possibilities' (although this is not attested in the Bank of English). The usual way of explaining the ordering of these combinations is in terms of three positions:

❑ predeterminers, which include *all, both, half,* and multipliers, *such, many,* exclamative *what, rather* and *quite.*

❑ central determiners, which include the most common determiners, such as articles (*the* and *a/an*), demonstratives (*this,* etc.) and possessives (*my,* etc.). Words such as *each,* which cannot be combined, are usually included here.

❏   postdeterminers, whose membership is somewhat uncertain (see above) but it includes *little*, *few*, *many*, *several* and numbers.

Of course, many combinations are not possible. Thus, *half* can occur before both *the* and *a*, while *all* cannot precede *a* and *such* cannot precede *the*.

Half the building was in flames.
I ordered *half a* pint of lager.
All the ironing is done.
Mother made *such a* fuss about it

Some of these restrictions can be explained away easily on logical grounds, but others cannot.

Beyond this, there are a number of exceptions to this three-position approach to determiner ordering, because some words can have different positions.

❏   *Every* can come before *few* but also after possessives, which makes it both a central determiner and a postdeterminer; there is, however, a difference in meaning:
Every few days there seemed to be another setback.
Television cameras would be monitoring *his every* step.
❏   *Such* can come after *many* (a postdeterminer) but can be a predeterminer before *a*.
Is this the last of *many such* occasions?
Mother made *such a* fuss about it.
❏   *Many* can be a predeterminer before *a* and a postdeterminer after definite determiners.
Many a successful store has paid its rent cheerfully.
None of *her many* lovers seemed to want to marry her.

Many a and *such a* are probably best accounted for as single units, in the same way that *a few* and *a little* generally are (because they do not behave as combinations; see Huddleston 1984: 234–5).

Definite and indefinite determiners

This distinction is somewhat problematic. First, these two groups are really rather different in referential terms. While the definite determiners (typically *the*, possessives and demonstratives) can clearly be said to 'determine' the noun group by referring to something familiar, established or identifiable in the listener/reader's consciousness, the indefinite determiners (typically *a/an* and the so-called 'quantifiers') only do so in a vague way, as Ducrot and Todorov point out (1981:253). This explains why Jespersen (1933) calls the indefinite article the 'article of incomplete determination'.

Second, while the distinction between definiteness and indefiniteness can help to understand the difference in meaning between certain pairs of words, such as *the* and *a/an*, and *which* and *what*, the borderline is not always clear. *Both*, for example is usually grouped with indefinite determiners, but it undoubtedly has an idea of definiteness; it refers to something in the text or the environment that is familiar, or established in the mind of the reader or listener. That is why *both* and *both the* mean the same thing.

Troubles for describers

This section looks at problems for the applied linguist/pedagogic grammarian when trying to interpret this analysis according to a particular purpose (most typically language teaching). There are some features that are not particularly problematic (at least for description), e.g. the association with type of noun (countable or not) which explains the (basic) difference between *many* and *much*, and between *(a) few* and *(a) little*, but others are.

The variety of patterns

One initial problem with some determiners is that they can occur in a number of patterns. To take *all* as an example, the following patterns are possible:

'*all boys*', '*all the boys*', '*all of the boys*'.

The structural aspect is not too hard to describe, but what about the meaning? The first is clearly different in meaning from the others (due to the absence of *the*), but is there any difference between the last two? The reader is invited to struggle with this one, as many people have before.

In addition, three determiners, *all*, *each* and *both*, can undergo the phenomenon known as 'quantifier float' or 'placement' where they occur after the noun they determine, typically in the so-called middle position, but also elsewhere. Here they have something in common with adverbs, as Giusti (1990) notes:

We'd <u>all</u> like to make easy money.

Liver and eggs are <u>both</u> good sources of natural iron.

The sergeants <u>each</u> carried one.

And although quantifier float is possible with nouns that follow the verb, there are restrictions. For example, *each* cannot come after a noun used as a direct object (you cannot say *I saw them each*) but can after an indirect object.

He handed them <u>each</u> a cup of tea.

Both and *all* are possible after direct objects (*I saw them all*, *I saw them both*).

Again, while the structural aspect can be described (if not fully explained), what of the meaning? Is there an extra emphasis to this use, as its label in the *Collins COBUILD English Dictionary* (1995) – 'emphatic pronoun' – would seem to suggest?

Assertion

This concept, that is, whether you are asserting the existence of a thing or not (see Quirk *et al.* 1985:83–84), is involved with a number of determiners. The case of *some* and *any* is well-known now in the literature (e.g. Lakoff 1969; see also Lewis 1986:33–37 for a clear account of why *some* and *any* are not suppletive forms). These two examples show how they can be in opposition:

I haven't found <u>some</u> of the money.

I haven't found <u>any</u> of the money.

A far less tractable case is that of *much* and *many*. As Quirk *et al.* point out (1985:384): '*Much* and, to a lesser extent; *many* have acquired some non-assertive force'. The problem is: how much? *Much* would seem to be rare in assertive circumstances in modern English unless it is being used with an intensifier (*so much*, etc), or is rather formal ('There is much confusion.')

Many is more debatable; again the reader is asked to ponder how formal *many* sounds in the examples below and whether there is a difference:

> *We have concluded <u>many</u> agreements.*
>
> *We haven't concluded <u>many</u> agreements.*

Coverage

One issue for the describer is how far to go in covering different uses of the same word. Given the similarity between the pronoun and determiner uses of these words pointed out above, it would seem to make sense to group them. However, many can also be adverbs, modifying verbs, adjectives or other adverbs. Generally their meaning is similar, although some are informal.

> *My back feels <u>all</u> achy.*
>
> *Lili opened her eyes <u>a little</u> wider.*
>
> *If you feel confident you will be <u>less</u> anxious.*
>
> *Landlords say they will not wait <u>any</u> longer.*
>
> *I can't believe he was <u>that</u> good an actor.*

With some of these, such as *more, less*, the adverb use is in fact the most common. In some cases, the adverbial meaning is not derivable from the pronoun/determiner.

> *In 1850 <u>some</u> fifty thousand women worked in such places.*

In addition, there are copious idioms in which determiners play a prominent part, where their individual meaning is not apparent.

> *It scarcely mentions women <u>at all</u>.*

The decision on what to include will depend on the underlying rationale of the work, not to mention the amount of space available.

Formality of some determiner and pronominal uses

Two problems involving formality were alluded to above: that of certain pronoun uses and that of *much* and *many* in assertive contexts. There are others. In particular, *few* and *little* are regarded as formal, whether as pronouns or determiners:

> *There is <u>little</u> hope.*
>
> *<u>Few</u> countries have accepted this claim.*

'Not much hope' and 'not many countries' would be non-formal alternatives here.

The problem with formality is, first, in identifying it – what is formal for one person may sound normal for another – and, second, in expressing it; its effects on use are so hard to quantify, how can advice be given? Beyond this, there is the issue of whether we have an adequate pedagogic metalanguage to describe it. It is not enough to talk only of formal vs informal, as my use of 'non-formal' above indicates.

Acceptability

There are three issues of acceptability I would like to raise. The first is a well-known one: the use of *less* with plural count nouns (instead of *fewer*). This use is widely attested and has apparently been a feature of English for a long time:

> *I did expect more food and <u>less</u> people.*

Against this we have claims that this usage is ungrammatical or incorrect. Even more frequent is the use of *less* followed by *than*:

> *It affects <u>less than</u> 70 children a year.*

When writing the book I was urged to indicate no restriction for *less*. I felt this would have been wrong; the writer has a position of responsibility towards the learner and to suggest both forms are interchangeable could be seen to be misleading. Also, it is my impression that most learners prefer a conservative approach to acceptability. Thus I chose the following formulation (Berry 1997a: 128):

'In informal English it is quite common to use "less" with count nouns in the plural. For some people, though, this is not acceptable.'

I am aware that this formulation will not suit everyone, but other writers have taken the same approach. Swan (1995) has a similar hedge.

Second, there has been an equally long dispute about which personal pronoun to recommend to refer back to an indefinite noun phrase (determined by e.g. *each*, *every* or *any*) where the gender is in doubt. Here I had no qualms in recommending *they* or *their* since the alternatives are awkward or problematic and since this usage is of some antiquity.

Each individual person thinks their case is justified.

The third issue is the position of the floating quantifier. Most pedagogic accounts give this as incorrect:

They all are just interested in making money.

However, analysis showed this to be fairly common, especially in spoken and American English, so it is at least worth noting.

[. . .]

Questions, suggestions and issues to consider

1. In what way might scientific and pedagogic accounts differ with respect to the notion of the 'zero article' (or 'zero determiner')?
2. Do you agree with the claim that determiners are not a separate class? Or do you feel that the 'prestidigitation' involved (making inconvenient exceptions disappear) is not valid?
3. What position should teachers adopt on the above-mentioned issues of acceptability? Namely:

   ❑ *less* with count nouns
   ❑ the use of *their* to refer back to indefinite noun phrases
   ❑ floating quantifiers placed in front of auxiliaries (*they all are interested* rather than *they are all interested*)

Should they be descriptive or prescriptive on these matters (see A1, Approaches to Grammar)? Note that the use of *their* to refer back to indefinite noun phrases reinforces what was said in B2 about the similar use of *they*.

PREPOSITIONS AND SPACE

David Lee

David Lee (2001) reprinted from Chapter 2 of *Cognitive Linguistics*, South Melbourne: Oxford University Press, pp. 137–145.

This is another chapter taken from David Lee's excellent book. This time the focus is on the use of prepositions to talk about the very basic concept of space.

Again, Lee is emphasising the personal element in language use, that what we say depends on how we view the world, and what we want to say about it — not on some grammatical absolute. We have choices, and can use language to make meaningful distinctions in areas of usage which teaching materials often simplify and portray as dependent upon automatic formal rules. Tense (see B5) and article usage (see C2) are often misleadingly explained in this way.

Gap-filling exercises are often part of this pedagogically inappropriate process. Students are presented with an incomplete sentence in which they are told there is only one possible answer. Yet in many cases (whether with articles, tenses or prepositions) there are alternatives which depend on the meaning the speaker wishes to convey. You can be 'in a bus' or 'on a bus' depending on how the situation is construed. Lee's paper convincingly demonstrates how the use of prepositions is not always determined by collocation with a particular noun.

Some specific terminology is used, such as 'trajectory' and 'landmark', but this is explained in the text.

2.1 Introduction

One of our earliest and most basic cognitive achievements as infants is to acquire an understanding of objects and of the way in which they relate to each other in physical space. The kind of concepts represented by words such as *up*, *down*, *in*, *out*, *on*, *off*, and so on are the building blocks on which we construct our mental models of the physical world. The Swiss psychologist Jean Piaget ([1936] 1952) recognised the fundamental importance of these concepts when he characterised the first stage of cognitive development as 'sensorimotor knowledge'. In other words, infants come to understand the world through grasping things, picking them up, dropping them, pulling them – and generally watching what happens when objects are manipulated by themselves and by others. Infants spend hours placing objects on top of each other or inside one another, so that these relationships are well established conceptually before the corresponding words are used.

It is no doubt because spatial relationships are so fundamental that we use space as a domain for structuring other less concrete aspects of our experience. For example, when we say that someone occupies a 'high' position in society, we are using the up-down axis as a means of talking about social status. If someone says that they are 'in trouble', they are treating 'trouble' as a container and themselves as a contained object. If I say that I have a 'close' relationship with someone, I am constructing the notion of intimacy in terms of physical proximity. The next chapter is devoted to a detailed discussion of this kind of application of spatial concepts to more abstract domains. Before this discussion is undertaken, we need to consider the ways in which we talk about space itself, since even in this very basic area, the relationship between language and reality is surprisingly complex. To illustrate this claim, three basic locative prepositions – *in*, *on*, and *at* – will be considered.

2.2 Example: *in*

The basic function of *in* is to refer to a situation where one object (the 'trajector') is contained within another (the 'landmark'). However, even if we focus only on those uses of *in* that are concerned with relations between objects in physical space (as opposed to examples such as *in trouble*), we find that *in* is used in a whole range of situations where there is only an approximation to this ideal meaning. Consider the following examples (Herskovits 1986).

1. *the cat in the house*
2. *the bird in the garden*
3. *the flowers in the vase*
4. *the bird in the tree*
5. *the chair in the corner*
6. *the water in the vase*
7. *the crack in the vase*
8. *the foot in the stirrup*
9. *?the finger in the ring*

Example 1 is a prototypical use of *in*, referring to a situation in which the trajector (TR) is wholly contained within the landmark (LM). Example 2 is similar, except that a garden is a less prototypical example of a container than a house, since it has no clearly defined upper boundary. Nevertheless, there is some notional boundary, since a sparrow can be 'in' a garden if it is flying around at a relatively low height, but we would not say that a hawk hovering at 200 metres above the garden was 'in' it. Already in this example, then, we see another example of the notion of 'construal'. Objectively speaking, a garden is not a well-defined three-dimensional container, but in our everyday use of a word such as *in*, it is construed as one.

Examples 3, 4, and 5 show that there is a good deal of flexibility in the way we apply the notion of containment to the real world. In 3 the fact that the flowers are not inside the vase does not prevent us from using *in* to refer to this situation (figure 2.1).

Figure 2.1 The flowers in the vase

In 4, in order to conceptualise a tree as a container, we have to construe it as a three-dimensional object, the boundaries of which are defined by the ends of the branches. In 5 the question of whether a chair is 'in' a corner is a particularly ill-defined issue, given the indeterminate nature of 'a corner'. The question can also be affected by the presence of other objects in the scene – we are much more likely to identify the chair in the diagram on the left of figure 2.2 as being in the corner than we are in the diagram on the right, even though it is in exactly the same position in both (Herskovits 1986: 47).

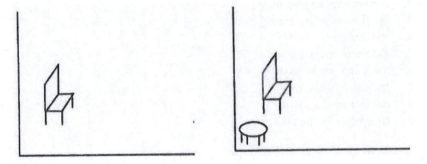

Figure 2.2 The chair in the corner

Examples 6 and 7 illustrate a rather different point – namely, the fact that the concept of 'containment' itself manifests a certain degree of flexibility. Example 6 constitutes a prototypical example of the concept, where a three-dimensional entity (the water) is entirely contained within the confines of a three-dimensional container, which surrounds it on all sides. But in 7 we interpret the notion of containment differently. Here, TR (the crack) is embedded in the surface of LM rather than in some hollow space inside it. In other words, there is some variation in the way LM is construed – as a volume in one case and an area in another. Similar examples of this latter use of *in* are found in such examples as *the weeds in the lawn, the wrinkles in his skin*.

Examples 8 and 9 are different again. The spatial configuration is similar in both cases (figures 2.3 and 2.4), yet there is a difference in how we identify the relationship between the two entities.

Figure 2.3 The foot in the stirrup   *Figure 2.4* The ring on the finger

In 8 we see the relationship as one of containment (even though only a small part of the foot is contained within the stirrup). In 9, it would be odd to conceptualise the situation in terms of the finger being 'in' the ring. The reasons for this have to do with a pragmatic asymmetry between TR and LM in each case. Since the function of a stirrup is to hold the foot in a particular position, it is naturally construed as LM, with the foot as TR. A ring does not have this function. The relationship here is the converse, with the finger functioning as a fixed entity (LM), with respect to which the ring is placed as TR. These examples show that, in order to explain the forms that we use to code these situations in language, we need to go beyond the level of surface topographical relationships. Background knowledge involving the relevant functional relationships is crucial to an understanding of the forms of coding, which reflect subtle aspects of everyday human experience.

The same point can be made about the following pair (Herskovits 1986).

10. *the bulb in the socket*
11. **the jar in the lid*

The topographical relationships are similar in each case (figures 2.5 and 2.6), but only in 10 is the relationship construed in terms of containment, since only in this case is the uppermost entity naturally construed as a fixed reference point. Again, our background knowledge concerning the functional relationships involved is crucial to an understanding of the relevant linguistic patterns.

Figure 2.5 The bulb in the socket   *Figure 2.6* The lid on the jar (*The jar in the lid)

2.3 Example: *on*

Similar points can be made about examples containing *on*. If native speakers are asked to give an example of a sentence containing the word *on*, they tend to give one such as 12, in which two entities are in physical contact with each other, with one positioned above the other and supported by it.

12. *the pen on the desk*

However, consider the following examples.

13. *the writing on the paper*
14. *the poster on the wall*
15. *the wrinkles on the face*
16. *the fly on the ceiling*

The situation described in 13 is different from that in 12. Since writing is not a physical object, the relationship between TR and LM in 13 is not one of physical support. From the point of view of a human conceptualiser, however, it seems entirely natural to see this situation as analogous to 12. Since the writing is applied to the paper in a manner that bears some similarity to the way in which a pen is placed on a desk, the objective differences between the two situations can be ignored for coding purposes.

Example 14 is judged by most speakers to be a slightly unusual use of *on*, because the wall is behind the poster rather than beneath it. (Other languages typically do not use the word corresponding to *on* in this case; French, for example, uses *à*, meaning 'at' in English, rather than *sur*, 'on' in English, in this case.) This example is perhaps closer conceptually to 13 than to 12 in that the wall, like the paper, forms a background, with the writing and the poster as foregrounded or displayed entities. Something similar can be said of 15, where the face is construed as a background against which the wrinkles are displayed, as opposed to *the wrinkles in his face*, which suggests that the wrinkles are etched more deeply into the skin and thus foregrounds the notion of embedding.

Example (16) is unusual in that the topological relationship between the ceiling and the fly is precisely the opposite of that which holds in the normal situation coded by *on*. As we move from the prototypical situation to cases such as 13, the notion of display seems to assume as prominent a role in the situation as that of support, and it is perhaps this factor that motivates the incorporation of 16 into the 'on' category (though the fact that the ceiling functions as a resting place for the fly is clearly also relevant). What this shows is that members of the same category may differ from each other quite markedly with respect to the characteristics that qualify them for their membership. This poses a critical problem for the traditional (Aristotelian) theory of category membership, according to which there is a necessary feature or features that all members of a category share (see Lakoff (1987: 161) for discussion). In chapter 3 it is noted that members of a particular category may in fact express meanings that are diametrically opposed to each other, since they connect to central (or 'prototypical') members by virtue of quite different features.

2.4 Example: *at*

The preposition *at* provides a particularly clear example of the flexibility and abstraction involved in the coding of spatial relationships. Herskovits (1986: 128–40) argues that the function of *at* is to locate two entities at precisely the same point in space and construe them as geometric points. This provides an elegant account of various characteristics of the use of *at*, but it clearly involves a considerable degree of abstraction and idealisation.

Consider 17 as a case in point.

17. *John is at the supermarket.*

This sentence would be an entirely natural utterance if I were at home telling someone where John was at that moment. However, I would be much less likely to say this if I were actually in the supermarket (or even just outside it), reporting the same situation. If I am close to or in the supermarket, it is difficult for me to conceptualise it as a geometric point in space. Given its size and salient materiality, it is much more natural to think of it in these circumstances as a container, as in 18.

18. *John is in the supermarket.*

As one moves away from the supermarket, however, it becomes progressively easier to conceive of it as a point. This may well have something to do with the fact that, as we move away from objects in our visual field, their image on the retina grows smaller, so that at a given distance they begin to approximate to a point.

A second piece of evidence supporting Herskovits's characterisation of the meaning of *at* is the fact that if I arrange with someone to meet me 'at the library', this can cause difficulties when the time of meeting actually comes, since it does not specify whether the meeting is to take place inside or outside the building. This distinction is lost when the building is construed as a point.

A third piece of evidence has to do with the situations in which it would be natural to use 19 rather than 20.

19. *The café is at the highway.*
20. *The café is on the highway.*

At first sight 19 appears to constitute a counterexample to the claim that *at* involves the construal of the two elements involved in the relationship as geometric points, since this seems incompatible with the fact that a highway is a long, straight object, more naturally conceptualised as a line in geometric terms. In fact, the typical context of use for 19 is when I am moving along a path (for example, driving a car) and I say that the café is located at the place where my path intersects with the highway at some point ahead – a location that is quite naturally conceptualised as a point. Similarly, there is an implicit notion of path in each of the following.

21. *The bomb exploded at 1000 feet.*
22. *We'll hold a lifeboat drill at the Equator.*
23. *The horse fell at the water jump.*

In 21 the point at which the bomb exploded is the point at which its trajectory (path) intersects with the 1000 feet altitude level; in 22 the lifeboat drill will be held at the point where the ship's path intersects with the line of the Equator; and in 23 the conceptualiser tracks the progress of the horse to the water jump, where it falls.

The concept of path is also present in the following examples, but in a more abstract form.

24. *The bird has a white band at its neck.*
25. *The bird is at the top of the tree.*
26. *There are bubbles at the surface.*

Whereas in 19–23 an actual physical movement is involved (that is, cars, ships, bombs, and horses follow paths through physical space), in 24–26 there is no such physical trajectory. Nevertheless, the cognitive claim is that there is movement in the following sense. What 24 implies is that the conceptualiser scans the body of the bird and comes across a white band when this scanning process reaches the neck; similarly, in 25 the scanning process moves across the tree, finding a bird when it reaches the top; and in 26 there is implicit movement through the liquid, encountering bubbles when it reaches the surface.

Further evidence for the notion that *at* involves some abstract notion of path in examples such as these is that the only circumstance in which a sentence such as *John is at London* is natural is if London is one of a series of points on a journey. Otherwise, it is more natural to conceive of London as a container than as a point.

Questions, suggestions and issues to consider

1. As with the paper in D2, we can ask to what extent the use of prepositions is a matter of creativity in each instance (as Lee suggests) or convention. Do we say we are 'in trouble' because we construe 'trouble' as a container, or because this is what we have heard other people say? What about being 'in need'? Is it not also plausible to suggest that these collocations exist because one of the 'meanings' of *in* is to suggest that something affects us ('trouble', 'need' or 'love')?

2. It could be argued that Lee's approach only works for the most basic prepositions, and only for their spatial and temporal meanings (and then maybe not all of those). Can you see how the idea of containment could be extended to the use of *in* in *I'll be there <u>in</u> a week*?

3. Look at Activity A4.5 in A4, concerning the preposition *for*. Can you think of a core meaning (in the same way that *in* refers to containment), and then ways in which the other meanings could be explained as different construals of this core?

4. The adjective *different* is usually followed by *from* in British English, but some-
    times it can be followed by *to* (also *than* in American English) as in these two
    sentences:

    > *She's very different from her mother.*
    > *She's very different to her mother.*

    Is there any difference in meaning between them? Are people construing
    the relationship between daughter and mother differently? Or might there be
    another reason for using *to*? (Hint: think of a similar word that might 'influence'
    different.)

5. Take another preposition which indicates a spatial relationship, e.g. *up*, *down*,
    and try to do the same as Lee: to find a core meaning which could explain some
    of its apparently idiomatic uses (e.g. *to walk up/down the road*).

FUTURE TIME – A SUMMARY

D5

Michael Lewis (1986) reprinted from Chapter 17 of *The English Verb*, Hove, Language
Teaching Publications.

Michael
Lewis

*This reading is pedagogically oriented (i.e. it aims to be intelligible to teachers) and provides
some interesting insights into ways of expressing future time in English. Lewis discusses some
forms already covered in this book, such as 'will' (A5) and the present progressive (B5 — which
he calls 'durative' as well as continuous), but other forms discussed are not related to tense
or aspect, such as '(be) going to', and 'be to'. His idea of conceptualisation is similar to that
of Lee's 'construing' (see D2 and D4): the importance of the way we perceive events and
states.*

English possesses no formal future tense but, of course, it is possible to talk about
Future Time. A number of different verb forms are possible and the choice of the
correct one is frequently a source of confusion for foreign learners. It is not possible
to give simple, easily accessible, comprehensive rules which describe the differences
between the different possible forms. Much of the discussion in this book has concentrated upon the fact that verb forms are frequently a matter of the speaker's choice.
This applies particularly to events in Future Time which are not, of their nature,
factually or objectively knowable in the same way that events in Past Time or Present
Time are.

Examination of the uses of those verb forms which sometimes refer to Future
Time and sometimes do not, shows that *all* uses of the form always have the same
primary semantic characterisitics. Those occasions when the verb form is used with
reference to Future Time are not different in kind. The consistency and regularity of
the use of the verb forms which is one of the central themes of this book are fully
preserved.

In several cases, uses of the forms which refer to Future Time are discussed in the appropriate chapters. Some of the contrasts are gathered together here for convenience. Six verb forms are common to refer to Future Time:

1. I'm going to leave tomorrow.
2. I'm leaving tomorrow.
3. I leave tomorrow.
4. I am to leave tomorrow.
5. I'll leave tomorrow.
6. I'll be leaving tomorrow.

Statements about Future Time are not statements of fact but predictions, guesses, etc. We expect the different forms chosen in some way to reflect the differing nature of the guesses, predictions, etc. Examination of how the forms are used, shows that they are used consistently and that the choices depend on how the speaker conceptualises the future event at the moment of speaking. It is helpful in considering the speaker's conceptualisation to ask *why* the speaker thinks the future event will occur.

Not 'degree of certainty'

Some readers may be familiar with the suggestion made by Leech (*Meaning and the English Verb, Longman, 1971*) that the choice of verb appropriate for a future event may be decided according to the degree of certainty ascribed to the future happening. He suggests:

1. Simple present (most certain)
2. { will/shall + infinitive
   { will/shall + progressive infinitive
3. { be going to + infinitive (least certain)
   { present progressive

   Even those marked 'least certain', however, convey at least a strong expectation of the future event.

Such an explanation is attractive because it is fairly simple for both teacher and student to grasp. There are, however, two difficulties – first, if the explanation is true, the difference between the various degrees of certainty is extremely subtle and, however simple the explanation is in theory, it is of little practical use. Second, however, there is a much greater problem – it is, quite simply, that the explanation is not true. I have on numerous occasions when speaking to native speaker audiences asked them to rate in order of 'degree of certainty' the sentences given at the beginning of the chapter. On every single occasion when I have done this with an audience of more than 12 the voting for 'most certain' and 'least certain' has split over at least three of the examples. Not infrequently some native speakers have voted one example 'most certain' while others in the same group have voted the same example 'least certain'. If native speakers cannot even agree on which is most or least certain, they are going to find it impossible to range the other examples between the two extremes. Such evidence seems to me to prove conclusively that 'degree of certainty' is not only an impractical classroom explanation, it is also completely without foundation.

The essential distinction between the different forms is the nature of the speaker's conceptualisation of the future act or event. Nobody except the speaker can *know* the speaker's conceptualisation. All we can do, is to point to parallels with other uses of the same form, or contrasts with the uses of different forms, to indicate the nature of the events described by particular verb forms.

1. (be) going to

This form is used if, at the moment of speaking, the speaker has *evidence* for the future event. That evidence may be either external (clouds or a tickle in the nose) or internal (a plan or decision):

> *It's going to rain.*
> *I'm going to sneeze.*
> *I'm not going to tell you.*

From the speaker's point of view such uses are similar; in each case the evidence is clear to the speaker, and the future act is seen as the culmination of a previous sequence of events or thoughts. The future event is a projection or extrapolation of events preceding, and up to, the point Now.

Statements of the 'internal evidence' type, will frequently begin with 'I'; questions using this form more frequently involve 'you' or a third person:

> *I'm definitely not going to take the exam in summer.*
> *Are you going to take the exam this summer?*
> *Is he going to go to university?*

Other combinations can occur.

> *What on earth am I going to do about it?*
> *You are definitely not going to borrow mine!*

but of course *my* internal evidence tends to be about me and *questions* about internal evidence are usually about other people.

(be) going to is non-modal. It does not involve the speaker's personal judgment and, in particular, is non-volitional. Events described using *(be) going to* are seen as arising out of a process which is already in progress at the time of speaking. This is clear from an example such as:

> *What do you think is going to happen next?*

where the listener's opinion is sought about something which happens independently of speaker or listener.

In some ways *(be) going to* forms are similar to *(be)* + . . . *ing* forms. There is, however, one important distinction.

2. The present durative

It is not always possible to use the present durative to refer to Future Time:

1.   **It's raining tomorrow.*
2.   *I'm playing tennis on Saturday.*
3.   **(?) I'm watching TV tomorrow evening.*

Example 1 is impossible; 2 seems natural and 3, although possible, is less likely than an alternative form, e.g. *I'm going to watch . . .* or *I'll be watching . . . .*

We need to think once more of the defining characteristics of the present durative. It is used if, at the moment of speaking, the speaker conceptualises the action as occurring between precisely two points in time, one before and one after the point Now. At the moment of speaking the speaker has in mind two points, one on either side of Now, between which the action, as far as the speaker is concerned, exists. It can be represented diagrammatically:

We see immediately why (1) is impossible. There is no way that the speaker can have in mind at Now some event which pre-dates Now and which is conceptualised as an intrinsic part of *It's raining tomorrow*. This contrasts with *I'm seeing him tomorrow* in which the arrangement of the meeting pre-dates Now and is seen by the speaker as an intrinsic part of the future act.

It is easy to see why *arrangements*, particularly made between the speaker and another person, may be expressed using this form. The speaker has in mind a precise event which pre-dates Now – the making of the arrangement – and an event which post-dates Now – the performing of the action itself, and, seeing these two events as linked and surrounding Now, chooses the verb form which expresses exactly those characteristics.

In example 2, we know that tennis involves playing with other people and that, therefore, some event must have preceded Now for the speaker to be able to make the statement about tomorrow. For this reason example 2 seems natural.

Example 3 feels a little unnatural; television watching is not usually arranged but, equally, on exactly those occasions when there is an event which pre-dates the moment of speaking and culminates in the performance of the action, example 3 will be appropriate.

The use of the present continuous to refer to Future Time is by no means random. The meaning of the *(be)* + *. . . ing* form interacts with the meaning of the verb itself. In some cases the combination is semantically impossible with Future Time reference, in others frequent, and in others rare. The form is used for precisely the same reasons to refer to Future Time as for all other uses. The frequently-used heading 'the present continuous used for the future' is an illusion; such uses are exactly like all others.

[. . .]

A pair such as:

What will you do when you leave school?

What are you doing when you leave school?

are both possible but suggest very different situations. The first suggests the speaker is inviting the other person to discuss the question and that the listener's present opinion is of immediate interest; the second suggests that the speaker would like to know the arrangements which the other person has already made, or thoughts he has already had; it is more a request for information.

As we have seen on several occasions in this book when considering contrasting pairs of this kind, the connotational differences understood by the hearer are a direct result of the meanings characteristically associated with the verb forms chosen.

The inclusion of *will* or *'ll*, being modal, concentrates on the precise moment of speaking, Now; the present durative associates the future event with a point which precedes Now.

The present durative with reference to Future Time resembles *(be) going to*, in that both relate the event in Future Time to something preceding Now. The distinction, sometimes slight, is that with the present durative there is usually a single event which pre-dates Now, whereas with *(be) going to* there is a sequence of events up to Now which the speaker projects forward to the future event. The contrast is clear with the pair:

What are you doing tomorrow?

What are you going to do tomorrow?

The first asks about the event you have already planned, and which will occur tomorrow; the second enquires about the listener's thinking *up to now* about tomorrow. With the present durative the event which pre-dates Now is more isolated from Now; with *(be) going to* there is something which pre-dates Now, but what is happening *at* the moment of speaking is also important.

3. The 'present simple'

The basic form is used when the lexical meaning of the verb alone is sufficient to convey the full message. With a pronoun, in 'the present simple', it is used when the speaker conceptualises the event as 'pure fact'. It is associated with 'simple facts', objective truth. Time reference is accidental to the occurrence of this form; it is appropriate precisely on the occasions that the questions *When?* and *On what occasion?* are not appropriate. (This was discussed in detail in Chapter 8.)

The form will be appropriate for events in Future Time when the speaker sees the future event as occurring quite independently of his understanding, perception, volition, etc. The event is determined by what the speaker sees as an external *force majeure*. This may be natural, or an appropriate timetable-making body:

Christmas Day falls on a Thursday this year.

What time does the sun rise next Saturday?

Arsenal play away next weekend.

We leave at 4 o'clock tomorrow afternoon.

It is comparatively unusual for this form to be used about *I* or *we* and notice that, in the example just given which contains *we*, the suggestion is clearly that we are catching a train or coach, rather than that we will be setting off with our own car, in which case *We're leaving about 4 tomorrow* or *We are going to leave at 4 tomorrow* would be more natural.

As we saw in Chapter 8 the verb form in: *We leave at 4 o'clock* is not intrinsically associated with a particular point in time. The occurrence of the phrase *at 4 o'clock* is coincidental, and not intrinsic to the choice of the form *leave*.

We have seen that the speaker can express a temporal view of the action by using the *(be) + ... ing* or *(be) going to* forms. If such marked forms are inappropriate, the speaker selects the basic form. In the case of Future Time reference, when the event is in no way dependent upon the speaker, the basic form is appropriate. Such uses are relatively rare, but entirely consistent with all other uses of this form.

4. (be) to

We have not considered this form elsewhere in this book. It is relatively rare in spoken English, but occurs in newspapers, and some relatively formal writing. Here are some examples:

> *The work is to be completed by the end of June.*
> *The Queen is to visit Canada in October.*
> *There's to be an enquiry into the whole affair.*

The form *(be) to* also occurs in the remote form:

> *At that time he did not know he was to be king.*
> *That wasn't the end of it – worse was to follow.*

Uses referring to Past Time provide an insight into the semantic characteristics of the form. *Worse followed* describes the event factually, and, from the speaker's point of view, as a remote fact. It is not, however, possible to make a similar transformation of the first sentence: *At that time he did not know that he was king.*

(be) to describes events which the speaker sees as facts, but as *future* facts, rather than pure, timeless facts, expressed, as always through the basic form.

With *was/were to*, in Past Time the events are seen as pure facts. They can, however, be described as future facts, from a point of view in the past. This is exactly the case with *At that time . . .* in the example. The introductory adverbial, placing the speaker's temporal point of view decisively at a point in Past Time, means a *(be) to* form is required by the meaning. With the example *Worse followed*, or *Worse was to follow* the difference, though less obvious, is the same; *followed* states the remote factuality of what happened for the speaker now, *was to follow* describes the past event factually, from a point of view in Past Time.

The same considerations apply to 'present' uses of *(be) to*. Like the basic form, the event is described as *fact* The distinction is made between future fact – *(be) to* and 'timeless' fact – the basic form. Not surprisingly, both forms are relatively rare and the difference between them often small.

Consideration of most 'present' uses of *(be) to*, however, reveals that the certainty about the future event is nearly always based on a formal announcement made by some authority which, through experience, is seen as irrevocable, and therefore certain. Events described by *(be) to* are nearly always based on an announcement of a single, particular event. The basic form is more frequent if the same impersonal *force majeure* is involved, but based on more regular, general and therefore timeless, information.

We are to leave at 4 suggests a guide or driver has just told me about a *particular* departure. *We leave at four this afternoon*, although apparently 'a future fact', is much more likely to be a reference to the *normal* timetable.

The basic form and *(be) to* share a sense of factuality. They differ in that the basic form is associated with timeless factuality, while *(be) to* is associated with future factuality. Because future factuality is unusual, *(be) to* forms are rare.

[. . .]

5. will/shall/'ll

We have noted that the essential characteristic of forms containing *will/shall/'ll* is that they are modal. This means they are essentially grounded in the moment of speaking. They express ideas which may be paraphrased as 'given the circumstances I see at the moment, I consider it is . . . that . . .'.

Both *will* and *shall* express the idea of the inevitable connection between two states, one pertaining at the moment of speaking and a second state. If the inevitable connection is a connection in time, *will* and *shall* refer to Future Time. The expression of Future Time with *will* and *shall* differs from the forms discussed above in its concentration upon the moment of speaking, Now, and in the speaker's involvement.

With two of the forms we have considered, the speaker sees the event factually. With the two others which include aspectual forms, the speaker interprets future events with reference to purely temporal characteristics. In both the present durative and *(be) going to* forms, the speaker sees something which pre-dates Now as a reason for the future event. In future forms involving a modal, the emphasis is on the speaker's judgment at the moment of speaking.

[. . .]

Questions, suggestions and issues to consider

1. One of Lewis's main themes in his book is that there is always a central meaning to any verb form. Do you agree? For instance, how convincing do you find his argument that the future use of the present progressive for arrangements and plans (*I'm seeing him tomorrow*) is no different from other uses? Here again is his description of the basic meaning of the present progressive:

    the speaker conceptualises the action as occurring between precisely two points in time, one before and one after Now.

    Do you feel this covers the meaning adequately? What about the idea of focusing on an activity or of something being in progress, as described in B5? Are these ideas compatible?

    Some grammarians would disagree with Lewis, claiming that there are meanings or uses which are mutually incompatible. For example, it is difficult to explain how the Groucho Marks joke in Activity B5.3 in B5 could work if there were not two separate uses of the present perfect.

2. Nevertheless, Lewis does have a point: grammarians often produce lists of meanings for verb forms that become so long as to be meaningless or useless.

    Look at the list of 'meanings' of the present simple in B5. Should we add the newspaper headline mentioned in the reading (*Government announces tax reductions*) as an extra meaning (referring to past time)? Or should we be looking to reduce these meanings? Is there any way you can rationalise them into one single meaning (or at least fewer meanings), and describe it in terms that are not too general?

3. Section A5 considers (and rejects) *will* as a candidate for the future tense. But Lewis also considers *shall*, reflecting the traditional view that *will* and *shall* together make up a paradigm for the 'future tense': *I will, we shall*, etc. Can you see what is wrong with this notion?

HEDGING AND BOOSTING

Ronald
Carter and
Michael
McCarthy

Ronald Carter and **Michael McCarthy** (2006) reprinted from *Cambridge Grammar of English*, Cambridge: Cambridge University Press, pp. 279–284.

This reading is different from previous ones in that it does not consist of continuous prose, like the articles and book chapters in other readings, but rather of an extract from a well-known reference grammar (a grammar which is intended primarily for finding answers to specific questions).

The information it contains is useful, as it relates to the grammatical areas described in B6 (modality) and elsewhere (e.g. the passive in A6), but it is also important for acquainting you with the nature of reference grammars and with how to use them as independent sources of information.

A third reason for adopting this reading is that it adopts a different approach to grammar by looking at it in one particular 'genre', in this case academic communication. The idea underlying this approach is that grammar operates differently according to the genre (e.g. business letters vs e-mails), as well as to the mode (speech vs writing). Whether this is more a matter of frequency and tendencies rather than different grammatical systems is discussed more fully in A12.

Note the use of sometimes lengthy authentic examples, and the use of glosses in brackets ahead of examples to describe the sub-genres involved. Bold is used for highlighted items (as opposed to underlining in this book).

Academic texts are most frequently characterised by a desire to avoid making claims and statements that are too direct and assertive, since academic discourse is often about theories, conclusions drawn from evidence, exchanging viewpoints, and so on, rather than hard, indisputable facts. Therefore, hedging (making a proposition less assertive) is very important in academic styles. Less often, it is sometimes also necessary to assert a claim or viewpoint quite directly and more confidently, a process we shall refer to as boosting.

Hedging and boosting are principally realised through modal expressions and through the use of simple tense forms. We also examine the role of adverbs and other constructions in asserting (boosting) and hedging.

Modality and tense-aspect   146a

Will is used to make confident predictions or to assert known or accepted facts:

> *Represented as a value between zero and one, X **will** approach unity in perfectly flat and open terrain, whereas locations with obstructions such as buildings and trees **will** cause X to become proportionally less (Oke, 1992).*

[pathology lecture]

*Right. Red blood cells leaving the capillaries and then entering the tissues. They'll break down there and haemoglobin **will** be released and the tissue **will** turn black and eventually **will** go.*

Must is used to make confident predictions or conclusions:

*Such changes **must** be due to changes in motivational organisation of social behaviour.*

Must is also used in boosted directives to the reader/listener to pay attention to particular points:

*We **must** remember, however, that migrants may not need information about more than one destination.*
(compare the weaker: We should remember, however, . . .)

*It is useful to try to apply these general stages when considering any piece of worked stone. As always, they are meant to help us understand the processes and as such are merely an intellectual framework. Therefore one **must not** apply them too rigidly.*

The unmodified simple forms of verb tenses are used to make non-hedged assertions:

*Attachment, then, **results** in close and prolonged proximity of bacterial digestive enzymes with the substrate.*
(compare the hedged: Attachment, then, may/can/could/might/should result in close and prolonged proximity of bacterial digestive enzymes with the substrate.)

*Adams **believed** that the Washington government must, for material as well as moral reasons, fight an aggressive war for American commerce.*
(compare: Adams may have believed/Adams probably believed . . .)

Hedging: modality   146b

Can, could, might and *may*

Broadly speaking, *can, could, might* and *may* are used in academic style in the same way as they are used in general English, but one or two usages which are more frequent in academic style are worth noting. Academic English often needs to state possibilities rather than facts, and academics frequently hypothesise and draw tentative conclusions.

   Can is often used to make fairly confident but not absolute assertions, in contrast with *could, might* or *may* (see below):

*These new insights into the multiple meanings of family **can** help us understand the experience of transnational migration.*
(asserting a claim of what is normal, i.e. almost equivalent to 'these new insights . . . help us understand . . .', but framed as 'usually/normally' rather than 'always')

Could and *might* are used for more tentative assertions:

*One **could** say that our concept of selfhood is radically contaminated by the mind-set of 'this is mine', 'I am this'.*

[consultant (A) tutoring a student doctor]

A: *Right. Very good. What do you think **might** have happened since he left hospital that caused this ulcer to break down yet again?*

B: *He **could** have either occluded his graft.*

A: *Yes.*

B: *Or the area **could** have become infected.*

A: *Okay. Now is there any clinical evidence that he **might** have occluded his graft?*

[on the behaviour of young birds]

*Thus, one **might** conclude that the predisposition to respond to pattern or flicker only affects the further development of a preference in that it **might** help to guide the young bird towards objects having these characteristics.*

A particular use of *may*, which is very common in academic texts, is to describe things which are likely to occur or which normally do occur. In this usage it is a formal equivalent of *can*:

*Parallel vertical pipes, several centimetres long and 1–2 mm thick, are common in much of the unit, but especially in the middle part, where there **may** be several in each cm horizontal section.*

[on mental health and mental retardation]

*The anger experience **may** culminate in a variety of behavioural reactions, including aggression or withdrawal.*

May is also widely used in a more general way in academic texts to make a proposition more tentative. *May* is less tentative than *could* or *might*:

*This change **may** also have been in progress in other counties.*

[CFS = chronic fatigue syndrome]

*Overall, one **may** conclude that the present study has shown that patients with CFS have psychomotor impairments, problems maintaining attention, and are visually sensitive.*

Would

Would is frequently used to hedge assertions which someone might challenge and to make argumentative claims less direct when used with speech-act verbs such as *advocate, argue, assume, claim, propose, suggest*:

*Given this, we **would argue** that the Iowa sample has provided a unique opportunity to examine a number of important questions regarding schizophrenia, including the issue of mortality.*

*Theoretically, one **would assume** that this increased bacterial mass would synthesise more enzymes.*

[lecture on the teaching of language and literature]

*And students think that by reading a text, getting the information from it, they have understood it. They are, **I would suggest**, full of the understanding of one level: the referential meaning.*

Would is also frequently used with *appear* and *seem*:

> It **would seem** that in this domain, as in so many others, the north was more
> favoured than the south.
> (compare the more assertive: It seems that in this domain . . .)

Should and *ought to*

Should allows the writer/speaker to describe desired or ideal situations. It is less strong
than *must*:

> However, to assess different advantages and disadvantages in other circumstances,
> the chosen method **should** be examined critically before use. (compare the stronger:
> . . . the chosen method must be examined . . .)

Ought to is occasionally used in this way in academic style, but is much less frequent
than *should*:

> Our use of the term 'stable' **ought to** be defined here.

Should is used to hedge conclusions and predictions, but it expresses confidence in
the probability that a situation will occur in a particular way:

> The overall agreement of the results **should** allow us to accept them with some
> confidence.
> (compare the more direct: . . . the results allow us to accept . . .)

> [English literature lecture]
> Okay. You **should** be able to see the connections already and hopefully you can see
> what Anderson is saying in this extract.

Hedging: other expressions 146c

Hedging in academic texts is often carried out by the use of a range of adverbial and
prepositional constructions (plus some other types of expression). Their full effect can
often best be observed by removing them from the example sentences quoted here.

Common hedging expressions include adverbs such as:

apparently	*generally*	*roughly*
arguably	*likely*	*seemingly*
broadly	*normally*	*surely*
evidently	*partially*	*typically*
frequently	*probably*	*usually*

> It was, **arguably**, the strongest leadership the department had ever had and it used
> its resources well.

> They are both from **roughly** the same period in the middle of the sixteenth century.

> Yet, **seemingly** for Bakhtin, though material forces no doubt exist, what determines
> that we know about them at all are intersubjective human relations.

Common prepositional phrases and other expressions used as hedges include:

as a (general) rule	in a way	in some respects/
broadly speaking	in most cases/in the	in many respects
generally speaking	majority of cases	more or less
in a sense	in principle	roughly speaking
	in some senses	

*Survey researchers have **as a rule** understandably preferred to make use of established diagnostic categories, rather than have to develop their own new ones and then try to persuade clinicians to accept these.*

[critique of a collection of political essays]
*Thus the essays were, **in a sense**, out of date when they appeared, yet the cultural tradition which they articulate and to which they contribute remains a part of the German scene to this day.*

*This summary **more or less** encapsulates the thesis advanced by Glynn in his new and wide-ranging history of arms races and arms control.*

Hedging and impersonal constructions   146d

Propositions may be hedged by the use of impersonal *it*-constructions with passive voice which enable the writer/speaker to avoid the more direct commitment to a proposition which a first person *I/we* + active voice may create:

*It **is suggested** that the analytic procedures illustrated in this paper be applied to more widely-used oral testing instruments in order to evaluate their utility in eliciting conversational interaction.*
(compare the more direct and personal: I suggest that . . .)

Such impersonal *it*-constructions may also be used simply to hedge a proposition by attributing it to other, unnamed experts:

*It **is claimed, or tacitly assumed,** in narrative studies that temporality should be explored in narrative texts where it functions as a dominant principle of organisation.*

A range of impersonal *it*-expressions are common in academic texts to attribute propositions to unnamed people. These include:

it is (widely) accepted	it is believed	it is /has been said
it is generally agreed	it is/has been claimed	it is/has been suggested

*It **is generally agreed** that one of the most influential reports published during the war was the Beveridge Report, published in 1942, which mapped out the future welfare state.*

*Literature, **it is claimed**, seeks to recapture and reconstruct tradition.*

The use of a raised subject as an alternative to, anticipatory *it*, similarly, enables the writer/speaker to make a less direct commitment to a proposition. Common passive expressions of this type include:

be believed to	be found to	be shown to
be claimed to	be said to	be thought to
be considered to	be seen to	

The value placed on children **is believed to have changed** *from pre-industrial societies to the present time.*

Operating practices **are said to have been** *a major obstacle to improvement.*

Boosting   146e

Boosting in academic texts, to make a claim more assertively, is often carried out by the use of a range of adverbial and prepositional constructions (plus some other types of expression).

Common boosting expressions include adverbs such as:

categorically	indisputably	plainly
certainly	inevitably	undeniably
clearly	irrefutably	undoubtedly
definitely	observably	unquestionably
emphatically	obviously	

This is **clearly** *a very restrictive hypothesis, which requires verification, and Lightfoot suggests that language change represents a useful testing ground.*

While most people were **indisputably** *poor, the economy had a considerable surplus above basic subsistence needs, although much of that surplus was concentrated in the hands of those in the top 10 per cent or so of the income distribution.*

Yet utilities and transport **unquestionably** *provide a service rather than a commodity.*

Other expressions used in boosting include:

for sure/for certain	there is/was no doubt that
it is/was clear/obvious/	that without doubt
indisputable/etc.	

It was clear that *the Danes would remain neutral, although they offered to approach Catherine II in order to sound her out on a possible settlement.*

In the early nineteenth century this was **without doubt** *true of much of the Nord region and the Normandy textile area.*

Questions, suggestions and issues to consider

1. In 146a it is said that both *must* and *will* are used for confident predictions. To what extent is this true? Look at the examples containing them and try replacing them with each other. Does this make a difference?

2. Look at the hedged statements below. Using your intuitions or the information above, explain the differences in meaning.

    We will
    We can   *argue that these results are an artefact of the methodology.*
    We might
    We would

3. Are the other hedging expressions listed in 146c equivalent in meaning to the modal auxiliaries in 146a and 146b? Try two tests:

    a) replacing the hedging expressions with modals
    b) adding modals to the hedging expressions

    for instance (using the last example):

    This summary <u>can</u> encapsulate . . .
    This summary <u>can</u> <u>more or less</u> encapsulate . . .

4. Consider the advantages and disadvantages of using the passive in academic writing as opposed to a personal construction, as for example in

    It can be argued that . . . vs We can argue that . . .

WORDS AND PHRASES

John Sinclair

John Sinclair (1991) reprinted from Chapter 5 of *Corpus, Concordance, Collocation*, Oxford: Oxford University Press, pp. 67–75.

Sinclair takes the reader through the process of analysing a particular verb to discover (some of) the ways in which it is used. It is an excellent example of how corpora can be used for grammatical/lexical analysis (Sinclair's final aim being to arrive at grammatically adequate dictionary definitions).

Sinclair appears to be using the term 'phrasal verb' in the more general sense identified in B7 (= 'multi-word verbs'), since he includes 'set about' (a prepositional verb in our narrower sense) under this heading. However, the two main multi-word verbs, 'set off' and 'set in', are both phrasal verbs in the narrower sense.

Some terms may be unfamiliar: lemma = 'word-family', and adjunct = 'adverbial'

Introduction

The studies of *decline* and *yield* in the previous two chapters open up the possibility of associating grammar and vocabulary in ways that can improve the description of both. They are both rich in semantic associations.

In this chapter and the next, we explore the use of concordances in the description of words that are much more frequent than so-called 'vocabulary words'. They are not normally expected to have a strong lexical environment, but are more associated with the grammatical end of the spectrum. The objectives are to demonstrate:

- how carefully the language is patterned;
- how the description is very sensitive to the number of instances of a form;
- how criteria for meaning (see Chapter 4) are applied in a specific case.

In addition, the relevance of this research to the teaching and learning of English is pointed up by the consideration of a feature of English much dreaded by learners – phrasal verbs.

Phrasal verbs

The choice of an example to illustrate the argument of this chapter was, as usual, partly accidental, and partly deliberate. I was looking for a fairly common, rather dull little word that was comparatively neglected in description and in teaching. I found out by chance that the word *set* was not well regarded by some experienced teacher–colleagues, and noticed that it got scant treatment in the syllabuses that I was able to examine. The immediate presumption was that it was a difficult word to isolate semantically. 'What does *set* mean?' is hardly a sensible question. It has to be put into context, because in most of its usage it contributes to meaning in combination with other words.

Among the many combinations of *set* are a number of phrasal verbs, such as *set about, set in, set off*, and these are picked out in language teaching as offering exquisite problems to the learner. The reason for their causing problems is easily explained. The co-occurrence of two quite common little words can unexpectedly create a fairly subtle new meaning that does not seem to be systematically related to either or both of the original words. The disposition of the words involved, and their syntax, is governed by complex and unpredictable rules.

The prospect sounds formidable even for native speakers, yet they not only manage phrasal verbs with aplomb, but seem to prefer them to single word alternatives. In fact, the whole drift of the historical development of English has been towards the replacement of words by phrases, with word-order acquiring greater significance.

Some recent work (Sinclair, Moon *et al.* 1989) shows that the semantics of phrasal verbs is not as arbitrary as it is often held to be. We usually cite phrasal verbs based on the verb element (*give up, give out, give over*, etc.). If, instead, we group them by the particle (*give over, get over, tide over*), it is possible to make sense groupings.

It will, however, be a long time before people will routinely look up *give over* in a dictionary under *over* rather than *give*. The presentation in this chapter emphasises the importance of the environment of *set* in determining the meaning. In the first instance, a particle following raises the prospect of a phrasal verb; then, the other words around help in indicating the precise meaning.

Some numerical facts

In the corpus of approximately 7.3 million words, used in Chapters 3 and 4, there are 2,320 instances of the different forms of the lemma *set*. We associate together the forms *set, sets,* and *setting* as instances of the word *set,* and the frequency of each is:

set	1885	(80%)
sets	219	(9%)
setting	246	(11%)

Other possible associates such as *setter* and *settee* are ignored.

Set is thus one of the commonest words in the language – the uninflected form is ranked number 272. However, if we compare the relative frequency of the inflected forms *sets* and *setting*, we see that they are not nearly as common as *set*, being approximately 9 per cent and 11 per cent of the lemma.

This is a commonly observed pattern, where one of the forms is much more common than any other. Similar, if less dramatic, tendencies are shown for *decline* and *yield* in Chapters 3 and 4 respectively. This means that if *sets* or *setting* has a use which is not shared by *set*, we have much less evidence to go on. Whatever criteria we use, there is nearly ten times as much evidence available for *set*.

It could be argued that, in one respect at least, the inflection of *set* is untypical, and that the frequency of forms of *set* will reflect the oddity. *Set* is one of a handful of verbs in English which do not have a separate past tense form. So whatever frequency is assigned to *walk* and *walked*, *say* and *said*, etc. is not differentiated in *set*. To complicate the picture further, all three forms of the lemma *set* are also readily available as nouns, and the picture is not at all straightforward.

However, compared to the vast majority of words, even the least common form *sets* is generously represented. But when we look for combinations of even these frequent words, the expectations are not promising.

If a corpus is held to be representative of the language as a whole, the probability of occurrence of a word-form can be expressed in general as a relation between the frequency of the word-form in the corpus and the total number of word-forms in the corpus.

In the case of *set* this is:

$$\frac{1855}{7,300,000} \text{ or } 0.0025$$

This means that the chance of *set* being the next word in the text is about 250 per million, or one occurrence in every 3,935 words.

Combinations of *set* + particle

How common are the phrasal verbs with *set*? *Set* is particularly rich in making combinations with words like *about, in, up, out, on, off*, and these words are themselves very common.

As an example, how likely is *set off* to occur, whether phrasal verb or not? Both are frequent words; *off* occurs approximately 556 times in a million words. Its probability of being the next word is 0.00055. We must now multiply the probabilities of *set* and *off*, because the question we are asking can be roughly rephrased as follows: how likely is *off* to occur immediately after *set*? This is approximately 0.00025×0.00055, which gives us the minute figure of 0.0000000001375.

Two important considerations are left out of this calculation, one linguistic and the other statistical.

a.   the phrasal verb *set off* can have a noun group inside it, for example: It was the hedge which *set* the garden *off*.

There are very few of these and so they have little effect on the general numerical argument.

b.   The assumption behind this calculation is that the words are distributed at random in a text. It is obvious to a linguist that this is not so, and a rough measure of how much *set* and *off* attract each other is to compare the probability with what actually happens.

In a text of 7.3 million words distributed at random, we might expect 0.0000001375 × 7,300,000 occurrences of *set off*, that is, one only. Since there are several different phrasal verbs with the form *set off* and no doubt some occurrences of *set* followed by *off* which do not provide an instance of a phrasal verb, we might require a fairly large number of occurrences of the combination of forms to show the characteristic patterns. At a frequency of about 1 in 7 million, we would require to collect large amounts of text, running into the hundreds of millions of words.

The gloomy picture thus projected by our arithmetic is, in fact, considerably relieved by what we find in actual texts. This is because our initial assumption, that the words are distributed at random, is false. *Set off* occurs nearly seventy times in the 7.3 million-word corpus, as against the random prediction of only one occurrence. The 70 instances give us enough evidence of the main patterning.

The combination *set in*

In this central part of the chapter, I shall consider all the instances of *set*, *sets*, and *setting* followed by *in*. The different ways in which the occurrence of these words together contribute to meanings will emerge, and the evidence will be found to be mainly in the surrounding language.

We begin by gathering all instances of the sequence *set in*. There are 90 of them. To this we add: *sets in* (16); *setting in* (6); and, for the sake of completeness, *settings in* (2). The total of instances of a form of *set* followed immediately by *in* is thus 114.

The first analysis combines several steps:

–   noting the word class of each example;
–   classifying the meaning roughly into word-meaning and phrase-meaning;
–   assigning the word-meanings to senses, where possible;
–   working out the phrases;
–   assigning the phrase-meanings to senses.

The distinction of word-meaning and phrase-meaning is of considerable importance in language study, and is explained in some detail in Chapter 8. Intuitively, we feel that some instances of a word are quite independently chosen, while in other cases we feel that the word combines with others to deliver a single multi-word unit of meaning. We shall call word-meaning *independent*, and phrase-meaning *dependent*.

In between these two fixed points is collocation, where we see a tendency for words to occur together though they remain largely independent choices. In what follows, the 114 instances are divided into:

- Nouns
- Verbs
  - sense (i)
  - sense (ii)
  - minor sense
  - sundry idioms
- Phrasal verbs

Let us first dispose of a few instances that do not fit into the above classification. There are five of these, one a typographical error (*as-sets*) and one where even the twenty-word citation does not give enough evidence of its meaning. Two are instances of other idioms with *set*, but in the passive so that *set* is immediately followed by *in*, for example:

> He was asking *a precedent* to be *set* in a field where . . .

The last is:

> . . . the controlled fires he *sets* in spring devastate shrubs . . .

We now go on to examine the first five categories in the above classification, before giving fuller attention to *set in* as a phrasal verb.

Nouns

The use of *set* as a noun includes all four forms of the lemma:

set	6 out of 90 (7%)
sets	4 out of 16 (25%)
setting	5 out of 6 (83%)
settings	2 out of 2 (100%)

Both instances of *settings* are nominal, of course. All but one of *setting* are nominal, which suggests that the verb is not much used in the progressive tense. Collocations include *work setting, social setting, a suitable setting*. *Sets* as a noun includes *television sets*, and *chemistry sets*. *Set* as a noun includes: *the social set, the Martini set, theatre set, a fishing set*, and *a TV set*.

These are all characteristic nominal uses of *set* which have been captured because they happen to be immediately followed by *in*. They would be best treated in a description of the whole nominal pattern of *set*. Here, we merely note them and clear them out of the way.

Verbs

Among the verbal uses, there are two principal independent senses and two minor ones. Only the form *set* occurs – not even *sets*, suggesting a preponderance of past-tense usage.

Sense (i)

There are 25 instances of *set* followed by *in* and meaning approximately 'placed'. Seven are to do with physical position (including one about someone who *had his bones set in an awmbry*; only the *OED* was able to tell me that an awmbry was a kind of cupboard, and this was not an instance of bonesetting). Twelve more are to do with the disposition of buildings, streets, etc. Three are abstract placings (for example, 'high expectations, set in the commercial future for nuclear power'); two are variations of a well-known quotation (including the remarkable 'no man, or woman, is an island, set in a silver sea'). One is a figurative extension, 'set in a haze of blue'.

Sense (ii)

There are 18 instances of *set* followed by *in*, meaning approximately 'located', and characteristically used of plays, films, and stories, such as:

Clearly, the film, set in Glasgow and the Highlands . . .

Minor senses

Of the two minor independent senses of *set*, one is to do with typesetting and the other is *set in my memory*, which means in context 'fixed in place' and not just 'placed'.

In all the above verbal instances, the words *set* and *in* make an important collocation, and not the casual co-occurrence that was found in the nominal uses.

Sundry idioms

There are 20 instances of uses which I have termed idiomatic, because in addition to *set* and *in* there are other restrictions as well.

a.   Of these, six have *set in* followed by a possessive pronoun and the word *ways*, such as: . . . too old and *set in her ways* ever to change.
b.   Five are of the phrase *set in motion*.
c.   The remainder are one or two instances of *set in train, set in hand, set in order, set in a traditional mould, set in front of, set in juxtaposition to*, and *set in the balance*.

This group of idioms comprises items for which a much larger text corpus would be needed to see if it was justifiable to pick them out as I have done here. They all seem common enough, and it is a slight shock to see how rare they are in a large corpus – one has to keep in mind the extreme unlikelihood, on statistical grounds, of any of them occurring at all.

Set in as a phrasal verb

Up to this point, we have been merely clearing the ground for study of the phrasal verb *set in*. The original 114 instances of *set* followed by *in* are reduced to 29. Three of the four forms are involved, as follows:

set	16 out of 90 (18%)
sets	10 out of 16 (63%)
setting	1 out of 6 (17%)

The phrasal verb meaning is that if something *sets in*, it begins, and seems likely to continue and develop.

One of the first things to note about the phrasal verb is that it seems to occur typically in a small and/or minor part of a sentence. It is not easy to say exactly what gives this feeling but the following may be factors.

1. The clauses in which *set in* is chosen are in general rather short – six words or fewer in the main. The longer ones are longer because of an adjunct rather than the subject, which is in most cases a single word or an article and noun pair.
2. A number of the clauses are subordinate. With the samples available, it is not possible to assign status in every case, and there are some of clear main clauses; but I think the tendency to lower status should be noted.
3. *Set in* is final in the clause in 22 of the 29 cases, and sentence-final in nine of them, showing a clear tendency to end structures.

Observations such as those above are difficult to evaluate because we lack comparative stylistic data, but the following is a very typical example:

> . . . where the rot *set in* . . .

Word-forms
As suggested in **1** above, the majority of verbal groups are simple, containing just the form of *set*. All the occurrences of *sets* (10) are, of course, in the present tense, and at least nine of these deal with general states of affairs rather than the here-and-now. None of them is unambiguously in a main clause, where the tense choice relates directly to time.

Of the others, the vast majority are in the narrative past – either simple past (9) or pluperfect with *had* (4). There are single instances of *would*, *has*, and *was*, and one complex verb *started to set in* which again shows the narrative past.

From this we can conclude that there is a tendency towards reference to things past or things which are not sensitive to the passage of time, which goes reasonably well with the meaning of the phrase; the phrasal verb is not used in speculation about the future, or in statements about the present. For example:

> It was no wonder that disillusion *had set in* . . .

Subjects
The most striking feature of this phrasal verb is the nature of the subjects. In general, they refer to unpleasant states of affairs. Only three refer to the weather; a few are neutral, such as *reaction* and *trend*. The main vocabulary is *rot, decay, malaise, despair, ill-will, decadence, impoverishment, infection, prejudice, vicious (circle), rigor mortis, numbness, bitterness, mannerism, anticlimax, anarchy, disillusion, disillusionment, slump*. Not one of these is conventionally desirable or attractive.

The subjects of *set in* are also, as can be seen above, largely abstractions: several are nominalisations of another part of speech.

A dictionary entry

These observations characterise the phrase and illustrate its use. In a dictionary, a great deal of information has to be compressed into a couple of lines and it must be reasonably easy to read. The explanation given in the *Collins COBUILD English Language Dictionary* is:

> If something unpleasant *sets in*, it begins and seems likely to continue or develop.

The three examples cited in the dictionary illustrate many of the points made in this section. *A feeling of anticlimax set in*; the subject is one of the longer ones, but is abstract and fairly unpleasant. *It must be treated quickly before infection sets in* illustrates the very short subordinate clause with the present tense verb. *The bad weather has set in for the winter* is one of a small but distinctive group of concrete subjects that would very likely be recognised as appropriate by native speakers.
[...]

Questions, suggestions and issues to consider

1. What problems does Sinclair identify with investigating a verb such as *set* using a corpus?
2. What reasons are there for treating *set off* as one unit lexically?
3. Why would this sentence be unlikely?
       From that moment happiness set in.
4. Do the same as Sinclair. Take a phrasal verb and investigate its use in a corpus. A number of corpuses are available online; a list of them is given on the Website. Remember to go through all the steps that Sinclair does.

SEMANTIC ROLES OF THE SUBJECT   **D8**

Lynn M. Berk (1999) reprinted from one section of Chapter One of *English Syntax: from Word to Discourse*, New York: Oxford University Press, pp. 14–23.   **Lynn M. Berk**

In this reading Berk identifies a number of different 'meanings' for the subject of clauses. These go beyond the traditional idea of the subject as the agent or doer of an action (see also the reading by Michael Halliday in D11).

Berk uses one unfamiliar term, 'predicate', to refer to anything in a clause after the subject (i.e. verb plus objects and / or predicatives). In this approach the clause is always divided into two parts, the subject and predicate, before the latter is further divided. Some grammatical phenomena are easier to explain on this basis, e.g. the use of certain proforms – see B11).

Lynn M. Berk

Berk also discusses empty (dummy) 'it' and cataphoric (anticipatory) 'it' as subjects; these are dealt with in A11 and B11.

It is of course the semantic component of the subject that is most salient to speakers. Even small children intuitively recognise some sort of division between a 'doer' and an 'action.' In *Jack yelled, Bonnie studied all night*, and *The child put the candy in her pocket*, Jack, Bonnie, and the child are all 'doers' engaging in some activity. This division between the doer and the action is often what people point to when they distinguish between the subject and the predicate. But to <u>define</u> the subject as a doer and the predicate as an action would be misleading. In the following sentences, the subject is in no way doing anything – *Susan is tall; The wall looked dirty; My mother was mugged last night.* If the subject is not necessarily a doer, what is it?

Subjects play a number of different **semantic roles** in English and 'doer of the action' is only one of them. (These roles are also called **thematic** or **theta** roles in some syntactic models.) I've identified below some of the most common semantic roles played by subjects in English sentences. While this list is not exhaustive, it will give you a good sense of the semantic variety.

Agent Subjects

The agent subject is the classic doer of the action. An agent subject is an animate being that acts deliberately, with intent. Most speakers consider the agent the most typical subject. If you ask someone to construct a sentence out of thin air, it is likely that s/he will utter one with an agent subject. All of the agentive subjects below are engaging in wilful, deliberate action:

(a)

Catherine's boss *fired her.*
Fred *threw the frisbee.*
Joan *built a birdhouse.*
My sisters *washed the car.*
The dog *tore up the newspaper.*
The mare *devoured her oats.*

(b)

The little boy *yelled.*
Those kids *are whispering.*
My niece *smiled.*
Mom *sat down.*
The choir *sang.*
The bulldog *growled.*

The agents in column (a) are acting on someone or something, i.e., the direct object, while the agents in column (b) are not acting on anyone or anything else. In other words, an agent subject can occur with or without a direct object. (Direct objects will be discussed shortly.)

Whether or not amoebas, slugs, and other lower creatures actually have agency is probably a biological question and not a linguistic one. They certainly don't do things deliberately but they do engage in some of the same activities that higher creatures do – crawling, eating, swimming, etc. It is probably reasonable to treat them as agents even though they are acting instinctively rather than deliberately.

Of course we often anthropomorphise machines and treat them as agents, even though they are technically inanimate – *The ATM machine refuses to return my card; My computer ate my term paper; The engine threw a rod.*

Causer Subjects

A causer is either an animate being who acts without volition or an inanimate entity. We distinguish causers from agents because the semantics of the two roles are quite different. A sentence like *Rob tripped Roy* is potentially ambiguous; if *Rob tripped Roy* just to see Roy fall, *Rob* is an agent but if *Rob tripped Roy accidentally,* then *Rob* is a causer.

All the sentences below contain animate causer subjects.

Mavis *inadvertently touched the wet paint.*

Benjamin *accidently cut his finger.*

Susanna *bumped her head.*

Sometimes animate causers inadvertently affect another person's psychological state.

The clown *(accidentally) frightened my daughter.*

Betsy *hurt Rene's feelings inadvertently.*

Michael Jordan *amazes me.*

Nan *depresses her mother.*

Michael Jordan certainly doesn't know that he amazes me, but he has that effect, nevertheless. Nan may depress her mother because her mother is worried about her lifestyle, in which case Nan might be totally unaware of the effect she is having.

It's not always easy to tell whether an animate subject is an agent or a causer. Out of context, we don't know whether the following subjects are acting deliberately or not.

Butch disgusts everyone.

The child amused the adults.

Professor Smith intimidates her students.

Of course inanimate entities lack intention or volition by their very nature. Causers can be things like rocks, forces like tornadoes, or abstract qualities like love.

Hail *cracked our windshield.*

Oil *stained the carpet.*

A hurricane *damaged the village.*

The wind *broke the window.*

The revolution *terrified the king.*

Determination *saved the family.*

Hate *destroyed her.*

Unlike agents, causers always act on something or somebody else; in other words, they are always followed by a direct object.

Instrument Subjects

An instrument subject, as the label implies, is an inanimate entity which acts on someone or something else because it is being used as an instrument. In a sentence like *The key opened the safe*, we can assume that some unnamed agent is wielding the key because keys don't operate by themselves; in *The tweezers removed the splinter*, an unspecified agent is using the tweezers.

Sometimes an instrument subject allows a speaker to avoid taking responsibility. A child might say 'My ball broke your window' rather than 'I broke your window with my ball.' Here the ball is the instrument used by the child in the breaking of the window. On the other hand, in *The hail broke your window*, *the hail* is clearly a causer, not an instrument.

Instrument subjects are fairly unusual in English. We most often find instruments in (adverbial) prepositional phrases – *Meredith opened the safe **with a key***; *The nurse removed the splinter **with the tweezers***; *I broke the window **with my ball***. I will discuss these constructions at some length in Chapter 4.

Experiencer Subjects

Experiencer subjects are always animate, usually human. An experiencer experiences a sensory perception or a psychological state. In other words, the experiencer is not <u>doing</u> anything but is instead experiencing something through the senses or the mental faculties. The verbs that co-occur with experiencer subjects relate to consciousness; they are verbs that reflect 'private' internal states.

Each of our five senses allows for an agent subject and an experiencer subject. When an agent engages in a sensory activity, the agent actively employs the sense in question. An experiencer, however, has a sensory experience that was unsought. An agent looks at or listens to something on purpose. An experiencer sees because an event passes before the eyes and hears because a sound occurs within earshot. When *Mary tastes the sauce*, she does so by putting her spoon in the bowl and then to her lips. But when *Mary tastes mold on the bread*, her taste buds simply register a sensation; she has taken no direct action to engage that sense.

Sensory verb with agent subject	Sensory verb with experiencer subject
Joan looked at the scar. [She examined it carefully.]	**Joan** saw some blood. [She didn't want to see it.]
Alex listened to the argument. [He put his ear to the wall.]	**Alex** heard the argument. [He couldn't help it; they were screaming.]
Maria smelled the tulips. [She leaned over to do so.]	**Maria** smelled smoke. [It wafted in through the open window]
Tony tasted the wine. [He put the glass to his lips.]	**Tony** could taste pepper in the soup. [Too much had been added.]
Margaret felt the cloth. [She ran her fingers over it.]	**Margaret** felt some pain. [It came on her suddenly.]

A sentence like *Gene smelled the perfume* is ambiguous out of context.

As you can see, sometimes the semantic difference between an experiencer sub-ject and an agent subject is reflected in the verb and sometimes it's not. In the case of *look at* versus *see* and *listen to* versus *hear*, this semantic difference is **lexicalised**; in other words, the difference in meaning is signaled by different words. In the case of agentive *smell* and experiencer *smell*, the semantic difference is not lexicalised; the verbs take the same form.

Mental state verbs, more often called **psych-verbs**, also take experiencer subjects. These subjects are not really engaging in action. Normally, when an agent acts, the direct object is directly affected by that action. But none of the experiencer subjects below has a <u>direct</u> effect upon the direct object.

Joan *wants a raise.*	**Susan** *loves stamp collecting.*
Brad *thinks about food constantly.*	**Ted** *adores Sally.*
Mary *can't tolerate liver.*	**I** *believe them.*
Rich *doesn't believe in love.*	**Eric** *is dreaming.*
She *admires her mother.*	**Sheila** *trusts her son.*

The fact that Ted adores Sally and that Sheila trusts her son might theoretically affect both Sally and the son in many ways, but the sentences above are silent on that issue. In fact, Sally may not even know that Ted exists and Sheila's son may be totally unaware of her feelings.

Later we will examine experiencers that are functioning as direct objects and prepositional phrases.

Patient Subjects (and Patient Direct Objects)

I'll approach the issue of patient subjects indirectly, by first previewing another category – the direct object. It is probably apparent to you that a noun phrase which follows a verb is often affected by the action of the verb. A noun phrase which follows the verb and is affected by the action of that verb is typically a **direct object**. Direct objects are structures inside predicates.

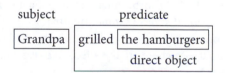

In *Jack dropped **the vase***, *Keisha opened **the door***, and *The insects killed the **plants***, the vase, the plants, and the door are the affected parties; they are also direct objects. In each of these sentences, an agent or causer subject has caused something to happen to the direct object. An event can also be expressed by eliminating the agent/causer and making the affected party the subject of the sentence. In ***The vase** fell*, the vase is not doing anything but rather is being acted upon by another unnamed force – somebody dropped it, the wind knocked it over, somebody kicked the table it was sitting on, etc. In ***The plants** died*, something killed the plants – insects, frost, the lawn mower, old age. In *The door* opened, someone or something caused this to happen – Keisha, the wind, a ghost. The traditional semantic label for an affected subject or an affected direct object is **patient**. (This label derives from the adjective *patient* which historically described one who 'bears or endures.') A patient is never volitional; a patient never exercises control; a patient is an entity to which things happen. You will find that most patient subjects co-occur with verbs that describe a change of state – *The water boiled; The chair broke; The water heater exploded; Rosa fell; The mirror shattered.*

In the examples below, you will find that none of the sentences with patient subjects contain direct objects.

Patient direct objects	Patient subjects
He laid **the book** on the table.	**The book** lay on the table.
The intruder opened **the door**.	**The door** opened.
Maria broke **the vase**.	**The vase** broke.
Dad thickened **the sauce**.	**The sauce** thickened.
We emptied **the pool**.	**The pool** emptied.
The soldier detonated **the bomb**.	**The bomb** exploded.
The earthquake shook **the house**.	**The house** collapsed.
The frost froze **my garden**.	**My garden** froze.
Alan darkens **his hair**.	**His hair** darkened.
Tom hung **the clothes** outside.	**The clothes** hung on the line.
The baby bounced **the ball**.	**The ball** bounced.

Semantically, a sentence like *Lance jumped* or *The woman rolled down the hill* is ambiguous out of context. Lance may be an agent subject who deliberately jumps or a patient subject who jumps involuntarily because something startles him. Similarly, *The woman rolled down the hill* can be interpreted as having an agent subject (she rolled on purpose) or a patient subject (something tripped her and she rolled). Usually when a sentence contains an animate subject which acts involuntarily, the agent/ instrument can be found elsewhere in the discourse, e.g., Lance jumped because someone set off a firecracker.

There can be only one patient in a simple sentence and if there is a direct object, it, not the subject, will carry that semantic role. In Susan *tripped the professor, Susan* must be an agent or a causer. Patient subjects occur only in intransitive or passive constructions. (Intransitivity will be explained shortly and the passive will be explained in Chapter 3.) In the sentence *Susan tripped* there is no direct object; Susan is clearly the affected party and thus a patient.

In his mystery novel *The Little Sister*, Raymond Chandler (1971) uses a series of patient subjects to underscore the fact that the hero has been knocked to the floor and cannot see his assailant, although he can hear the results of her activities. 'The door opened. A key rattled. The door closed. The key turned' (p. 54).

Described and Located Subjects

Some subjects are simply being characterised or described by the information in the predicate. These subjects always co-occur with copulas, verbs that have little independent meaning but relate the information in the predicate back to the subject. (Copulas will be discussed in detail later.)

> **Michael** is tall.   [*Tall* describes Michael]
> **Marty** seems pleasant.   [*Pleasant* describes Marty]
> **This food** is French.   [*French* characterises the food]
> **The bread** was stale.   [*Stale* describes the bread]

Other subjects are simply located in space. In the following sentences the location is double underlined.

> **Samson** is <u>in his doghouse</u>
> **The pots** are <u>in the bottom cupboard</u>
> **Tomi** is <u>on the porch</u>
> **The Centrust Building** stands <u>on Miami Avenue</u>.

Some Other Semantic Roles

Subjects play other semantic roles in the sentence and linguists don't always agree on how far to go in categorising these. For example, some of the empty *it* subjects above can also be paraphrased with subjects that express place.

> **Seattle** is foggy.
> **Alaska** is cold.
> **This bar** is smoky.

These are usually called **locative subjects** because they simply name a location. (Don't confuse locative subjects with <u>located</u> subjects.)

Subjects that express time are sometimes categorised semantically as **temporal subjects**.

> **Wednesday** is the baby's birthday.
> **Tomorrow** is our anniversary.
> **Weekends** are lonely.

Subjects like these have an adverbial quality and can in fact be paraphrased with adverb constructions – *It is rainy in Seattle; The baby's birthday is on Wednesday.* (We will discuss adverbs in Chapter 4.) Some grammarians (e.g., Quirk, Greenbaum, Leech, and Svartvik, 1972, p. 42) also establish an **event** category for subjects – *The party is at 9pm; The concert is over.*

It isn't clear just how far we should go in creating semantic categories for subjects or any other grammatical construction. Meaning is a continuum and we could go on forever creating ever finer semantic distinctions, but such an exercise has limited utility. You will find that different grammarians sometimes employ different labels and grammarians don't always agree on just what should be included in a given category, but the roles agent, instrument, experiencer, and patient are quite standard. The semantic categories discussed above can encompass a large number of English sentences and, as you will see later, most of these categories have important grammatical implications.

<table>
<tbody>
<tr><td colspan="2"><u>Summary of subject semantic roles</u></td></tr>
</tbody>
</table>

Agent subject	**Tom** threw his socks on the floor.
	My dog ate my term paper.
Causer subject	**Walter** stubbed his toe.
	The water damaged the furniture.
Instrument subject	**The key** opened the door.
	The chain saw felled the tree.
Experiencer subject	**Benny** wants a new sports car.
	I smell smoke.
Patient subject	**Our pipes** froze last night.
	The chair broke.
Described subject	**That hairdo** is hideous.
	The room grew dark.
Located subject	**Marlene** is in the yard.
	Terry was on the boat.

Questions, suggestions and issues to consider

1. a) Look at the verbs that are associated with described subjects. Do you notice anything about them? (See B8.)
   b) Look at the verbs that are associated with patient subjects. Do you notice anything about them? (See C7.)
2. Where would you fit a subject such as *the book* in
   The book talks about many topics
   into Berk's classification?
3. On page 237 Berk mentions the existence of direct objects (rather than subjects) in the role of experiencer. Can you think of some examples?

D9 **SPEECH ACTS**

Ronald Carter and Michael McCarthy

Ronald Carter and **Michael McCarthy** (2006) reprinted from *Cambridge Grammar of English*. Cambridge: Cambridge University Press, pp. 680–684.

The reading below is another extract from the Cambridge Grammar of English *(see also D6). It comprises the first part of the chapter on speech acts. It first of all describes the concept of speech act and then goes on to discuss how this relates to the clause types that were discussed in B9. As in the previous extract modals are again involved, showing just how versatile this group of auxiliaries is in English.*

Note that 'speech acts' do not only refer to speech, though they are more obvious there because of their interpersonal nature; they can also be identified in writing.

INTRODUCTION 408

This chapter (408–423) is concerned with interpersonal meanings of grammar, that is, how language enables us to get things done by ourselves or by others.

The term speech act refers to what the speaker or writer is doing in uttering a particular form of words. For example, an imperative form such as *Come here!* usually has the meaning of directing the listener to act in a certain way, and a clause such as *Can you pass me that book?* is likely to be a request to someone actually to pass the book, rather than an enquiry about the person's physical ability. Speech acts are concerned with the speaker's intention rather than the content-meaning of the utterance.

In everyday written and spoken interactions, common speech acts occur such as informing, directing, questioning, requesting, exemplifying, offering, apologising, complaining, suggesting, promising, permitting, forbidding, predicting and so on.

Speech acts may be divided into five broad types:

- Constatives:
  The speaker asserts something about the truth of a proposition, associated with acts such as: affirming, claiming, concluding, denying, exclaiming, maintaining, predicting, stating beliefs.
- Directives:
  The speaker intends to make the hearer act in a particular way, associated with acts such as: advising, asking, challenging, commanding, daring, forbidding, insisting, instructing, permitting, prohibiting, questioning, requesting, suggesting, warning.
- Commissives:
  The speaker commits to a course of action, associated with acts such as: guaranteeing, offering, inviting, promising, vowing, undertaking.
- Expressives (or acknowledgements):
  The speaker expresses an attitude or reaction concerning a state of affairs, associated with acts such as: apologising, appreciating, complimenting, condemning, congratulating, regretting, thanking, welcoming.
- Declarations:
  The speaker performs the speech act solely by making the utterance, for example: *I pronounce you man and wife; I declare this meeting closed; I name this ship x.*

This chapter focuses particularly on directives and commissives, as these are the speech acts in which grammatical choices figure most prominently, especially involving modal verbs and clause types (e.g. declarative versus interrogative).

The chapter describes how the clause structure contributes to different kinds of speech act (such as statements, questions, directives, etc.) (→ 410). We also consider the role of modal verbs in constructing speech acts such as requesting (*Would you hold this for me?*), offering (*I'll carry that for you*), promising (*I'll buy you one for your birthday*), suggesting (*We could stay in a bed-and-breakfast place*), permitting (*You can stay up till ten o'clock*), and so on (→ 411–420).

There are also verbs, referred to as speech act verbs, which a speaker can use to label a speech act explicitly (*I **promise** you I'll be there; He **denied** that he was involved in any way*) (→ 422). When these are used actually to perform the speech act (e.g. *I apologise*), they are called performative verbs (→ 422a).

The way speech acts are realised also involves politeness and the efforts speakers make to avoid loss of face, or dignity, for themselves and their interlocutors. For instance, a speaker who says *I **was wondering** if **I could** have a word with* you? will be heard as less direct, more polite and less imposing than one who says *I **wonder** if I **can** have a word with you*, which in turn is more polite and less imposing than someone who says *I **want to** have a word with you*. Tense and aspect choices are therefore also implicated in speech acts (→ 423).

On the larger scale, speakers need to perform functions such as opening con-versations, closing them, making sure they get their turn to speak, and so on. These are referred to in passing in this chapter (→ 423d) and are dealt with in greater detail in 104–122 'From discourse to social contexts'.

Speech acts can only be interpreted in context, and so it is often necessary to use quite long examples to illustrate how particular acts are realised, especially in face-to-face conversation, where speech acts such as requests, invitations, advice, etc. have to be carefully negotiated between speakers and listeners and are not necessarily realised in one phrase or clause.

Although we also exemplify speech acts in written texts, and although there are a potentially huge number of possible speech acts which could be discussed, our emphasis in this chapter will be on the performance of the most common, everyday, frequent speech acts which occur in spoken contexts, using grammatical resources. We focus particularly on those speech acts which are interactive, involving getting others to act in a particular way.

Typical speech acts which occur in academic contexts are covered in 140–154 'Grammar and academic English'.

WAYS OF REALISING SPEECH ACTS   409

Principally, speech acts are realised using the following resources:

- formulaic utterances (fixed expressions conventionally associated with particular speech acts): greetings such as *Hi, Goodbye*; expressions of reaction to events such as *Congratulations, Gosh!, Sorry, Excuse me, Pardon*.
- explicit lexical items (speech-act verbs or speech-act nouns) to perform or to label the speech act: *I **pronounce** you man and wife; My **advice** is not to use olive oil*.
- syntax (e.g. clause types, tense and aspect choices): *Was I surprised!* as an exclamation; ***Did** you want to say something?* as a polite invitation to someone to take the speaking turn.
- modal constructions (typically modal verbs): ***Can** I get you a drink?* uttered as an offer; *You **must** be patient* as a directive.
- prosodic means: a declarative clause plus rising intonation may indicate a question rather than a statement, e.g. A: *You'll be arriving late?* B: *Yes*.

CLAUSE TYPES AND SPEECH ACTS 410

The chapter **Clause types** (290–303) described the basic types of clause. The clause types most directly correspond to common speech acts as shown in the table below.

Typical correspondences between clause types and speech acts

clause type	typical speech act	examples
declarative	statement	*He works in Barsham.*
interrogative	question	*How long did it take?*
imperative	directive	*Put it all in a pile here.*
exclamative	exclamation	*How nice you look!*

However, such a direct correspondence is not always the case, and the clause types, especially declarative and interrogative, are used to perform other speech acts too, as shown in the table below.

Other possible correspondences between clause types and speech acts

clause type	possible speech acts	examples
declarative	question	A: *So you're going to be here about quarter past?* B: *Yeah quarter past, twenty past, yeah.*
	command	*You sit there.*
	offer	*I'll hold that for you.*
	exclamation	*There's a rat!*
interrogative	command	*Will you be quiet!*
	request	*Could you carry this for me?*
	intensified statement, or exclamation	*Was I embarrassed when I realised what had happened!* (I'm telling you I *was* embarrassed)
imperative	intensified warning about a particular course of action	*Do that again and I'm going to smack you.*
	offer	*Have a banana.*

Declarative clauses functioning as questions 410a
A declarative clause may function in context as a question. Although these are less frequent than interrogative questions, a common type of declarative question is when

a speaker checks an assumption or inference drawn from the ongoing conversation. Initial *so* and/or final *then* are common in such questions:

> [speaker A is recounting how an elderly relative has found a good place to live in her old age]
> A: *It's a little terraced house. And sort of very old fashioned but spotlessly clean and very cosy.*
> B: *Oh well.*
> A: *New kitchen new whatnot.*
> B: *Yeah.*
> A: *And a thousand and something a month.*
> B: *Yeah. **So you're pleased?***
> A: *Oh I'm relieved. Yes. Yes.*
> A: ***So you had a good day at work then?***
> B: *Yes it was all right.*

The declarative question may also be used as a comprehension check:

> [speaker A is on the phone to a printing company to check on the progress of a print job]
> A: *I'm ringing just to see if everything was okay with the job when Dave got it opened up and printing out and everything.*
> B: *Ah. No, he said this morning there were some fonts missing, Chris.*
> A: ***There were some fonts missing?***
> **B:** *Yes.*
> → **430 Declarative questions** on the intonation of declarative questions

Modal verbs and interrogative clauses as directives   410b

Because the bare imperative is considered extremely forceful and in many cases impolite in English, many directive speech acts (commands, instructions, requests, etc.) involve interrogative clauses and modal verbs:

> ***Will you*** *look at your handouts, now, please.*
> ***Can you*** *shut that door?*

These will be dealt with more fully in **412–413**.

Interrogative clauses as exclamations   410c

Occasionally, clauses with affirmative or negative interrogative structure can also be used as exclamations:

> [speaker is recounting a long and problematic journey]
> *Oh God, **was I** exhausted by the time I got home!*

> [looking at a small child]
> *Gosh! **Hasn't she grown!***

> *Sometimes life played cruel tricks . . . **Didn't it just!***

Imperative clauses as *offers and invitations* 410d

Friendly offers and invitations, which are commissive speech acts (→ 417–419), often occur in the imperative form:

A: *Have another drink.*
B: *Oh, no thanks, I've had enough thanks.*
A: *Come and see us some time if you're in the area.*
B: *Mm, yeah, that'd be nice. I will.*

MODAL EXPRESSIONS AND SPEECH ACTS 411

When modal expressions concerned with necessity, obligation, permission, etc. (→ 377–407 'Modality') are used in declarative and interrogative clauses, they often function as directives (realising speech acts such as commanding, instructing, suggesting, advising, warning, requesting) and commissives (promising, offering, inviting).

The modal verbs *can/could, will/would, shall/should, may/might, must, ought to* are used frequently in this way:

[swimming instructor to learner]
*You **shouldn't** be looking at me Joseph, you **should** be looking out of the window.*
(*should* is heard as a directive: the swimmer must do what the instructor says)

***Could** you just hang on a second, Joan?*
(*could* is heard as a directive; Joan can hardly refuse to do what the speaker asks)

*Here, I'**ll** carry that for you.*
(*'ll* is heard as an offer)

*We'**ll** get it done for you by Friday, no problem.*
(*'ll* is heard as a promise)

It is not just which modal verb is used but which clause type it occurs in that affects the speech act being performed. In the subsequent sections on modal verbs (412–420), declarative and interrogative uses are distinguished as the speech acts they signal may vary.

Each type of speech act is described in terms of its modal verb choices and its occurrence in declarative and interrogative clauses.

Questions, suggestions and issues to consider

1. Are speech acts really part of grammar?
2. What is the difference between declaratives and declarations in the above text?
3. Take a speech act such as suggesting and try to think of all the possible ways of realising it in English. Then analyse them according to their clause type.
4. Think of all the ways in which a modal auxiliary such as *can* can be used and think of all the possible speech acts it can be involved in.

D10 CONDITIONALS

In this section there are two readings. They are on the same topic, sentences expressing conditions, and both are pedagogic in nature, being aimed at teaching materials which present a misleadingly simple (and, at the same time, complicated) picture of this area of English grammar.

Conditional sentences are generally equated with sentences with 'if', i.e. multiple complex sentences with a subordinate, adverbial clause introduced by 'if', for example:

'If you listen carefully, you can hear the sea.'

However, there is a mismatch between form and function here (cf. B9). On the one hand, 'if' does not always signal conditions. Sometimes it can have an idea of 'concession' (i.e. similar to 'although'), especially when used in a verbless clause:

'They were happy, <u>if exhausted</u>.'

On the other hand, there are many ways of expressing conditions that do not use 'if': other conjunctions such as 'provided that', 'as/so long as'; other constructions, such as an imperative plus 'and' (i.e. a compound rather than a complex sentence):

'Do that and you'll be sorry.' ('If you do that . . .')

or inversion:

'Had I known about the problem earlier, I could have done something.' (See A11)

Nevertheless, it is clearly sentences with 'if' that are the subject of the two readings.

Michael Lewis

D10.1 Michael Lewis (1986) reprinted from *The English Verb*, Hove: Language Teaching Publications, pp. 148–150.

2 Conditional Sentences

It is the verb phrase not the sentence which is the fundamental unit requiring analysis. Certain combinations are, for semantic reasons, highly frequent, while others are less frequent or even impossible.

A particular misunderstanding frequently arises in the teaching of so-called conditional sentences. It is common to teach three 'basic' kinds:

1.   *If he comes I'll ask him.*
2.   *If he came I'd ask him.*
3.   *If he'd come I would've asked him.*

These are frequently referred to as:

1.   The first conditional, or *likely* conditions.
2.   The second conditional, or *unlikely* conditions.
3.   The third conditional, or *impossible* conditions.

The three examples given are all well-formed sentences of types which would be relatively frequent in much written English. Readers may care, however, to examine the following list and mark the sentences which they consider to be well-formed:

1. If he would come, I'd ask him.
2. If he'll come, I'll ask him.
3. If he's come, I'll ask him.
4. If he's going to come, I'd ask him.
5. If he could come, I'd ask him.
6. If he can come, I'll ask him.
7. If he might come, I'll ask him.
8. If he comes, I'm going to ask him.
9. If we hadn't been going to ask him, he wouldn't have been invited.
10. If he hadn't been invited by us, he wasn't going to get an invitation at all.

In fact *all* of these examples are well-formed English sentences. If students are taught *only* the first, second and third conditionals, they will know only a small, admittedly highly frequent, sub-set of the possibilities. It is not necessary to teach the fourth conditional, the fifth conditional, etc., but it is important to recognise that the possibility arises from the *meaning* of the individual clauses and that there are many more possibilities than those frequently presented in language teaching textbooks. The explanation of the use of a form in a conditional sentence is exactly the same as that of its occurrence in any other utterance. The underlying principle behind this is that each main verb phrase is treated independently.

An understanding of the importance of the verb phrase rather than the sentence has two important practical consequences, one at lower levels and one for more advanced students.

As soon as we turn our attention to the spoken language we note that interchanges such as the following are common:

A   *Are we going to ask him?*
B   *If we have to.*

A   *Are you going to bring your car?*
B   *If it would help.*

A   *Are you going on Saturday?*
B   *If it doesn't rain.*

In traditional structuralist courses 'the conditional' is taught at a relatively late stage. In a communicative syllabus this is most unsatisfactory – it is by no means true that because one is a comparative beginner one only wishes to make unqualified remarks. The teaching of 'the conditional' as if it were a special form is theoretically unsound. There is no reason at all why expressions introduced by *if* or *unless* cannot be introduced into a course at a comparatively early stage. This increases the student's communicative ability, and provides an introduction to the more complex conditional structures which are comparatively common in the written language.

Teachers should also note that introducing *would* as 'the English conditional' is extremely, and unnecessarily, confusing. *Would* frequently occurs in conditional sentences but, as we have seen with the Principle of General Use, it is important to avoid teaching a partial truth as a generally applicable rule. The following are in no sense 'conditional':

Would you like a cup of tea?

It would take about three days.

It is not uncommon to argue that such sentences contain a 'covert' condition but, if that is the case, so does: *I'm taking my umbrella* (*even if it isn't raining yet*).

Incidentally, like many conditional clauses in English, this clause does not contain *would* – further evidence that *would* is not 'the conditional' in English. English simply does not have 'a conditional tense'. These difficulties are avoided quite simply if *would* is treated as a modal auxiliary, and not referred to as 'the conditional'. With modern functional methodology this is not a very radical suggestion. It is clear that expressions such as *Would you like a cup of tea?* are best explained as 'when you want to offer somebody something, or invite them to do something, use *Would you like . . .* or *Would you like to . . .*'. The functional description is a sufficient explanation of the meaning *and* use of the form. It is confusing and unnecessary to dissect its structural characteristics.

For many school students the main problem with conditionals is one of manipulating the various auxiliaries which occur. Most mistakes are mistakes of form. This suggests that school students do require practice of the forms of such highly occurrent uses as the so-called first, second and third conditionals.

At higher levels, however, students are frequently inhibited from forming natural expressions of their own because of the restrictive rules with which they have been presented. For such students it would be helpful to present them with a large list similar to that presented above and invite them to:

(a) divide the list into those forms which are possible and those which are not
(b) discuss together the *possible* patterns.

The truth towards which they should be led is that the possibilities in conditionals are identical to those in 'non-conditional' uses.

Dave Willis

D10.2 Dave Willis (1994) reprinted from 'The Lexical Approach', in M. Bygate, A. Tonkyn and E. Williams, *Grammar and the Language Teacher*, Hemel Hempstead: Prentice Hall International, pp. 59–60.

(b) The 'second conditional'

Many ELT grammars and coursebooks talk about the 'three conditionals':

1. *If it rains we'll get wet.*
2. *If it rained we would get wet.*
3. *If it had rained we would have got wet.*

These patterns are highlighted for the learner and offered as paradigms. This is done, presumably, in the belief that the learner will be able to generalise from these patterns. Of course other modals can be used in conditionals; for example:

4. *If it rains, we could/may/might get wet.*
5. *If it rained, we could/might get wet.*
6. *If it had rained, we could/might have got wet.*

There are 'mixed' conditionals:

7. *If United had won they'd be top of the table.*
8. *If they caught the train they'd be here any minute.*

There are many sentences in which *if* marks a condition but in which the subordinate clause is not conditional:

9. *Even if I had the time, I feel too tired.*
10. *If you want a beer there's one in the fridge.*

Conditionals are simply the sum of their parts. The second conditional contains a main clause with the modal *would*. The COBUILD 7.6 million corpus, which was used for the early research which went into the production of the *Collins COBUILD English Dictionary* (1987) contains just under 15,000 occurrences of the word *would*. It is the forty-fourth most frequent word in the corpus and the most frequent modal, much more frequent than *will*, for example, which has 8,800 occurrences. In around half of its 15,000 occurrences, *would* is used to talk of events which are of a hypothetical nature at the time of being mentioned, either because they are in the future, or because they depend on events which may or may not occur. Examples include:

A picnic wouldn't be any fun without you.
Wouldn't it be quicker to chop it down?
The Tempest would make a wonderful film.
I suspect that the West Germans would still be a bit cautious.

In these examples a condition has been established earlier in the text, or is implicit in the word *would*. This accounts for around 7,500 of the occurrences in the corpus. A subcategory of this, accounting for a further 1,200 occurrences, is *would* used in explicitly conditional sentences; for example:

I would be surprised if sterling strengthened.
It would be funny if it wasn't so sad.

In these sentences *would* is combined with the past tense. Hypothesis is also one of the meanings carried by the past tense; for example:

I wish I lived in a caravan.
Suppose you got lost.

The second conditional does not create these meanings, it simply brings them together.

It is clear that all the modals, not only *will* and *would*, are commonly found in conditionals, and that *would* used to talk of hypothetical events and situations is much more commonly found without *if* than with *if*. Most modals are taught lexically. Students learn that *might* and *could*, for example, are used for possibility. It is not thought necessary to teach as standard patterns conditionals like 4, 5 and 6 above. Provided that learners know what *if* means, and they know what *might* and *could* mean, and they know that the past tense is used for hypothesis, it is assumed that they can create for themselves sentences like 4, 5 and 6. In exactly the same way, if *would* is taught lexically with its main meaning of hypothesis, learners will be able to generate for themselves sentences like 2.

The strategy of highlighting word meaning is a much more productive one than the strategy of teaching structural patterns. If the second conditional is taught as a means of introducing learners to the meaning of the word *would* and the hypothetical meaning of the past tense, this seems to me to be an economical teaching strategy. Learners may then be led to the generalisation that *would* also occurs in all sorts of environments without *if*. But this is not generally what happens. The second conditional is normally taught as if it had some life of its own, as if there were something unique about this combination of the past tense and the modal *would*. But both these elements carry the meaning of hypothesis quite independently of the second conditional. In fact, *would* in conditionals is no more difficult than *might* or *could* in conditionals. It is simply more common.

Questions, suggestions and issues to consider

1. What are the criticisms that Lewis and Willis make of the three-conditional model?
2. What differences are there between the two readings? For example, which supplies more evidence?
3. If you learnt English formally in school, were conditional sentences presented to you in this way? Were any 'exceptions' mentioned? What labels were used for the three types? Some accounts mention another conditional, the 'zero' conditional, where both tenses are present: (*If he is given the role, I quit.*) but this does not help to solve the basic problem.
4. Select a sentence from the Willis reading that could be used as a quote attacking the three-conditional approach.
5. Compare this pedagogic problem with others mentioned in the book, for example the 'rule' for second mention article usage (see B3). How similar are they?

SUBJECT, ACTOR, THEME

Michael Halliday (2004) reprinted from *An Introduction to Functional Grammar* (3rd edition, revised by Christian Matthiessen), Arnold: London, pp. 53–57.

This reading takes us into some new areas: grammatical theory (how do we go about describing grammar, what are the possibilities?), the history of grammatical description, and so on. However, its main aim is to discuss the ambiguity of the word 'subject'. There is a popular interpretation of this word as well as a terminological, grammatical, one. Compare

What is the subject of this paragraph?

What is the subject of this verb?

The two possibilities come together in

What is the subject of this sentence?

But Halliday goes further than this, identifying three possible meanings that are relevant to language description.

His psychological subject, which he later calls 'theme' was referred to briefly in A11 as 'topic'. Note that this concept, whatever it is called, does not correspond to the idea of 'given' information as described in A11, though the two often coincide.

'Actor' here refers to what we have called 'agent' elsewhere.

One of the concepts that is basic to the Western tradition of grammatical analysis is that of Subject. Since this is a familiar term, let us take it as the starting point for investigating the functions in an English clause.

Consider the clause:

the duke gave my aunt this teapot

In accordance with the syntactic principles established by medieval grammarians, which were themselves based on the grammarians of ancient Greece and Rome, each clause contains one element that can be identified as its Subject (see e.g. Covington, 1984; Seuren, 1998: 34–7) and in this instance, the Subject would be *the duke*.

Here are some other clauses with the Subject shown in italic:

Oh, *I'm* just starving and *all* [[*you'll feed me*]] is something rotten, or something [[*I hate*]]. *I* hate lasagne and *I* don't want rotten carrots – *I* only want salted carrots. (Text 76)

I wasn't making a cubby house; *that* wasn't a cubby house. – What were *you* making with it, then? (Text 76)

Adam, do *you* like red or white? – *I* would like red but only if *you're* opening it. (UTS/Macquarie Corpus)

(S04:) *That's* [[how *my nan* used to do them in Manchester]] – parboil them. – (S02:) What parboil them? – (S04:) Yeah. – (S01:) Did *she*? – (S04:) Yeah. (UTS/Macquarie Corpus)

They fit me. – Do *they*? – *They* will. (UTS/Macquarie Corpus)

The thought occurred to me on Air Force One a few weeks ago when *I* was escorted into President Clinton's cabin for a farewell interview. (Text 110)

[. . .]

It is possible to conclude from these examples that 'Subject' is the label for a grammatical function of some kind (*subject* being the Latin translation of a word in Greek, *hypokeimenon*, used as a grammatical term by Aristotle in the sense of 'that which is laid down, or posited'). There seems to be something in common, as regards their status in the clause, to all the elements we have labelled in this way. But it is not so easy to say exactly what this is; and it is difficult to find in the grammatical tradition a definitive account of what the role of Subject means.

Instead, various interpretations have grown up around the Subject notion, ascribing to it a number of rather different functions. These resolve themselves into three broad definitions, which can be summarised as follows:

(i)   that which is the concern of the message
(ii)   that of which something is being predicated (that is, on which rests the truth of the argument)
(iii)   the doer of the action.

These three definitions are obviously not synonymous; they are defining different concepts. So the question that arises is, is it possible for the category of 'Subject' to embrace all these different meanings at one and the same time?

In *the duke gave my aunt this teapot*, it is reasonable to claim that the nominal group *the duke* is, in fact, the Subject in all these three senses. It represents the person with whom the message is concerned; the truth or falsehood of the statement is vested in him; and he is represented as having performed the action of giving.

If all clauses were like this one in having one element serving all three functions, there would be no problem in identifying and explaining the Subject. We could use the term to refer to the sum of these three definitions, and assign the label to whichever element fulfilled all the functions in question. But this assumes that in every clause there is just one element in which all three functions are combined; and this is not the case. Many clauses contain no such element that embodies all three. For example, suppose we say

     this teapot my aunt was given by the duke

– which constituent is now to be identified as the Subject?

There is no longer any one obvious answer. What has happened in this instance is that the different functions making up the traditional concept of Subject have been split up among three different constituents of the clause. The duke is still represented as the doer of the deed; but the message is now a message concerning the teapot, and its claim for truth is represented as being vested in my aunt.

When these different functions came to be recognised by grammarians as distinct, they were first labelled as if they were three different *kinds* of Subject. It was still implied that there was some sort of a superordinate concept covering all three, a general notion of Subject of which they were specific varieties.

The terms that came to be used in the second half of the nineteenth century, when there was a renewal of interest in grammatical theory (*see* Seuren, 1998: 120–33, on the subject–predicate debate that lasted from the nineteenth century until the 1930s), were 'psychological Subject', 'grammatical Subject' and 'logical Subject'.

(i)   Psychological Subject meant 'that which is the concern of the message'. It was called 'psychological' because it was what the speaker had in his mind to start with, when embarking on the production of the clause.

(ii)   Grammatical Subject meant 'that of which something is predicated'. It was called 'grammatical' because at the time the construction of Subject and Predicate was thought of as a purely formal grammatical relationship; it was seen to determine various other grammatical features, such as the case of the noun or pronoun that was functioning as Subject, and its concord of person and number with the verb, but it was not thought to express any particular meaning.

(iii) Logical Subject meant 'doer of the action'. It was called 'logical' in the sense this term had had from the seventeenth century, that of 'having to do with relations between things', as opposed to 'grammatical' relations, which were relations between symbols.

In the first example, all these three functions are conflated, or 'mapped' on to one another, as shown in Figure 2-11.

The duke	gave my aunt this teapot
psychological Subject grammatical Subject logical Subject	

Figure 2-11 Same item functioning as psychological, grammatical and logical Subject

In the second example, on the other hand, all three are separated (Figure 2-12). In *this teapot my aunt was given by the duke*, the psychological Subject is *this teapot*. That is to say, it is 'this teapot' that is the concern of the message – that the speaker has taken as the point of embarkation of the clause. But the grammatical Subject is *my aunt*: 'my aunt' is the one of whom the statement is predicated – in respect of whom the clause is claimed to be valid, and therefore can be argued about as true or false. Only the logical Subject is still *the duke*: 'the duke' is the doer of the deed – the one who is said to have carried out the process that the clause represents.

this teapot	my aunt	was given by	the duke
psychological Subject	grammatical Subject		logical Subject

Figure 2-12 Psychological, grammatical and logical Subject realised by different items

As long as we concern ourselves only with idealised clause patterns, such as *John runs* or *the boy threw the ball*, we can operate with the label Subject as if it referred to a single undifferentiated concept. In clauses of this type, the functions of psychological, grammatical and logical Subject all coincide. In *the boy threw the ball*, *the boy* would still be Subject no matter which of the three definitions we were using, like *the duke* in the first of our examples above.

But as soon as we take account of natural living language, and of the kinds of variation that occur in it, in which the order of elements can vary, passives can occur as well as actives, and so on, it is no longer possible to base an analysis on the assumption that these three concepts are merely different aspects of one and the same general notion. They have to be interpreted as what they really are – three separate and distinct functions. There is no such thing as a general concept of 'Subject' of which these are different varieties. They are not three kinds of anything; they are three quite different things. In order to take account of this, we will replace the earlier labels by separate ones which relate more specifically to the functions concerned:

psychological Subject: Theme
grammatical Subject: Subject
logical Subject: Actor

We can now relabel Figure 2-12 as in Figure 2-13.

this teapot	my aunt	was given by	the duke
Theme	Subject	Actor	

Figure 2-13 Theme, Subject and Actor

In *the duke gave my aunt this teapot*, the roles of Theme, Subject and Actor are all combined in the one element *the duke*. In *this teapot my aunt was given by the duke*, all three are separated. All the additional combinations are also possible: any two roles may be conflated, with the third kept separate. For example, if we keep *the duke* as Actor, we can have Theme = Subject with Actor separate, as in Figure 2-14(a); Subject = Actor with Theme separate as in (b); or Theme = Actor with Subject separate as in Figure 2-14(c).

In any interpretation of the grammar of English we need to take note of all these possible forms, explaining how and why they differ. They are all, subtly but significantly, different in meaning; at the same time they are all related, and related in a systematic way. Any comparable set of clauses in English would make up a similar **paradigm**. Often, of course, there are not three distinct elements that could carry the functions of Theme, Subject and Actor, but only two, as in Figure 2-15 (**not included**). [. . .]

And often no variation at all is possible, if there is only one element that can have these functions; for example *I ran away*, where *I* is inevitably Theme, Subject and Actor. (Even here there is a possibility of thematic variation, as in *run away I did* or *the one who ran away was me*; see Chapter 3.) On the other hand, while explaining all these variants, we also have to explain the fact that the typical, **unmarked**

(a)

my aunt	was given	this teapot by	the duke
Theme			Actor
Subject			

(b)

this teapot	the duke	gave to	my aunt
Theme	Subject		
	Actor		

(c)

by	the duke	my aunt	was given	this teapot
	Theme	Subject		
	Actor			

Figure 2-14 Different conflations of Subject, Actor and Theme

form, in an English declarative (statement-type) clause, is the one in which Theme, Subject and Actor are conflated into a single element. That is the form we tend to use if there is no prior context leading up to it, and no positive reason for choosing anything else.

Questions, suggestions and issues to consider

1. What does 'unmarked' (on the last line of page 254) mean?
2. How does 'actor' relate to the semantic roles of subject that Berk discusses in D8?
3. Look at the rearrangement in this example. What names have we given to the processes involved?

    This teapot my aunt was given by the duke.
4. Take a short text and try to identify the subjects, actors and themes in it.

GRAMMAR IN THE CONSTRUCTION OF ONLINE DISCUSSION MESSAGES

Ann Hewings and Caroline Coffin **Ann Hewings** and **Caroline Coffin** (2004) reprinted from *Applying English Grammar*, Caroline Coffin, Ann Hewings and Kieran O'Halloran (eds), London: Arnold, pp. 137–143.

In this research article, Hewings and Coffin investigate computer-mediated communication (CMC). Although it is written language, it has many of the features of speech, and their basic aim is to see to whether it is more similar to speech or writing. For this purpose they compiled a corpus of conference messages posted by students regarding an assignment, and a corpus of the essays written for that assignment. For the sake of comparison, they also used data from the conversation and academic prose corpora from the Longman Grammar of Spoken and Written English *(Biber et al. 1999).*

These were then compared according to two measures thought to be indicative of the spoken/written distinction: the frequency of personal pronouns, and the frequency of coordinating conjunctions. The results are shown below.

The paper has been greatly shortened; two general sections from the beginning — 8.1 (Introduction) and 8.2 (Background to this Study) — have been omitted, as well as further findings and the conclusion.

8.3 A Hybrid Medium

The premise on which this research project was based was that communication between tutors and students using CMC would be influenced by the medium itself and that CMC as a new and evolving medium would affect the way learning took place. At its simplest, the medium of communication is characterised in terms of whether the language is spoken or written. Studies such as those by Biber and associates (1999), Carter and McCarthy (e.g. 1995), Brazil (1995) and Halliday (2002: 323–52) describe grammatical differences that result from the contexts of spoken interaction as opposed to written. Carter and McCarthy go furthest in identifying grammatical realisations associated not just with speech but with specific contexts of use, such as the language used in telling stories, recounting experiences, or casual conversation. Writing too displays grammatical differences which are context-dependent. The choices of both grammar and lexis are likely to be very different between, for instance, a letter to a friend and an essay written for assessment purposes. It is not enough then just to focus on writing or speech as the descriptive categories for 'medium'.

If we are able to identify grammatical choices that are more commonly associated with writing or speech, we should also be able to characterise the grammatical choices made in CMC. However, this is complicated by the fact that CMC can be influenced not just by the medium but by other variables as we mentioned earlier (how well the CMC contributors know each other, their communicative purpose, and the subject matter being discussed). In addition, as Baron notes in relation to e-mail, the speed at which the technology is evolving suggests that people are having to familiarise themselves with a medium that is not yet stable:

> Email is more a moving linguistic target than a stable system, thereby complicating the problem of constructing a unified grammar of email. Three major sources of fluidity in email bear note: evolution of the *technology*, growth in *usership*, and partial *maturation* of the genre.
>
> (Baron, 1998: 144)

Despite this lack of stability there are now some studies looking at the grammar of emails and other forms of CMC. Table 8.1 indicates a variety of features differentiated on the grounds of their typicality in speech or writing. The letter C indicates which of these features have also been found commonly in emails/CMC.

Table 8.1 Email/CMC grammar in relation to spoken and written modes

Lexico-grammatical feature	Mode	
	Speech	Writing
Lexical:		
Pronouns (e.g. *I, you, we* vs *he, she, it, they*)	heavily first, second person C	heavily third person
Adjectives and adverbs	Heavier use of attributive adjectives and amplifiers C	Varied
Type/token ratio:	Low	high C
Sentential/syntactic:		
Lexical/grammatical density	Lower	higher C
Adverbial subordinate clauses (e.g. since . . . , while . . .)	Less frequent	common C
Disjunctions (e.g. however . . . , in contrast . . .)	Less frequent	common C
Tense	present C	present, past, future
Contractions	many C	few

Source: Adapted from Baron (1998: 153)

The features listed in Table 8.1 were identified by Collot and Belmore (1996) and Yates (1996) (both cited in Baron, 1998) and were based on an analysis of 'one to many dialogues', that is, where a message is sent out to a number of recipients such as is the case in computer conference discussions. We followed up this work by examining the grammatical features of our CMC data to help us understand how people are utilising the new medium and to what extent their interaction more closely resembles speech as it would in a face-to-face tutorial or whether it is more like written academic prose.

8.4 Methodology 1: Corpus Analysis

To answer the question 'Does CMC exhibit differences in grammatical choices from conventional speech or writing?' we made use of an electronic corpus of texts and concordancing software. We aimed to give an empirical basis to our informal impressions that electronic messages in the conference environment show similarities with speech even though they are in fact written text.

To make comparisons between speech, writing, and CMC we collected both CMC messages and conventional written essays from students and made use of a published source of conversational data described below. The messages sent to the conferences and written as essays formed a 'corpus', a collection of texts, that could be examined using the computer software *WordSmitH Tools* (Scott, 1996). Two sub-corpora were prepared – the conference messages (142,078 words) and the essays (110,112 words). Texts in both sub-corpora were prepared for analysis by first converting them into rich text format which is readable by the software, and then by tidying up the resultant files. For example, some HTML characters had become embedded in the conference text messages and these were deleted. Where people had sent messages as attachments these were opened and also included in the sub-corpus. The corpus as a whole was left as plain text, that is, it was not grammatically tagged so only words and not parts of speech could be searched for.

In addition to this corpus we also made use of the detailed corpus analysis carried out by Biber *et al.* (1999) published as the *Longman Grammar of Spoken and Written English* (LGSWE). The LGSWE is prefaced on the understanding that grammatical features vary in different contexts and under different circumstances. This is illustrated throughout by comparing the distribution of different grammatical features among groups of texts classified as the registers of *conversation, fiction, news* and *academic prose*. For the purposes of this study, we use the LGSWE findings for conversation to allow comparisons across spoken, written, and CMC interactions. We also give their figures for grammatical structures in academic prose as representative of writing similar to, or more formal than, our student essay data.

The first task was to ascertain whether or not the written conference compositions represented the spoken-written hybrid reported in emails/CMC by Baron. This would enable us to see whether communication in the conferences showed any evidence of the dialogue and interaction that take place in face-to-face tutorials or whether they were more typical of academic writing. In general, tutorials are seen as more successful if students interact with each other as well as the tutor and reflect on their learning. Two simple measures of interactivity were used relating to pronouns and coordinators. The first was based on the findings of Collot and Belmore (1996) and Yates (1996) (summarised in Table 8.2) on personal pronoun usage. In spoken interaction there is greater use of personal pronouns such as *I* and *we*, so if the interaction taking place has spoken-like qualities, pronoun usage is likely to be higher than in traditional written academic prose. A second comparison was based on the findings reported in the LGSWE, which identified marked differences in the distribution of common coordinators (*and*, *but* and *or*) between conversation and academic prose. Both pronouns and coordinators are relatively easy to measure numerically using corpus analysis software and comparisons were made between the CMC and essay data collected for this research and between the findings reported in LGSWE.

8.5 Results and Discussion 1

All personal pronouns and corresponding possessive and reflexive forms (with the exception of *it*, *its*, *itself*) were counted in the conference messages and essays subcorpora. The raw figures were converted into frequencies per million words to make them comparable with each other and with the data provided by graphs in LGSWE. Table 8.2 shows the comparison between first and second person pronoun usage between the conferences and essays sub-corpora.

Table 8.2 Frequencies of first and second person personal pronouns

First and second person pronouns	Conference messages	Essays
Total no. of occurrences	6515	1544
No. per million words	45,862	14,022

The findings support the summary of evidence given by Baron in Table 8.1 above: that first and second person pronoun use is much higher in email/conference messages than in academic prose. Despite the writing being by the same people and on the same topics, first and second person pronouns are three times more common in the conference messages, indicating that interpersonal interactivity in the conference is high.

Biber *et al.* (1999) in LGSWE do not break down their data on pronoun usage in conversation and academic prose to first and second person versus third person. Their statistics indicate only overall usage of personal pronouns. LGSWE data contains all personal and reflexive pronouns, including *it*, *its* and *itself*. To make our data more comparable it was therefore necessary to include third person pronouns. However, we stopped short of including *it*, *its*, and *itself* for two reasons. First, personal pronouns are used as an indicator of the more personal and involved stance of the author. Pronouns such as *I* or *you* are therefore of importance, whereas *it* is likely to be less significant. Second, *it* has functions other than just as a personal pronoun (see Chapter 6 by Hewings and Hewings, this volume). It would have been necessary to edit concordance lines manually for non-personal pronoun uses of *it* and then to run the frequency counts. Had the corpus been grammatically tagged, as was that used by Biber *et al.* (1999), this procedure could have been automated. The personal pronoun comparison with our corpora needs therefore to be treated as a very rough guide only.

Table 8.3 Frequencies of personal pronouns

Personal pronouns	Conference messages	Essays conversation	LGSWE academic	LGSWE prose
Total no. of occurrences	8657	3692	–	–
No. per million words	60,931	33,529	138,000 (approx)	18,000 (approx)

The results in Table 8.3 show the same general trends in the data as we observed in Table 8.2, but the variation between conference messages and essays is not as great as that between conversation and academic prose. This finding supports the description of CMC messages as a spoken–written hybrid. The conference messages show features of speech in that pronoun usage indicates a personal dialogue between participants. However, as they are written forms and the interactants are not in a face-to-face context, the contrasts are not as marked as the LGSWE findings.

The research by Biber *et al.* also identities a difference in the use of common coordinators (*and*, *but*, and *or*) in different registers. *And* is the most frequent coordinator, linking both phrases and clauses throughout their corpus, but it is, surprisingly, less frequent in conversation than in academic prose. Example 1 from the academic prose sub-corpus used by LGSWE (Biber *et al.*, 1999: 83) shows both uses. The first and third uses serve to link phrases (*and* potassium, *and* iron) whereas the second and fourth uses serve to link clauses (*and those which are, and are transferred*).

1. A distinction is needed between elements, which include nitrogen, phosphorus and potassium, which are mobile in the phloem and those which are comparatively immobile, for example, calcium, boron and iron, and are transferred only slowly to the developing organ.

The authors of LGSWE suggest that *and* is less frequent in conversation than in academic prose because in conversation phrases are simpler and do not need coordination. In contrast, *but* occurs more frequently in conversation because, although it cannot be used to coordinate noun phrases, it serves to string together clauses in which ideas are contrasted without too much pre-planning. *But* allows the speaker to modify a statement (example 2) and others to disagree (example 3):

2. I think he will have salad but he doesn't like tomatoes.
3. A: The golden rule is if you're reversing you must look behind you!
    B: Yeah, but she said she did.

(Biber *et al.*, 1999: 82)

Or is the least frequent of the coordinators but is relatively more common in academic prose. This may be because academic discourse frequently considers alternatives (example 4) and explains terminology (example 5):

4. Such movements may come from local or regional deformation of the land or from a global rise or fall of sea level.
5. According to Chamberlain and Moulton, these broke into small chunks, or planetesimals, which went flying as cold bodies into orbits around the Sun.

(Biber *et al.*, 1999: 82)

Frequencies for *and, but,* and *or* were obtained in our two sub-corpora and the results made comparable with those in LGSWE (see Table 8.4).

Table 8.4 Frequencies of simple coordinators (per million words)

Occurrences/ million words	Conference messages	Essays	LGSWE conversation	LGSWE academic prose
and	24,000	34,783	20,000 (approx)	27,000 (approx)
but	4237	2942	7000 (approx)	3000 (approx)
or	3829	5030	2000 (approx)	6000 (approx)

Again, we found that trends are similar. *And* and *or* are used less frequently in conference messages and conversation than in essays and academic prose. *But* is used more frequently in conference messages and conversation than in essays and academic prose. However, as would be expected, given the differences between the corpora, the proportions differ.

In interpreting these comparisons we need to be careful regarding the findings concerning *and*. LGSWE notes that in conversation 80 per cent of occurrences of *and* are to link phrases (single nouns or noun phrases) such as in 'individual personalities **and** learning styles'. In contrast, in academic text 35 per cent of occurrences are as clause-level connectors, 'Does it only happen in a formal framework **and** is it only something experts deal with'. As neither clauses nor noun phrases were tagged within our corpus, it was not possible to verify statistically whether this was the case in the data examined here. However, qualitative observation of the data suggests that *and* does function in this contrasting fashion in different types of conference message. This is returned to in the qualitative analysis discussed below.

Use of a corpus methodology enabled us to observe quantitative trends in the use of certain key grammatical indicators. Analysis of pronouns and coordinators confirms a difference in grammatical choices between the sub-corpora. Personal involvement as indicated by pronoun usage is more significant in conference messages. However, it is still higher in student essays than in the LGSWE academic prose sub-corpus, perhaps indicating that essays in applied linguistics have a more personal dimension than in non-disciplinary specific texts composed by professional academics.

With regard to coordination, we can say that the frequency of *and, but* and *or* in conference messages lies somewhere between its frequency in conversation and academic prose, as represented by the LGSWE corpus evidence. This suggests that conference messages are indeed a hybrid form.

Questions, suggestions and issues to consider

1. How do the findings fit in with what was said in A12 about the use of *and* for coordination in spoken English?
2. The authors do not discuss whether ellipsis was present in their data. How might this have affected their findings?
3. Do you think the evidence from personal pronouns and coordinating conjunctions is enough to prove that CMC is different from other forms of writing? What other linguistic forms could be investigated to provide further evidence?
4. Look at some emails or other forms of CMC that you receive in English. How far do they correspond to informal speech or formal writing? What features are prominent, for example, ellipsis?
5. Is there any variation between or within the different types of CMC that you write and receive? What factors are involved in differences? For example, do you write differently when addressing friends, or parents, or teachers? And are there differences in what they write to you?

SOURCES OF TEXTS USED

Christie, Agatha. 1972. *Elephants Can Remember*. London: Collins Crime Club. (B3)

Cornwell, Bernard. 2009. *Azincourt*. London: Harper. (C2)

'Proving your identity to a bank can be like proving you were abducted by aliens', by Sandi Toksvig. In *Seven Magazine, Sunday Telegraph*, September 19, 2010. (C11)

'Sample of General American'. 2008. Reprinted from *Practical Phonetics and Phonology*, by Beverley Collins and Inger M. Mees, p. 157. London: Routledge. (C12)

Tan, Amy. 1989. *The Joy Luck Club*. New York: G.P. Putnam's Sons. (C9)

'The A to Z of Englishness'. *Women Journal*, September 1988. (C10)

REFERENCES

Baron, N.S. 1998. Letters by phone or speech by other means: the linguistics of email. *Language and Communication* 18: 133–70.

Berry, R. 1997a. *Collins COBUILD English Guides 10. Determiners and Quantifiers*. London: HarperCollins.

Biber, D., S. Johansson, G. Leech, S. Conrad and E. Finegan. 1999. *Longman Grammar of Spoken and Written English*. Harlow: Longman.

Brazil, D. 1995. *A Grammar of Speech*. Oxford: Oxford University Press.

Carter, R. and M. McCarthy. 1995. Grammar and the spoken language. *Applied Linguistics* 16/2, 141–158.

Chandler, Raymond. 1971. *The Little Sister*. New York: Ballantine Books.

Christopherson, P. 1939. *The Articles: a Study of their Theory and Use in English*. Munksgaard: Copenhagen.

Collins COBUILD English Dictionary. 1987/1995. London: HarperCollins.

Collot, M. and N. Belmore. 1996. Electronic language: a new variety of English. In S. Herring (ed.) *Computer Mediated Communication: Linguistic, Social and Cross-Cultural Perspectives*. Philadelphia: John Bejamins, pp. 13–28.

Covington, M.A. 1984. *Syntactic Theory in the High Middle Ages: Modistic Models of Sentence Structure*. Cambridge: Cambridge University Press.

Ducrot, O. and T. Todorov. 1981. *Encyclopedic Dictionary of the Sciences of Language*. Oxford: Blackwell.

Gleason, H.A. 1961. *An Introduction to Descriptive Linguistics*. Chicago: University of Chicago Press.

Giusti, G. 1990. Floating quantifiers, scambling and configurationality. In *Linguistic Inquiry* 21, 633–641.

Halliday, M.A.K. 2002. *On Grammar*. London: Continuum.

Herskovits, A. 1986. *Language and Spatial Cognition: an Interdisciplinary Study of the Prepositions in English*. Cambridge: Cambridge University Press.

Hilpert, Martin. 2008. The English Comparative – Language Structure and Language Use. *English Language and Linguistics* 12/3, 395–417.

Huddleston, R. 1984. *Introduction to the Grammar of English*. Cambridge: Cambridge University Press.

Hudson, R. 1990. *English Word Grammar*. Oxford: Blackwell.

Jespersen, O. 1933. *Essentials of English Grammar*. London: George Allen & Unwin.

Lakoff, G. 1987. *Women, Fire and Dangerous Things: What Categories Reveal about the Mind*. Chicago: Chicago University Press.

Lakoff, R. 1969. Some reasons why there can't be a 'some/any' rule. *Language 45*, 608–615.

Lewis, M. 1986. *The English Verb*. Hove: Language Teaching Publications.

Piaget, Jean. [1936] 1952. *The Origins of Intelligence in Children*, trans. by M. Cook. New York: International Universities Press.

Quirk, R., S. Greenbaum, G. Leech and J. Svartvik. 1972. *A Grammar of Contemporary English*. London: Longman.

Quirk, R., S. Greenbaum, G. Leech and J. Svartvik. 1985. *A Comprehensive Grammar of the English Language*. Harlow: Longman.

Saussure, F. de. [1915] 1974. *Course in General Linguistics*, trans. by W. Baskin. London: Fontana/Collins.

Scott, M. 1996. *Wordsmith*. Oxford: Oxford University Press.

Seuren, P.A.M. 1990. *Western Linguistics: an Historical Introduction*. Oxford: Blackwell.

Sinclair, J., R. Moon *et al.* 1989. *Collins COBUILD Dictionary of Phrasal Verbs*. London: Collins.

Swan, M. 1995 (second edition). *Practical English Usage*. Oxford: Oxford University Press.

Thompson, Geoff. 1994. *Collins COBUILD English Guides 5: Reporting*. London: HarperCollins.

Ware, R.X. 1979. Some bits and pieces. In F.J. Pelletier (ed.) *Mass Terms: Some Philosophical Problems*. Dordrecht: D. Reidel, pp. 15–29.

Yates, S.J. 1996. Oral and written aspects of computer conferencing. In S. Herring (ed.) *Computer Mediated Communication: Linguistic, Social and Cross-Cultural Perspectives*. Philadelphia: John Benjamins, pp. 29–46.

INDEX OF TERMS AND CONCEPTS

You can use this index to find explanations of important terms and concepts. Only major locations are listed; the most important ones are in bold where there is more than one. Only a few key terms introduced in the C and D sections are included.